Doing Disability Research

Edited by

Colin Barnes and Geof Mercer

The Disability Press

Leeds

First published 1997
The Disability Press
Disability Research Unit
School of Sociology and Social Policy
University of Leeds
Leeds LS2 9JT.

Output from disk supplied and printed by University Print Services, a division of Media Services at Leeds.

British Library Cataloguing in Publication Data
A catalogue record for this book is available from the British Library

Library of Congress Cataloguing in Publication Data
A catalogue record of this book has been requested

ISBN 0-9528450-2-4 (pbk)

Contents

The Disability Press

The Disability Press aims to provide an alternative outlet for work in the field of disability studies. The Disability Press draws inspiration from the work of all those countless disabled individuals and their allies who have, over the years, struggled to put this particular issue onto the political agenda. Its establishment is a testament to the growing recognition of 'disability' as an equal opportunities and human rights issue within the social sciences.

Funding for this third volume has been provided by the Disability Research Unit. The editors also wish to record their thanks to the School of Sociology and Social Policy at the University of Leeds for its continuing support.

Contributors

Michael Bach is Director of Research at the Roeher Institute, Toronto, Canada.

Colin Barnes is a Senior Lecturer in the School of Sociology and Social Policy at the University of Leeds, where he is also Director of the Disability Research Unit.

Sarah Beazley is a Senior Lecturer in the Department of Psychology and Speech Therapy and a member of the Disability Studies Team.

David Benzie is a Research Assistant in the Department of Psychology and Speech Therapy and a member of the Disability Studies Team.

Peter Beresford works with Open Services Project, teaches at Brunel University and is a member of Survivors Speak Out.

Tim Booth is Professor of Social Policy in the Department of Sociological Studies at the University of Sheffield.

Wendy Booth is a Research Fellow in the Department of Sociological Studies at the University of Sheffield.

Cameron Crawford is Vice-President at the Roeher Institute, Toronto, Canada.

Neil Lunt is a lecturer in the Department of Social Policy and Social Work at Massey University, New Zealand.

Geof Mercer is a Senior Lecturer in the School of Sociology and Social Policy and a member of the Disability Research Unit at the University of Leeds.

Michele Moore is a Senior Lecturer in the Department of Psychology and Speech Therapy and Co-ordinator of the Disability Studies Team.

Mike Oliver is Professor of Disability Studies at the University of Greenwich.

Mark Priestley is a Research Fellow in the Disability Research Unit at the University of Leeds and administrator of the e-mail discussion list *disability-research@mailbase.ac.uk.*

Marcia H. Rioux is President at the Roeher Institute, Toronto, Canada.

Tom Shakespeare is a University Research Fellow in the School of Sociology and Social Policy at the University of Leeds.

Emma Stone is completing her PhD on disability in China at the University of Leeds, and is also a Research Officer in the Disability Research Unit.

Patricia Thornton is a senior researcher in the Social Policy Research Unit, at the University of York.

Miriam Ticoll is Director of Information Services at the Roeher Institute, Toronto, Canada.

Ayesha Vernon is a Research Fellow in the Social Policy Research Unit, at the University of York.

Jan Wallcraft is a research student at South Bank University and a member of Survivors Speak Out.

Linda Ward is a Senior Research Fellow at the Norah Frye Research Centre, University of Bristol, and Programme Adviser (Disability) to the Joseph Rowntree Foundation.

Gerry Zarb is a Senior Fellow responsible for the Disability Programme at the Policy Studies Institute, London.

CHAPTER 1

Breaking the Mould? An introduction to doing disability research

Colin Barnes and Geof Mercer

BACKGROUND

Over the last two decades disability activists have established the social model of disability as a comprehensive critique of mainstream academic theories and policy approaches. The disillusionment of disabled people and their organisations has also extended to research on disability. In a trenchant attack, Oliver (1992) condemns it as a 'rip-off' that has done little, if anything, to confront the social oppression and isolation experienced by disabled people or initiate policies which have made a significant improvement in the quality of their lives.

The significance of disability theory and practice lies in its radical challenge to the medical or individual model of disability. The latter is based on the assumption that the individual is 'disabled' by their impairment, whereas the social model of disability reverses this causal chain to explore disadvantages were ignored by academic social researchers. Witness the lack of impact of the collection of essays by disabled women and men entitled *Stigma: The Experience of Disability* (Hunt, 1966), or Campling's (1981) volume on disabled women. In contrast, the 'socio/medical model of disability' has been dominated by interpretative studies of the experience of 'illness', which focus on individual coping mechanisms, including the management of 'stigma', and other perceived threats to 'self' and 'identity' (Bury, 1996).

For their part, disability theorists have criticised this socio/medical model for not breaking the causal link with impairment, or at most, providing a 'social model of impairment'. The latter reinforces the view that disability is studied as a 'personal tragedy' rather than as social oppression. In Paul Hunt's (1966) words those with an impairment are treated as 'unfortunate, useless, different, oppressed and sick'. They represent everything that the 'normal world' most fears – 'tragedy, loss, dark, and the unknown' (p. 155).

The impact of the ICIDH/individual model is also very evident in policy-oriented research, most notably in the national disability survey conducted by OPCS in the 1980s (Martin *et al.*, 1988; Martin and White, 1988). Although officially presented as the most comprehensive account of the social conditions and needs of disabled people, its reception by disabled people has been highly critical. If anything, the study has become synonymous with a lack of consultation with organisations of disabled people, a denial of the social model, a reduction of disability to simplistic, 'objective' measures, the dissemination of disputed findings, and few positive policy outcomes (Abberley, 1991; Oliver, 1992).

As the 1980s drew to a close, some disability researchers undertook studies which turned the spotlight on the experience of disablement and away from individualistic explanations. Examples include: Mike Oliver *et al's* (1988) *Walking into Darkness;* Jenny Morris' (1989) *Able Lives*; and Colin Barnes' (1990) *Cabbage Syndrome*. The disabled people's movement (through BCODP) also commissioned research in support of its campaign for anti-discrimination legislation which led to the publication of *Disabled People in Britain and Discrimination* (Barnes, 1991).

At the same time, there was a burgeoning literature on the possibilities of 'critical social research', including work by feminists, Black writers and educationalists, which positively allied itself with oppressed groups. This complemented charges by disabled activists and their organisations that existing research had been a greater source of exploitation than liberation. The scene was set for disability research to break completely with mainstream approaches.

DOING EMANCIPATORY RESEARCH

Although not a unitary body of thought, 'critical social research' has achieved a pre-eminent influence on disability researchers, at least in its emphasis on emancipatory goals, and its calls for openly partisan and politically committed research. It became an 'article of faith' that social researchers adopting a critical perspective should take the side of the oppressed (Becker, 1967). Traditional claims to be 'objective' and 'neutral' were dismissed on the grounds that all knowledge is socially constructed and culturally relative (Kuhn, 1961).

A crucial opportunity for disabled people to debate the possibilities of developing new ways of 'doing disability research' was provided by a series of seminars funded by the Joseph Rowntree Foundation in the late 1980s and early 1990s. These brought together a variety of interested individuals and organisations and resulted in a national conference and a special issue of the journal *Disability, Handicap and Society* in 1992 (Ward and Flynn, 1994) Probably the most influential contribution was Mike Oliver's call for disability research to follow 'what has variously been called critical inquiry, praxis or emancipatory research' (1992: 107). At its heart is a political commitment to confront disability by changing: the social relations of research production, including the role of funding bodies; the relationship between researchers and those being researched; and the links between research and policy initiatives.

For Oliver, emancipatory research must be located in the social model of disability. It must reject the individual or medical model view that impairment is the root cause of disabled people's problems. This includes giving proper recognition to disability and disabled people in social research (e.g. in studies of the family, employment, sexuality, education and the like) but more ambitiously, it is suggested that disability research presents a radical alternative to mainstream research theory and methods.

The idea that research should be about changing the world, not simply describing it, goes back at least to Marx. Contemporary critical theorists have argued that research is inherently 'political' (rather than 'objective'), and must be guided by the 'purpose of emancipation' (Gitlin *et al.*, 1989). Needless to say, the political challenge must have particular targets in the research process. Uppermost in the minds of most disability writers has been the need to transform the 'social and material relations of research production'. With respect to the latter, it is argued that the main funders of disability research have a considerable potential to influence its direction and character. Similar concerns have been expressed about the role of the large research institutes and units which dominate 'contract' policy research.

The primary issue for those who have focused on 'social relations' has been the asymmetrical relationship between researcher and researched. This is seen as a major reason for the alienation of disabled people from the research process. The power of the researcher-experts is enshrined in their control over the design, implementation, analysis and dissemination of research findings. As a consequence, the 'subjects' of research are treated as 'objects', with little positive input to the overall research process. The emancipatory paradigm rejects this notion of researcher-experts moving between projects like 'academic tourists', and using disability as a commodity to exchange for advancing their own status and interests. The response of disabled people is quite simple: 'no participation without representation' (Finkelstein, 1985).

The role of the non-disabled researchers has raised similar questions. For some, their lack of personal experience of disabling barriers means that their contribution lacks authenticity; for others, disabled and non-disabled researchers live in a disablist society and can both contribute to disability theory and research.

A striking feature of the call for a new approach in disability research has been the lack of alignment with particular research methods or techniques, although this may now be changing. Oliver suggests that the new paradigm should highlight 'reciprocity, gain and empowerment' (1992: 111), but there has been relatively little discussion on what these entail or how they should be achieved. In contrast, feminist criticism of 'malestream' research has prioritised the validity of personal experience as opposed to 'scientific methods'. This has been translated into an enthusiasm for unstructured research methods (Morris, 1996).

This is highlighted in the emphasis on reciprocity in the relationship between researcher and researched as an attempt to give due recognition to those being researched as 'expert-knowers'. It also means that the 'expert-researchers' place their skills and knowledge at the disposal of those being researched. However, this objective has proven difficult to translate into practice. Is the elimination of power differences always necessary or feasible? Is the relationship to be reversed or equalised in some way? In addition, the presumption that the social world is divided neatly between oppressors and oppressed has been challenged. Studies with black people, for example, have pointed to the cross-cutting sources of oppression – such as gender, 'race' and disability. The designation of oppressors and oppressed varies across social contexts.

There is a parallel dilemma for researchers who try to convey the experience of disability if the 'oppressed' group resists non-hierarchical research relationships or alternatively takes contrary lines by explaining their 'disability' in terms of their impairments. At the same time, there are concerns that research findings are misrepresented or used to reinforce disablist notions, for example by describing disabled people as helpless 'victims'. One solution is to distinguish between the structural position of disabled people and their own experiences. According to one feminist researcher:

'This enabled me to see that evidence of women successfully accommodating to various structural features of their lives in no way alters the essentially exploitative character of the structures in which they are located' (Finch, 1984: 84).

An associated issue is the significance that should be attached to people's subjective experiences of disability and impairment. As described by Finkelstein (1996), the choice is between an 'outside in' or an 'inside out' approach. In the former, disability research and political activity concentrates on the barriers 'out there' (e.g. Oliver, 1996), while the latter adds an emphasis on disabled people's subjective reality – their experience of physical pain, fatigue and depression – (Morris, 1991; 1996; Shakespeare et al., 1996; Crow, 1996).

In summary, emancipatory research in the disability context should be enabling not disabling. It must be 'reflexive' and self-critical lest a new orthodoxy is established which turns 'doing disability research' into a technical routine. Disability research must not deteriorate into propaganda: it must be politically committed but rigorous.

REFLECTIONS ON DOING DISABILITY RESEARCH

Mainstream social research has long recognised the potential divergence between 'theory' and 'practice': as is illustrated by such volumes as *Doing Sociological Research* (Bell and Newby, 1977), and *Doing Feminist Research* (Roberts, 1981). Following these examples, the contributors to this volume have been encouraged to explore the promise and possibilities of 'doing disability research', as well as its problems and pitfalls. This collection includes established writers on disability as well as 'new recruits'. The chapters span the theory and practice of disability research, from the preparatory stages through to dissemination of findings.

The first contributor is Mike Oliver who has been central to debates about the character and objectives of disability research. He delivers a 'critical reflection' on his recent research on the history of disability politics which he undertook with Jane Campbell (Campbell and Oliver, 1996), as well as making general observations on the state of disability research. Oliver expresses grave doubts about the extent to which the social and material relations of research production have been changed, and highlights the impact of major research funders. He concludes that, in seeking to make a contribution to the emancipation of disabled people, disability researchers must be more explicit about the ideological position which they are adopting.

A less pessimistic perspective on what has been achieved this far is provided by Linda Ward, based on her experience working with the Joseph Rowntree Foundation (JRF) and the Norah Fry Research Centre. She argues that JRF has become committed to the social model of disability and has supported very innovative research that has made significant advances in involving people with learning difficulties and disabled children in the research process from interviewing to dissemination. Ward contends that an organisation which is idealistic in its goals, and open to persuasion about new ways of doing research, has been a catalyst for change in shifting the balance of power between researchers and those being researched. She concludes that a constructive dialogue between funders and disability researchers is possible and has had a positive impact on disability research.

One obvious research project suggested by the social model of disability is to measure disability by investigating disabling barriers. This is now the subject of an ESRC-funded study entitled *Measuring Disablement in Society*.

Its director, Gerry Zarb, outlines the steps it has taken to change the social and material forces of research production. The project has been particularly ambitious in the significance attached to enabling disabled people to guide the research agenda. A further commitment has been to the recruitment and role of disabled researchers. Zarb examines various problems encountered in the course of the research, including the constraints imposed by research funders and employers that do not always take into account the particular circumstances of disabled researchers.

In their chapter, Beresford and Wallcraft consider the applicability of disability research to the survivors' movement – those with experience of the psychiatric system. Not all survivors consider themselves 'disabled' despite the similarities in social disadvantage and social oppression. This in part explains why the survivors' movement has been far less united on its theoretical and research agenda. In research terms, there has been a slower movement down the emancipatory path and survivors have been used more as a resource for experiential data rather than the 'creators of our own analysis and theory'. However, the authors detail the gathering tradition of survivor-led research which is seeking alternatives to the medical control of definitions of mental illness and of psychiatric treatments and institutions.

Mark Priestley's discussion of doing disability research centres on a collaborative project with Derbyshire Coalition of Disabled People and Derbyshire Centre for Integrated Living. The discussion spans issues associated with being a non-disabled researcher, setting up the project, agreeing the research questions, and devolving control to those being researched. All parties were committed to breaking down the traditional researcher-researched hierarchy, but found that compromises had to be made. Not least, Priestley's position as a postgraduate student provided considerable potential for conflicts of interest between his 'academic' and 'political' self. Indeed issues of power and control are central to his discussion. Not that disabled people always wanted to take the research over, rather their concern was to equalise the relationship and ensure researcher accountability.

Lunt and Thornton's chapter on disability and employment policies in different countries diverges significantly from most others in the book in that it relies on secondary analysis of published literature. The research also took its cue from national governments, rather than disabled people. However, its focus on the policy establishment allows discussion of the social and material relations of contract research production. The authors argue that they were not constrained by their funders as much as disability theorists might suspect. Indeed, funders were not always clear what they wanted and on occasions did not speak with one voice. Nevertheless, time and resource pressures meant that the research was very reliant on official sources for information and policy evaluation.

Tim and Wendy Booth have an established reputation for conducting research with people with learning difficulties. Their contribution identifies a range of technical, ethical and conceptual difficulties encountered in a recently completed project on parenting. Innovative data collection methods were employed which stemmed from a narrative method of 'life review'. They describe how they sought to ensure that the processes of data collection were determined by the respondent's subjective interpretation of their own experience and development of their storyline. Various devices were employed to generate the necessary rapport, including writing stories, and shared interviews between siblings. The overall goal was to facilitate the interviewee taking control of the interview. The study throws new light on taken-for-granted assumptions about parenting by focusing on those who 'break the rules', but in so doing, the Booths illuminate parenting processes in general.

Beazley, Moore and Benzie began their study determined to provide as much control as possible to their disabled subjects. However, the lack of time and resources, the involvement of other 'stakeholders' with differing interests and commitments, plus other unforeseen interruptions, represent not untypical complications. The researchers describe how their attempts to maintain the direction and progress of the project were frustrated in various ways and by different people and groups. Even the involvement of other disabled people did not mean 'emancipatory' research objectives were easily sustained. There were further tensions to be sorted out in terms of different interest within the research team. The path of disability research requires considerable skills as well as the commitment to emancipatory goals!

Ayesha Vernon provides an 'insider's perspective' on researching the oppression experienced by disabled Black women. She placed particular significance on devising ways to break down the researcher-researched hierarchy. Her discussion explores a wide range of issues confronting the researcher committed to achieving respondent control and researcher accountability. These include: setting the research focus; getting the researcher-researcher relationship 'right' before interviews began; involving interviewees in checking/changing their answers; and commenting on the researcher's commentary on their experiences. The dilemmas posed extended from practical constraints of time and resources through to differences of interpretation: how does the disability researcher respond to 'disablist' views from disabled respondents? Her emphasis on reciprocity reinforced the importance of interviewees taking something positive from the research experience, but 'intent is no guarantee of outcome'.

Tom Shakespeare's chapter draws on research which led to the jointly-authored book *The Sexual Politics of Disability* (Shakespeare *et al.*, 1996). He raises many issues about the approach to researching people's experiences of disability and sexuality, which he sets within the twin considerations of intellectual and political commitment. He notes the diverse reasons which underpin disability projects by academics: personal ambition and advancement; intellectual curiosity, political commitment and perceived need; and a dose of pragmatism. So is it emancipatory research? 'To be honest, I don't know and I don't care' is Tom's response. He espouses a 'free spirit' view of the researcher. 'I don't follow recipes when I cook'. He also distances himself from the 'stronger' claims for emancipatory research, and argues that the tension between researching disability and researching disabled people's lives must be recognised.

Marcia Rioux and her colleagues discuss their research into inequality, citizenship and human rights, through the specific prism of the abuse and violence experienced by disabled people in Canada. The authors outline the limitations in existing theory and methodology in this area. They argue for both a re-interpretation of 'violence and abuse' as well as more appropriate research methods. The emphasis is on creating the right climate for interviewees. Although using disabled researchers was not a priority, careful training in interviewing the research subjects was. Indeed, the study relied heavily on an enhanced role for the interviewers in interpreting the experience of interviewees. (British readers will note that the editors have resisted the temptation to change the authors' use of terms such as 'people with disabilities' which prevail North America.)

Emma Stone brings the volume to a close with an account of her experiences as a postgraduate research student embarking on a disability research project in China. As a non-disabled researcher and a 'foreign devil' researching a contentious subject, she was confronted by searching questions from her hosts. Compromises had to be made. The social model did not travel easily: at times it seemed culturally and linguistically untranslatable. Chinese views of doing research also conflicted with the emancipatory paradigm. Stone was obliged to devise strategies to satisfy these different research and political sensibilities. She concludes that emancipatory research must relinquish some of its wider claims: for example, in her experience, participatory and action research does not necessarily mean acting as an oppressor.

REVIEW

One aim of this book is to explore what 'doing disability research' really means. The contributors to this volume take us down this path. By adopting a 'confessional' and 'reflexive' approach, they help to put flesh on the bones of the emancipatory model. They convey a sense of the vitality and diversity of disability research, and what is possible with commitment and perseverance. They provide a picture of innovative disability research that encourages optimism about the way forward, while also recognising that much more work needs to be done.

REFERENCES

ABBERLEY, P. (1987) 'The Concept of Oppression and the Development of a Social Theory of Disability', *Disability, Handicap and Society*, 2 (1): 5-21.

ANDERSON, R. and BURY, M., eds. (1988) *Living with Chronic Illness: the experience of patients and their families*. London: Unwin Hyman.

BARNES, C. (1990) *Cabbage Syndrome: The Social Construction of Dependence*. Lewes, Falmer.

BARNES, C. (1991) *Disabled People in Britain and Discrimination*. London: Hurst & Co.

BARNES, C. and MERCER, G., eds. (1996) *Exploring the Divide: Illness and Disability*. Leeds: The Disability Press.

BECKER, H. (1967) 'Whose side are we on?', *Social Problems*, 14: 239-47.

BELL, C. and NEWBY, H., eds. (1977) *Doing Sociological Research*. London: Routledge and Kegan Paul.

BURY, M. (1996) 'Defining and Researching Disability: Challenges and

Responses' in C. BARNES and G. MERCER, eds. *Exploring the Divide: Illness and Disability*. Leeds: The Disability Press, pp. 17-39.

CAMPBELL, J. and OLIVER, M. (1996) *Disability Politics: Understanding Our Past, Changing Our Future*. London: Routledge.

CAMPLING, J. (1981) *Images of Ourselves: Women with Disabilities Talking*. London: Routlege and Kegan Paul.

CROW, L. (1996) 'Including all of Our Lives: renewing the social model of disability' in C. BARNES and G. MERCER, eds. (1996) *Exploring the Divide: Illness and Disability*. Leeds: The Disability Press, pp. 55-74.

DISABILITY, HANDICAP & SOCIETY (1992) Special Issue: 7 (2).

DISABLED PEOPLES' INTERNATIONAL (1992) *Proceedings of the Third World Congress of Disabled Peoples' International*. Winnipeg: Disabled Peoples' International.

FINCH, J. (1984) ' The ethics and politics of interviewing women', in C. Bell and H. Roberts, eds. *Social Researching: Politics, Problems, Practice*. London: Routledge and Kegan Paul.

FINKELSTEIN, V. (1985) Unpublished Paper given at World Health Organization Meeting, 24-28 June, Netherlands.

FINKELSTEIN, V. (1996) 'Outside, "Inside Out" ', *Coalition*, April, pp 30-6.

GITLIN, A. D., SIEGEL, M. and BORU, K. (1989) 'The politics of method: from leftist ethnography to educative research', *Qualitative Studies in Education*, 2 (3): 237-53.

HUNT, P. (1966) 'A Critical Condition' in P. Hunt, ed. *Stigma: The Experience of Disability*. London: Geoffrey Chapman

HUNT, P. (1981) 'Settling Accounts with the Parasite People', *Disability Challenge*, 2: 37-50.

KUHN, T. (1961) *The Structure of Scientific Revolutions*. Chicago: Chicago University Press.

MARTIN, J. and WHITE, A. (1988) *The Financial Circumstances of Disabled Adults*. London: HMSO.

MARTIN, J., MELTZER, H. and ELLIOT, D. (1988) *OPCS Surveys of Disability in Great Britain: Report 1 – The prevalence of disability among adults*, London: HMSO.

MILLER, E. J. and GWYNNE, G. V. (1972) *A Life Apart*. London: Tavistock.

MORRIS, J. (1989) *Able Lives*, London, The Women's Press.

MORRIS, J. (1991) *Pride Against Prejudice*. London: The Women's Press.

MORRIS, J., ed. (1996) *Encounters with Strangers: Feminism and Disability*. London: The Women's Press.

OLIVER, M. (1992) 'Changing the Social Relations of Research Production?', *Disability, Handicap & Society*, 7 (2):101-114.

OLIVER, M. (1996) 'Defining Impairment and Disability: Issues at Stake', in C. Barnes, and G. Mercer, eds. *Exploring the Divide; Illness and Disability*. Leeds: The Disability Press, pp. 39-54.

OLIVER, M., ZARB, G., SILVER, J., MOORE, M. and SAINSBURY, V. (1988) *Walking into Darkness*. London: Macmillan.

ROBERTS, H., ed. (1981) *Doing Feminist Research*. London: Routledge and Kegan Paul.

SHAKESPEARE, T. GILLESPIE-SELLS, K. and DAVIES, D. (1996) *The Sexual Politics of Disability: Untold Desires*. London: Cassell.

UPIAS. (1976) *Fundamental Principles of Disability*. London: Union of Physically Impaired Against Segregation.

WARD, L. and FLYNN, M. (1994) 'What Matters Most: Disability, Research and Empowerment', in M. H. RIOUX and M. BACH, eds. (1994) *Disability is Not Measles. New Research Paradigms in Disability*. North York, Ontario: Roeher Institute, ch. 2.

WOOD, P. (1980) *International Classification of Impairments, Disabilities and Handicaps*. Geneva: World Health Organization.

ZARB, G. (1992) 'On the road to Damascus: first steps towards changing the relations of disability research production', *Disability, Handicap & Society*, 7(2): 125-38.

CHAPTER 2

Emancipatory Research: Realistic goal or impossible dream?

Mike Oliver

INTRODUCTION

After much critical reflection on my own work (is this what we mean by reflexivity?) during the 1980s provoked by my involvement in the disability movement, I came to the inescapable and painful conclusion that the person who had benefited most from my research on disabled people's lives was undoubtedly me. It also became apparent that there was increasing anger, hostility and suspicion amongst organisations of disabled people that much that passed for 'disability research' was nothing more than a 'rip-off'.

In 1990 I was invited to give a paper on disability research to a conference of academic researchers in Sweden and this gave me the opportunity to reflect on the issues involved. To this day I remember entering the conference room on the first morning with the other researchers, none of whom were disabled, and finding the words 'what do you think you are doing talking about us in this way?' written on the board. No-one except me thought it referred to us; those who even noticed the comment at all simply assumed the board hadn't been cleaned by whoever had used it the day before.

What did we think we were doing: pursuing knowledge for the benefit of humankind? Informing policy and practice? Helping disabled people? Building networks? Developing our own careers? Having a freebie at someone else's expense? All of those things probably and more; but also much less.

In the following year Len Barton and myself were able to persuade the Joseph Rowntree Foundation to fund a project which literally locked disability researchers and disabled people into the same room for a series of seminars which culminated in a national conference and a special edition of the journal *Disability and Society,* 1992, Vol 7, No 2. The personal experience of this was profound for most, if not all of us, leading one of the researchers to confess as much on Radio 4.

In this paper I'm not going to attempt to provide a comprehensive analysis of what's happened since nor a reinterpretation of the ideas and issues that emerged. Instead I want to discuss my own subsequent research work in relation to what I called for both in my paper published in the special edition and from the conference platform; namely for the development of an emancipatory paradigm in respect of disability research. This is, I suppose, what sociologists would call an exercise in reflexivity, if I have understood the term correctly. In order to make this more than an exercise in self-indulgence, I shall attempt to consider some of the issues this reflexivity raises for disability research in general and for 'would be' emancipatory researchers in particular.

WHAT IS EMANCIPATORY RESEARCH?

In the previous paper I contextualised the emerging paradigm in the following way:

> 'The development of such a paradigm stems from the gradual rejection of the positivist view of social research as the pursuit of absolute knowledge through the scientific method and the gradual disillusionment with the interpretive view of such research as the generation of socially useful knowledge within particular historical and social contexts. The emancipatory paradigm, as the name implies, is about the facilitating of a politics of the possible by confronting social oppression at whatever levels it occurs' (Oliver, 1992: 110).

This was never intended to be an argument against the pursuit of knowledge *per se*, whether that knowledge be absolute, socially useful or whatever; but rather an assertion that it is not possible to research oppression in an objective or scientific way. As Barnes (1996) has recently argued, you cannot be independent in researching oppression; you are either on the side of the oppressors or the oppressed.

In seeking to describe what the emancipatory research project was, I suggested that it might be seen as an emerging new paradigm for undertaking research. The reason for this was simple:

> 'The issue then for the emancipatory research paradigm is not how to empower people but, once people have decided to empower themselves, precisely what research can then do to facilitate this process. This does then mean that the social relations of research production do have to be fundamentally changed; researchers have to learn how to put their knowledge and skills at the disposal of their research subjects, for them to use in whatever ways they choose' (Oliver, 1992: 111).

Thus what made it a new paradigm was the changing of the social relations of research production – the placing of control in the hands of the researched, not the researcher.

Building on previous feminist work (e.g. Lather, 1987; Ribbens, 1990), I went on to suggest that there were three key fundamentals on which such a paradigm must be based; reciprocity, gain and empowerment. However, merely attempting to base research on these fundamentals did not necessarily mean working in ways very different from some positivist work and much interpretive work. But changing the social relations of research production meant that it was impossible to incorporate emancipatory work into existing research paradigms.

In this paper I do not wish to review the progress that has or has not been made in developing an emancipatory paradigm for disability research. Instead I want to consider how the only piece of major research I have completed since I outlined the criteria for emancipatory research meets those very criteria. In sum I shall use my own criteria to judge my own work, not the work of others.

A BRIEF HISTORY OF 'DISABILITY POLITICS'

The research to be discussed was jointly undertaken by Jane Campbell and myself (Campbell and Oliver, 1996). Chapter 1 of that book provides both a description of and a rationale for the work we undertook. At this point however, I should make it clear that this paper represents my own views and not those of my co-researcher. Nevertheless, in describing the work undertaken in the following paragraphs, I switch to the use of 'we' rather than 'I'.

The book was neither a complete history of the disability movement nor a comprehensive account of the issues facing the movement today. Instead, based on in-depth interviews with around thirty key activists who have participated in the rise of the movement since the 1960s, it was a series of accounts of why the movement emerged when it did, the issues it faced during its transition from emerging to emergent movement and the directions it might take in the future.

Crucial to the production of the book were our own roles as both activists and researchers. This we tried to summarise in the following way:

> 'We approach the research task as activists trying to make sense of our actions, not as researchers trying to be where the action is' (Campbell and Oliver, 1996: 24).

WERE THE SOCIAL RELATIONS OF RESEARCH PRODUCTION CHANGED?

In order to examine this key issue, I need to consider first where the idea for the book originated. While it is true that at no point did the movement, however that might be defined, formally commission us to undertake the research, it was an issue that many disabled people and their organisations had suggested was of crucial importance. With a few notable exceptions, little work on the movement had been undertaken and as participants in the movement, we were often part of discussions which articulated the need for such work to be undertaken.

The decision to proceed was an individual one and we negotiated a contract with a publisher. The choice of how to proceed was also ours alone; we decided who to interview, how to interview them and how we would proceed with the analysis. We were aware of the contradictory nature of our position and this was further brought home to us in lengthy correspondence with the then General Secretary on behalf of the Greater Manchester Coalition of Disabled People (GMCDP).

They asked a series of appropriate but difficult questions about who controlled the research, who had commissioned it, what was going to be done with it and where the royalties were going. We answered as honestly as we could; we were in control although participants would be given every opportunity to comment on and change working drafts, no-one had formally commissioned the research, ultimately we were in control and as we had not managed to attract any substantial funding we would jointly share the royalties in order to offset the costs we would incur.

While we wanted the work to be an integral part of the collective movement of disabled people rather than an external commentary on it, we neither had the time, energy or money to make it a wholly collective production. This was less than satisfactory to us and almost certainly so to GMCDP. While they never formally opposed the work, they did not participate either and an unfortunate though understandable gap remains.

Almost all the other people we approached readily agreed to be involved although changes in personal circumstances meant that not everyone approached eventually participated. In choosing to use unstructured methods, what was discussed was as much in the control of our participants as it was us and was located within their own personal biographies.

Finally, we offered all the participants the opportunity to see both their words and drafts of the complete manuscript before publication. The fact that only 2 took us up on this offer could be seen either as alienation from our emancipatory project in exactly the same way as disabled people have been alienated from most non-emancipatory research or as testament to the trust that the participants had in our commitment not to exploit them! The truth is probably more complex than that and falls somewhere in between these extreme positions.

WHO GAINED?

It is undeniable that we, as researchers, gained. We have an extra publication to our names, whatever that is worth. We will eventually receive royalty cheques though whether they will defray our costs remains an open question. We have been invited to present our work at national and international fora. We have also gained a better understanding of our own personal biographies and our collective history and the relationship between the two.

We hope that our participants would also sign up to the last point. While the feedback we have had so far suggests that is not an unreasonable hope we have not systematically contacted everyone involved. Whether disabled people generally have gained is even more difficult to determine. A review in *Disability Now* (Vernon, 1996) laments our failure to even consider the role of organisations like SCOPE while GLAD News is much more appreciative.

WAS IT EMPOWERING?

This question is perhaps a false one. As I have argued elsewhere (Oliver, 1992; 1996) empowerment is not in the gift of the powerful; albeit whether they are politicians, policy makers or researchers; empowerment is something that people do for themselves collectively. Disabled people have decided to empower themselves therefore the question that needs to be asked is whether our work makes a contribution to this process. The question could also be asked in a negative way – is our work likely to contribute to the disempowerment of disabled people?

However, in an anonymous review in Disability Arts in London (DAIL), the reviewer does describe the book as empowering:

> 'It...got me back in touch with my strong self, my peers, our shared politics. This book's a contribution to my liberation' (DAIL, 1996: 32-3).

WAS IT PART OF AN EMANCIPATORY RESEARCH AGENDA?

Building on the work of Bourne (1981), I suggested six ways in which this new research paradigm can make a contribution to the combating of the oppression of disabled people:

1) a description of experience in the face of academics who abstract and distort the experience of disabled people;
2) a redefinition of the problem of disability;
3) a challenge to the ideology and methodology of dominant research paradigms;
4) the development of a methodology and set of techniques commensurate with the emancipatory research paradigm;
5) a description of collective experience in the face of academics who are unaware or ignore the existence of the disability movement; and
6) a monitoring and evaluation of services that are established, controlled and operated by disabled people themselves.

In evaluating our own research against this agenda, I should perhaps deal with the easy ones first. I would hope that our work is a faithful account of the experiences of those disabled people who participated and also of those people who would self-identify as part of a collective movement (1). I would also suggest that our book redefines the problem of disability away from it being an individual or welfare one, transforming it into a political one (2), albeit with individual and welfare dimensions. It is also a description of the collective experience of some, though of course, not all disabled people (5). It is not, and was never intended to be, an attempt to monitor and evaluate services controlled by disabled people unless I argue that the disability movement provides a political service to disabled people (6).

While I would hope that our work provides a challenge to the ideology of the dominant research paradigms, I can be less certain what challenge, if any, it poses to dominant methodologies (3). In eschewing objectivity and neutrality and embracing partisanship, we were clearly confronting many of the canons of scientific and social scientific approaches to research. I remain unclear as to whether the methodology and techniques of our work challenge anything at all (3) and (4). If methodology is defined as nothing more than a set of appropriate techniques, then I am not sure whether interviews, questionnaires, participant observation, transcript analysis, etc., are compatible or incompatible with emancipatory research. I am convinced however, that such techniques can only be part of an emancipatory project where, and only where, the social relations of research production have been changed.

So, our work and my own reflexivity requires two key questions to be addressed. The first is – did the research succeed in changing the social relations of research production? My own reflexive answer would be 'nearly but not quite'. On the basis of reading the above and perhaps the book itself, others may come to a less comfortable conclusion. The second key question is – has or is the research contributing to the emancipation of disabled people? I would like to leave the answer to this until the end of the chapter.

CHANGING THE MATERIAL RELATIONS OF RESEARCH PRODUCTION?

At the seminar series referred to earlier, Zarb (1992) argued that it was not simply the social relations of research production that needed to change if disability research was to be an integral part of a process of collective empowerment, but the material ones also. In other words, it was not simply control of the research process which was an issue but also control of the resources needed to undertake research in the first place which must change. Until then, he argued, only participatory research was possible.

These material relations cannot be reduced simply to money but if we look at the specific issue of funding, we can see that control of the resources remains in the hands of major funding bodies; of which three, the Economic and Social Research Council (ESRC), the Department of Health and the Joseph Rowntree Foundation were, and remain, the most important. By considering each in turn, I will argue that the material relations of research production (as Zarb called them) have not changed very much at all, even if superficially they may appear to have done so.

The ESRC has funded several major research projects on disability but, in the main, these have been located within existing research paradigms The exception is the project on 'disabling environments' currently being undertaken at the Policy Studies Institute (PSI) and directed by Gerry Zarb. The idea for this emerged from a joint conference organised by British Council of Disabled People (BCODP) and Social Science Research Group (SSRG) and was published in a paper the following year (Oliver, 1987). This was worked into a specific proposal jointly by Gerry Zarb and myself and submitted to 2 different ESRC research initiatives from the University of Greenwich. On both occasions, the proposal was rejected but subsequently, when Zarb moved to PSI, a revised (though essentially similar) proposal was accepted for funding.

There are, of course, a number of possible explanations for this; the final proposal was the strongest, research priorities have changed, it was considered by different committees and so on. One central fact however is pertinent to our discussion here; while the radical idea and methodology of the original proposal has been retained, the project only achieved funding when it was located within a relatively 'conservative research organisation', one which has a reputation for being a safe pair of hands.

The recent history of disability research emanating from the Department of Health offers another interesting case study of the complexities of the relationship between the social and material relations of research production. The Department, it seems, has discovered the 'user' for in the 'Foreword' to a recently published set of documents on Consumers and Research in the NHS (1995), Professor Sir Michael Peckham, Director of Research and Development in the NHS spells out his position:

> 'The NHS is attaching increasing importance to seeking out and acting upon the views of its users on the coverage and delivery of the services it provides' (unpaged).

As far as disability research is concerned, the Department has established and implemented a National Research and Development Programme for People with Physical and Complex Disabilities. When such a programme was established, a steering group was appointed to oversee the drawing up of the research agenda. The only disabled person invited to join the group was the Director of RADAR, although he is not generally accepted within the Disabled People's Movement as a legitimate representative of disabled people, and is not known within the academic research community for his research experience or expertise.

When the research agenda was drawn up, a new body was constituted to oversee the programme and allocate the funds. None of the members of this Commissioning Group are disabled or representatives of the disability movement but they 'advise the Programme Director on the scientific merit and value to the NHS of research proposals submitted for funding'. Belatedly the Department did offer to set up a consultative group of disabled people although they were to have no role in the decision making. Quite what they were to be consulted on remains a mystery and not surprisingly, disabled people declined the offer to participate and no such group was ever established. Emancipatory research might still have been on the agenda however, as next to the top of the identified priorities to which the programme was supposed to be working was 'consumer views' and potential applicants were explicitly directed to my original paper on emancipatory research (Oliver, 1992). So far the programme has spent £3.9 million on 30 projects; not a single one of those is located outside the University sector or the Health Service. Despite 'consumer views' being ranked second in order of priority, disabled people have not been involved, no organisations of disabled people have received any of the funding and none of the projects could be called emancipatory; they are all located within the positivist or interpretive paradigms.

The Joseph Rowntree Foundation is the other major funder of disability research. Since it established its Disability Committee in 1988, it has been committed to consulting disabled people and to funding research which is designed to develop initiatives that disabled people themselves think are important. And as has already been mentioned, the JRF funded the seminars linking disabled people and researchers together. While initial and subsequent research has remained rooted in what disabled people regard as important, little funding has gone to research which could genuinely be called emancipatory.

This is perhaps most disappointing of all. At the end of the series, a set of detailed guidelines were produced (see *Disability and Society*, 1992, Vol 7, No 3). These guidelines have been virtually ignored by the research community and even the Rowntree Foundation itself has failed to make explicit use of them in its subsequent funding activity.

This appears to support Zarb's argument that the 'objective constraints' imposed by the material relations of research production are beyond the control of both researchers and researched. He concludes that 'we can still go some way towards changing the social relations of research production' (Zarb, 1992: 127) and suggests that participatory research is the way to do it. My own problem with this is that participatory research, while it can be used as a vehicle for changing social relations, all too often leaves the relationship between the social and material relations of research production untheorised and untouched. In trying to say something about the complexities of this relationship the issues of politics and praxis need to be considered and it is to these issues that I shall now turn.

THE POLITICISATION OF THE RESEARCH PROCESS

The two central issues so far discussed can be summarised in political terms as control over process and control over resources. Both are of fundamental importance and the difficulties of achieving either should not be underestimated.

By now it should be clear that even defining the terms on which the research should proceed is not simply a matter of language or science (Oliver, 1996b); it is also a matter of politics. Altman captures this in respect of the definitional battles surrounding AIDS:

> 'How AIDS was conceptualised was an essential tool in a sometimes very bitter struggle; was it to be understood as a primarily bio-medical problem, in which case its control should be under that of the medical establishment, or was it rather, as most community-based groups argued, a social and political issue, which required a much greater variety of expertise' (Altman, 1994: 26).

The ways in which disabled people have been systematically excluded from the definitional process has recently been described in one incident which captures the nature of this exclusion more generally:

'It is a hot summer day in London in the late 1980s. Gathered together in one of the capital's most venerable colleges is a large number of academics, researchers and representatives of research funding bodies. Their purpose? A symposium on researching disability comprising presentations on a variety of different methodological and other themes, given and chaired by a panel of experienced disability researchers.

Those convening the seminar are proud that it will shine a spotlight on a usually neglected area of social science research. But some in the audience (and one or two others who have chosen not to attend) hold a different view. What credibility can such a seminar muster, they ask, when none of those chairing or presenting papers are themselves disabled? What does it say about current understanding of disability research issues that such an event has been allowed to go ahead in this form, when a Symposium on researching gender issues given entirely by men, or race relations research given entirely by white people, would have been laughed out of court?' (Ward and Flynn, 1994: 29).

It should be pointed out that this exclusion has been systematic and disabled people have not been properly consulted by organisations such as the World Health Organization (WHO) and the Office of Population Censuses and Surveys who have been most heavily funded in Britain to undertake such work. Nor has this exclusion been significantly addressed, as I have argued above, by organisations such as the ESRC, Department of Health and the Joseph Rowntree Foundation in more recent times.

However, disabled people have begun to resist this situation by producing their own research based upon their own definitions (Barnes, 1991; 1992), the British Council of Disabled People has established its own research sub-committee and in Canada disabled people have produced their own guidelines on what is acceptable and not acceptable research for disability organisations to be involved in (Woodiwill, 1993).

RESEARCH PRAXIS OR 'HOW DO WE DO EMANCIPATORY RESEARCH?'

As I indicated earlier, the question of doing emancipatory research is a false one, rather the issue is the role of research in the process of emancipation. Inevitably this means that research can only be judged emancipatory after the event; one cannot 'do' emancipatory research (nor write methodology cookbooks on how to do it), one can only engage as a researcher with those seeking to emancipate themselves.

Because of the difficulties this involves, even the most committed of researchers, echoing Zarb (1992), have settled for doing participatory or action research. The problem with participatory and action approaches is that they have tended to reinforce existing power structures rather than challenge or confront them let alone change them. For example, much action research in education is concerned to allow teachers to do their existing jobs better, rather than confront the oppressive power/knowledge structures that currently constitute the practice of education. In a provocatively titled essay 'Whatever happened to action research?', one commentator concludes:

> 'Everybody knows what action research is against. But the important and still unresolved question is: what is it for?' (Carr, 1995: 102).

Thus participatory and action approaches, it seems to me, share a limited vision of the possible. To use a game metaphor, these approaches are concerned to allow previously excluded groups to be included in the (research) game as it is whereas emancipatory strategies are concerned about both conceptualising and creating a different game, where no one is excluded in the first place.

Zarb (1992), however, has argued that the distinction between participatory and emancipatory research is a false one in that the latter will only be achieved when the material as well as the social relations of research production are overthrown: in other words when disablist late-capitalism has been replaced by a different kind of society. Until then, participatory research is all we have got, unless we want to return to positivist or interpretive approaches.

My problem with this approach to research (e.g. Lather, 1987) is that its challenge to existing structures of power is all; it becomes the end in itself and not the means to something better. Participatory and action research is about improving the existing social and material relations of research production; not challenging and ultimately eradicating them. The inevitable result of this, as I pointed out at the beginning, is that we as researchers gain, but mainly at the expense of those whose lives we have researched. While our intentions have been honourable, we remain on the wrong side of the oppressive social and material relations of research production.

SHOULD WE GIVE UP RESEARCH ALTOGETHER THEN?

We all, as researchers, have developed personal strategies to cope with two inescapable facts; that we are the main beneficiaries of our own research activities and that we are usually between a rock and a hard place; trapped between the social and material relations of research production with only politics or praxis to help us.

Diagram 1

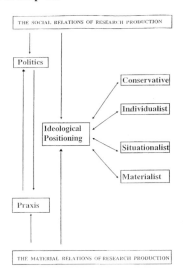

These strategies always are located within particular ideological positions which we as individuals adopt; whether we admit to them or not. There are four main ones, I would suggest, and I shall call these the conservative, individualist, situationalist and materialist positions. These are not intended to be pejorative labels and indeed, if I had wished to be polemical I would have called them positivist, renegade, opportunist and radical positions.

The classic recent statement of the conservative position can be found in Hammersley (1995) where he provides an extensive critique of newer approaches to social research before mounting a defence of 'objective research within the liberal university' (see Oliver, 1996a, for a critical review of this position). Bury (1996) adopts a similar position specifically in respect of disability research.

Some like Ray Pahl (1995) take an individualist position and characterise much that passes for sociological research as applying 'increasingly sophisticated methods to what seem increasingly irrelevant topics' (Pahl, 1995: 14-15) and thereafter confines himself to saying 'I am my research instrument', my sample is confined to 'chums of chums' and 'my research - is as much about my own life as it is of others'. Clough takes a similar stand in respect of disability and special needs research:

> 'An organising concept....is that of identity: my identity as a researcher and the identities of the teachers who occupy the ground of the research' (Clough, 1995: 126).

Most researchers however, have not sought such individualistic solutions to their difficulties, seeking instead to develop situationalist responses. Such responses often locate themselves within the shelter of the safe harbour of the postmodernist worldview which champions deconstruction in the here and now as the only possible research strategy. But as Mary Maynard points out in respect of feminist research:

> 'If one major goal of feminist research is to challenge patriarchal structures and bring about some kind of social change, however conceived, then the postmodern approach, which eschews generalisations and emphasises deconstruction, can only have a limited role in that endeavour' (Maynard, 1994: 22).

Skritc (1995) in his book on special education, certainly does not recognise the limits of deconstruction, claiming that postmodernists can be the architects of reconstruction, saving not only education in America but democracy itself. Shakespeare (1996) makes a more sensible and serious case for situationalist research stressing the need to be independent in certain circumstances but without confusing this with objectivity or neutrality. He concludes:

> 'I defend the right of researchers to undertake research and develop theory for its own sake' (Shakespeare, 1996: 118).

In my view, the realities of the impact of oppression on the lives of the oppressed make it essential that researchers do not merely resort to individual responses or set sail for the safety of postmodernism. Reflexivity, as I implied earlier inevitably means that, however painful, we must ensure that we examine our own research practice in the context of the current oppressive social and material relations of research production.

This reflexivity may lead to uncomfortable conclusions as one Australian educational researcher explains:

'After some years of struggling with education departments in Victoria, Queensland and New South Wales to develop inclusive educational programmes I feel like an accessory after the fact, like an accomplice in exclusion' (Slee, 1996: 112).

For, as Len Barton succinctly puts it 'intent is no guarantee of outcome' (Barton, 1996: 6).

CONCLUSION

Finally then, the second key question I posed earlier needs answering – has my own research been emancipatory? While I would not seek to describe it as such, when disabled people have emancipated themselves (as one day they surely will), I hope the book will be seen as having made a small contribution to that emancipation. To those who would see this as an example of utopian thought used to justify my own work I conclude with a comment from Paul Abberley:

'The Utopias implicit in social theories read themselves back into current analysis and consequent political theorising and (research) practice' (Abberley, 1996: 67).

To those who would seek to dismiss not just my own utopianism but my critique of much that passes for social research as nothing more than the ramblings of someone who can personally afford to say such things – after all I am a professor and I am not interested in gaining big research grants, with or without strings, then the question still remains – which ideological position are you going to admit to adopting?

REFERENCES

ABBERLEY, P. (1996) 'Work, Utopia and Impairment' in L. Barton, ed. (1996) *Disability and Society: Emerging Issues and Insights.* London: Longman.

ALTMAN, D. (1994) *Power and Community: Organizational and Community Responses to AIDS.* London: Taylor and Francis.

BARNES, C. (1991) *Disabled People in Britain and Discrimination.* London: Hurst & Co/BCODP.

BARNES, C. (1992) *Disabling Imagery: An Exploration of Media Portrayals of Disabled People.* Halifax: Ryburn/BCODP

BARNES, C. (1996) 'Disability and the Myth of the Independent Researcher', *Disability and Society,* 11 (1): 107-10.

BARNES, C. and MERCER, G. eds. (1996) *Exploring the Divide: Illness and Disability.* Leeds: The Disability Press.

BARTON, L., ed. (1996) *Disability and Society: Emerging Issues and Insights.* London: Longman.

BOURNE, J. (1981) 'Cheerleaders and ombudsmen: a sociology of race relations in Britain', *Race and Class,* 21: 331-52

BURY, M. (1996) 'Disability and the Myth of the Independent Researcher: a reply', *Disability and Society,* 11 (1) 111-13.

CAMPBELL, J. and OLIVER, M. (1996) *Disability Politics in Britain: Understanding Our Past, Changing Our Future.* London: Routledge.

CARR, W. (1995) 'Whatever happened to action research' in W. Carr, *For Education: Towards Critical Educational Enquiry.* Buckingham: Open University Press.

CLOUGH, P. (1995) 'Problems of identity and method in the investigation of special education needs' in P. Clough, and L. Barton, eds. (1995) *Making Difficulties: Research and the Construction of SEN.* London: Paul Chapman Publishing.

CLOUGH, P. and BARTON, L., eds. (1995) *Making Difficulties: Research and the Construction of SEN.* London: Paul Chapman Publishing.

DISABILITY ARTS IN LONDON (1996) 'Explaining the politics of disability', anonymous review, Issue 119: 32-3.

HAMMERSLEY, M. (1995) *The Politics of Social Research.* London: Sage.

LATHER, P. (1987) 'Research as Praxis', *Harvard Educational Review,* 56 (3): 257-73.

MAYNARD, M. (1994) 'Methods, Practice and Epistemology: The Debate about Feminism and Research', in Maynard, M. and Purvis, J., eds. *Researching Women's Lives from a Feminist Perspective.* London: Taylor and Francis.

OLIVER, M. (1987) 'Re-defining Disability: Some Implications for Research', *Research, Policy and Planning*, 5: 9-13.

OLIVER, M. (1992) 'Changing the Social Relations of Research Production' *Disability, Handicap, & Society*, 7 (2): 101-115.

OLIVER, M. (1996a) *Understanding Disability: From Theory To Practice.* Basingstoke: MacMillan.

OLIVER, M. (1996b) 'Defining Impairment and Disability: issues at stake' in C. Barnes and G. Mercer, eds. (1996) *Exploring the Divide: Illness and Disability.* Leeds: The Disability Press.

PAHL, R. (1995) *After Success: Fin de Siècle Anxiety and Identity.* Cambridge: Polity Press.

PECKHAM, M. (1995) 'Foreword' in *Consumers and Research In The NHS.* Leeds: Department of Health.

RIBBENS, J. (1990) 'Interviewing - an "Unnatural Situation"?', *Women's Studies International Forum*, 12 (6): 579-92.

RIOUX, M. and BACH, M., eds. (1994) *Disability Is Not Measles: New Research Paradigms in Disability.* North York, Ontario: Roeher Institute.

SHAKESPEARE, T. (1996) 'Rules of Engagement: doing disability research' *Disability and Society*, 11 (1): 115-19.

SKRTIC, T. (1995) *Disability and Democracy: Reconstructing [Special] Education for Postmodernity.* London: University of Columbia Teachers Press.

SLEE, R. (1996) 'Clauses of conditionality: the "reasonable" accommodation of language' in L. Barton, ed., *Disability and Society: Emerging Issues and Insights.* London: Longman.

VERNON, G. (1996) 'Disability Politics by J. Campbell and M. Oliver: a review', *Disability Now*, September, p. 24.

WARD, L. and FLYNN, M. (1994) 'What Matters Most: Disability, Research and Empowerment' in M. Rioux and M. Bach, eds., *Disability Is Not Measles: New Research Paradigms in Disability.* York, Ontario: Roeher Institute.

WOODIWILL, G. (1993) 'Independent Living and Participation in Research'. Toronto: Centre for Independent Living in Toronto (CILT).

ZARB, G. (1992) 'On the Road to Damascus: First steps towards changing the Relations of Research Production', *Disability, Handicap, & Society*, 7 (2): 125-38.

CHAPTER 3

Funding for Change: Translating emancipatory disability research from theory to practice

Linda Ward

INTRODUCTION

Like most of the people contributing to this book, I do so wearing multiple hats. Each has a strong influence on what I have to say about 'doing disability research' and, in particular, about how we can make it more emancipatory in practice; I want to start by saying a bit about each hat to put my contribution into context.

The first hat is as Programme Adviser on Disability for the Joseph Rowntree Foundation, the largest single independent funder of applied research and development projects in the fields of housing, social care and disability in the UK. Joseph Rowntree was a Quaker; his beliefs and values have a continuing influence on the Foundation and its work. His goal was to 'seek out the underlying causes of social evil' (by research amongst other things) and in this way 'to change the face of England'. In other words, he could see the importance of research, but only in so far as it provided the tools and the impetus for change towards a more just society, particularly for those most disadvantaged within it.

The second hat is that of Senior Research Fellow at the Norah Fry Research Centre at the University of Bristol. The Frys were also Quakers like the Rowntrees and the research and other work carried out at the Centre is similarly informed by a human rights perspective and geared towards changes in the support and opportunities available to people with learning difficulties as equal members of the society in which they live.

Finally there is the 'personal' hat, made up of multiple strands – past experience in community development and welfare rights work, in the women's movement and feminist research and teaching; personal involvement with people with learning difficulties and other disabled friends within the disability movement.

All these hats affect my understanding of, and involvement in, the development of more empowering disability research aimed at bringing about positive changes in disabled people's lives. In this chapter I want to draw particularly on recent experiences within the Foundation and the Norah Fry Research Centre to ask:

1. How far have we moved towards a more emancipatory disability research in practice over the last 5 years?

2. What progress has been made in involving people with learning difficulties in research that affects their lives?

3. What have we learned about ways of involving disabled children in projects?

4. What can we learn from all this about ways to promote positive change?

1. HOW FAR HAVE WE MOVED TOWARDS A MORE EMANCIPATORY DISABILITY RESEARCH IN PRACTICE?

Mike Oliver, in his contribution to this book, reviews progress in the funding policies and practices of the major funding bodies in this area: the Economic and Social Research Council (ESRC), the Department of Health, and the Joseph Rowntree Foundation. His verdict is that little has changed in reality even if superficially some gains appear to have been made. As far as the Joseph Rowntree Foundation is concerned, he argues that 'little funding has gone to research which could generally be called emancipatory.' Not surprisingly, given the Foundation's key role in funding the seminal 'Researching Physical Disability' series, he views this as 'perhaps most disappointing of all' (Oliver, 1997, p24). I would agree with Oliver that progress remains frustratingly slow; but, as a pragmatist, I would point to a significant number of small steps which have been taken by the Foundation in recent years to ensure that the research that it funds moves closer to the criteria set out by him and others for more empowering or emancipatory disability research.

First, there is the avowed commitment to only funding research which locates itself within the social model of disability, a policy deriving from the inception of the Foundation's Advisory Group on Disability of which Oliver was an original, key, member, and significant resource and ally to the author. Nowadays, an avowed commitment to the social model of disability is relatively commonplace (in principle if not in practice) but in 1988 this was far from true. As a major funding body, the Foundation was able to play a significant consciousness-raising role in firmly stating its commitment to the social model of disability and its expectation that those seeking funding would follow suit.

Second, with the advent of the NHS and Community Care Act and the official commitment to 'user involvement' came the requirement of the Foundation's then Community Care and Disability Committee that all proposals submitted to it should strive for appropriate user involvement at all stages of the research or development process. Thus the stage was set for searching questions to be asked of non-disabled researchers who had not sought partnerships with organisations of disabled people in putting forward their research proposals.

Third was the commitment to ensuring that at least one person on the Foundation committee handling funding proposals for disability projects should themselves be a disabled person (with relevant experience) involved with disabled people's organisations and the disability movement.

Fourth, the Foundation's general commitment to only funding projects which have clear potential for bringing about policy and practice changes which will be positive for people's lives, and its commitment to 'staying with' projects funded (ensuring that their findings are promoted widely to a variety of different audiences and that questions are asked about 'what should happen next' to take things further) have been closely applied to disability projects. Thus, for example, a whole programme of work around independent living and direct payments has developed from the original work by Jenny Morris comparing disabled people's experiences of different kinds of community care services and how far they were facilitative of their independence (Morris, 1993); through Gerry Zarb and Pamela Nadash's work for BCODP, comparing the costs and quality of services provided by local authorities as compared with those purchased by people through direct or indirect payments (Zarb and Nadash, 1994); to a continuing programme of work exploring how direct payments can be made to work for people with learning difficulties (Holman and Collins, 1997) and, in the future, perhaps, older people.

Foundation staff have also had access to some Disability Equality Training. As a result of all these developments the Foundation – officers, Committee and Trustees – are all significantly more aware of disability research issues than they were 5 years ago. Traditional (positivist) research proposals will simply not get funded. Nor will research proposals masquerading as more emancipatory because of token references to 'consultation' with individual disabled people. Where proposals originate from non-disabled people and their organisations, then the assumption is that a proper partnership with organisations of disabled people should be in place. Where the Foundation commissions disability research then the means of involving disabled people and their organisations within the proposed is explicitly required to be outlined. Within our new Disabled Children's Programme (to which I return below) the involvement of disabled children as consultants, and in other ways is similarly expected. The experiences of disabled young people are placed centre stage. There are equivalent expectations of meaningful user involvement in research concerning people with learning difficulties (see below). There is increasing attentiveness to the need to support more appropriate and emancipatory research methodologies (as, for example, in the research on Deaf and hearing people working together, currently being undertaken at the Centre for Deaf Studies at the University of Bristol) and the need to ensure that key messages from research are shared in ways which make them easily accessible to their intended audience, as, for example illustrated leaflets to disabled children and illustrated magazines and tapes for people with learning difficulties (see below). Where the target audience is those involved with disabled people rather than disabled people themselves – as, for example, in a Foundation funded project to encourage people to 'hear the voice of people with dementia' – then imaginative strategies for disseminating ideas are being pursued – in this case via a card quiz game (Kindred and Goldsmith, 1997).

Clearly, there is still a long way to go. Not all of the disability projects funded by the Foundation meet all the criteria set out by Oliver (chapter 1 in this volume) but, I would suggest, that all of them address some. It remains true that the number of research projects conceived and undertaken by disabled people's organisations remains small but this is not surprising. Many organisations of disabled people would rather 'do' than 'research'. They are, moreover, almost always better equipped to do the former than the latter. Sometimes, the Foundation can have an important role in marrying up the separate and complementary skills and expertise of an organisation of disabled people which knows which issues need to be researched, with those of a consultant or non-disabled researcher, who has the skills required to ensure that the work undertaken satisfactorily meets both the goals of the disability organisation and the requirements of methodologically robust research. Thus, the Foundation was instrumental in ensuring that the crucial research on direct payments for disabled people was undertaken by researchers with unarguable research expertise but working to the agenda of disabled people (BCODP) who knew what the appropriate issues were to be explored (Zarb and Nadash, 1994). Similarly the Foundation has been instrumental in funding consultancy to support REACT (Preston Research Action on Learning Disability), a group of young people with learning difficulties, to carry out a research project of their own.

Increasingly, the Foundation is able, through its privileged position in networks of researchers, professionals and disabled people and their organisations, both to learn how things might be done better and to educate others to act accordingly. In the wake of a substantial amount of work which has successfully involved people with learning difficulties in research we are now encouraging those who wish to undertake work with other marginalised and traditionally silenced groups to think of how they could do this in an empowering way within our 'Promoting voices and choices' programme.

Innovative projects on 'hearing the voice of people with dementia' (Goldsmith, 1996) and on issues confronting people with aphasia (being undertaken at City University) are to be joined by exciting work with children with autism, where research has almost exclusively been located to date within the medical model of disability. While there is still a long way to go before the work that the Foundation funds meets all the criteria of Oliver's ideal emancipatory research agenda, it is important not to overlook some of the significant progress that has been made. Below I look in turn at developments in research involving people with learning difficulties and research involving disabled children, as positive examples of change.

2. INVOLVING PEOPLE WITH LEARNING DIFFICULTIES IN RESEARCH

The research process – relying heavily as it does on intellectual skills – is, by definition, less easily accessible to people with learning difficulties than it is to people with other kinds of, non-intellectual, impairments. But the debate about the emancipatory research paradigm which was fuelled by the seminar series on researching physical disability has largely ignored the particular issues which arise in relation to research involving people with learning difficulties. Those actively pursuing more empowering research strategies as allies of people with learning difficulties have yet to add their experiences to the emancipatory research paradigm debate, though they have clearly much to contribute (e.g. Rodgers, 1996). Nonetheless, there has been a positive sea change in ideas and expectations about appropriate ways of understanding and undertaking research involving people with learning difficulties (at least in some quarters) which seeks to respect and further their agenda for empowerment.

The most basic and fundamental change has been the recognition that people with learning difficulties, like non-disabled people and people with other kinds of impairments, might appropriately be involved in research as participants and respondents. While Oliver and others have, quite appropriately, commented on the negatives associated with research which 'rips off' disabled participants, by simply using them to obtain information without involving them in constructing or implementing the research agenda, for people with learning difficulties the recognition that they are appropriate respondents in research about their lives and the services that they use is a victory won only in the last 10 years. Before that 'user views' if sought at all were solicited from parents or professionals rather than people with learning difficulties themselves. In the intervening decade or so significant progress has been made in recognising that people with learning difficulties are the best commentators on their experiences and that it behoves researchers to acquire and develop innovative research skills which can access the views of people with learning difficulties who may only have limited verbal communication skills or may communicate in other ways entirely (see, for example, Atkinson, 1988; Beresford, 1997; Marchant and Page, 1993; Minkes *et al*, 1995; Simons, 1994; Ward, 1997a; 1997b). Of course, there is real scope here for inappropriate exploitation of people with learning difficulties by seeking their views in the 'rip off' research tradition appropriately condemned by Oliver, which is of primary benefit to researchers and professionals rather than people with learning difficulties themselves. But there are positive signs of funding bodies, like the Foundation, and researchers (e.g. McCarthy, 1997 amongst others) paying careful attention to ensuring that research undertaken is potentially empowering and, certainly not disempowering or exploitative of the participants with learning difficulties involved.

But beyond this basic right – to be consulted in research which affects your life – there have been more important gains. The Foundation, in its expectations about research involving disabled people, states clearly that they should be involved in all stages of the research process. We now have positive models of practical ways in which people with learning difficulties can, and have been, involved in research in a variety of ways: as originators of the research idea; as advisers or consultants to a research project; as research workers or interviewers; and as disseminators of research findings (see Ward (1997a)).

ORIGINATING RESEARCH IDEAS

A recent project funded by the Foundation and undertaken by researchers at the Norah Fry Research Centre originated in the concern of people with learning difficulties in the Bristol area about the extent to which they were involved in the recruitment of staff in their homes and day centres. The local self-advocacy group had written to the Social Services Committee about the importance they attached to this. Through a small survey of 11 local day centres, they found that opportunities for involvement in recruiting staff existed in principle but in practice were limited. Researchers at the Norah Fry Research Centre were alerted by them to this issue. The researchers sought funding for a more substantial research project on user involvement in recruitment with a view to encouraging better practice in the area. The research workers were non-disabled but were advised throughout by four panels of people with learning difficulties. They gave advice on the content and design of an accessible leaflet about the project; tested out the materials for the pictorial interview schedule for people with learning difficulties in the study and gave their own experiences of involvement in staff recruitment to guide the researchers in their formal interviews. Outputs from the project included a resource pack for supporters working with people with learning difficulties on how to facilitate involvement at all stages of the recruitment process (Townsley et al, 1997) and an accessible leaflet with factsheets giving clear ideas for action for people with learning difficulties themselves (Townsley and Macadam, 1996). The Foundation has now supported further work to help implement developments in this area in a variety of local organisations.

UNDERTAKING RESEARCH AND ACTING AS ADVISERS

The last few years has seen a gradual increase in the number of research projects which have been undertaken by people with learning difficulties themselves, not just as advisers or consultants (see, for example, Whittaker et al, 1991; Whittaker, 1997). In Bristol, for example, a group of people attending a local day centre were approached by a local NHS Trust to find out where gender issues were particularly significant in service provision. The group of 11 men and women and their supporter took responsibility for deciding the questions to be asked, the format in which information would be collected and the design of the illustrated questionnaire, with support from a member of staff at the Norah Fry Research Centre. The researchers divided up the work involved in mailing out 400 copies of the questionnaire and analysing the material returned. They agreed the rates of pay for the work involved and were involved in disseminating the information they collected (see Minkes et al, 1995; and Townsley 1995, for further details).

In London, the organisation of people with learning difficulties, People First, was involved, with the support of the Joseph Rowntree Foundation, in a study of the experiences of people with learning difficulties moving from long stay institutions into homes in the community. With support from an adviser from Charities Evaluation Services, two interviewers from People First were trained to undertake the evaluation from carrying out the interview to analysing and presenting the material in a report, a summary and a tape (see People First, 1994). Elsewhere, the Nottingham-based Advocacy in Action group has helped the Notting Hill Housing Trust survey the views and experiences of tenants in their supported housing, including those tenants who could not respond to a written survey but could contribute their views with the aid of pictures, sounds, symbols and audio tapes (Notting Hill Trust, 1994). Other examples of service evaluation by people with learning difficulties are given in Whittaker (1997).

In other projects people with learning difficulties are increasingly playing a crucial role as consultants and advisers. At the Norah Fry Research Centre it is becoming the norm for research projects involving people with learning difficulties to recruit an advisory panel to help researchers formulate their projects appropriately. Thus, for example, in a recent Foundation funded project on the impact of legislative changes on opportunities for adult education for people with learning difficulties a group of six students with learning difficulties met during the lifetime of the project to design the letter which went out to self-advocacy groups with a tape inviting their views and experiences and guiding the questions which were used by interviewers in visits to particular colleges. Their involvement highlighted significant aspects of adult education (for example bullying by non-disabled students) which might otherwise not have been included in the research (Macadam and Sutcliffe, 1996a; 1996b). In another research project on the impact of changes in the law on registered homes for people who lived with other families – adult placements – the consultants with learning difficulties were able not only to advise on key words and important topics to include, and to test out the pictures which were used to enable people with learning difficulties to take part in the study, but also to articulate to the researchers the positives and negatives of adult placements from their perspective: often very different from those of the practitioners and policy makers involved (Robinson and Simons, 1996a; 1996b).

As a funder of research involving people with learning difficulties, the Foundation would now expect all research projects in this area which were not undertaken by people with learning difficulties themselves to demonstrate firm evidence of partnership with their organisations and their involvement as interviewers or consultants and advisers with appropriate payment of fees (with due attention being paid to the method of payment so that rights to state benefits are not affected).

DISSEMINATION

The Foundation, because of its commitment to ensuring that the findings from the projects it funds become part of a process of change, places an enormous emphasis on dissemination. Traditionally, this has been aimed at policy makers and practitioners, who were seen to be in a position to bring about change. Now, however, there is recognition that people with learning difficulties are effectively disempowered by research if its findings are not accessible to them. As a result, the Foundation has funded an ongoing series of short, illustrated magazines (accompanied by tape) conveying key messages for people with learning difficulties from projects which it has funded. These are sent free to 1,100 self-advocacy groups and day centres in the UK and are also available on a subscription basis to other organisations and individuals. An evaluation of the pilot series was overwhelmingly positive; ideas for further improving the series on the basis of comments received from people with learning difficulties are now in hand and a guide for others on producing information in a simple and illustrated form is now available (Townsley and Gyde, 1997).

The development of the series has been aided by an advisory group of people with learning difficulties and the expectation is that every researcher producing a draft Plain Facts will test out the appropriate key findings or messages to be included within it with people with learning difficulties in their local area. This is critical. Experience shows that even those most committed to making information accessible can unwittingly produce information which is not. Andrew Bright, of People First, London, for example, found in his evaluation of information produced by Southwark Inform (which was set up to provide accessible information to people with learning difficulties) that posters with photographs were best understood by people with learning difficulties and that video also worked well. However, information using symbols did not because people with learning difficulties did not understand them. His conclusion?

'We felt that people with learning difficulties should have been involved from the beginning, both in the day-to-day running of the project and in testing out the materials. This could have resulted in more people understanding more of the information' (Bright, 1997: 44).

It is, of course, also important that people with learning difficulties should be actively involved in the dissemination of research findings, as well as being enabled to have access to them. Over the last few years, there have been increasing, often powerful, examples of people with learning difficulties playing a key role in seminars and conferences based on project findings and in generating material in non-traditional or printed ways. Thus, for example, a Foundation funded project on crime against people with learning difficulties resulted not only in a report aimed at policy makers and practitioners (Williams, 1995) but also, as a result of pressure from the people with learning difficulties involved in the project, in a video in which they participated and a skills pamphlet to accompany it (Gyde *et al,* 1995). More recently, the messages from that project have been shared even more widely with people with learning difficulties as the Strathcona Theatre Company of people with learning difficulties have embarked on a nation-wide tour of their play 'Error of Judgement' and accompanying educational workshops.

INVOLVING DISABLED CHILDREN AND YOUNG PEOPLE IN RESEARCH

Just as people with learning difficulties have, traditionally, been liable to exclusion even from voicing their views in research which affects their lives, so too have the voices and experiences of disabled children and young people been ignored and silenced. The Children Act 1989 and the UN Convention on the Rights of the Child have slowly begun to change this in their embodiment of key principles that demonstrate respect for the views of children and paved the way for them to be consulted about decisions which affect them (Lansdown, 1995; Alderson, 1995). Organisations like The Who Cares? Trust have successfully promoted the perspective of young people themselves and their right to participate in policy and practice decisions affecting their lives. Other key organisations like the Save the Children Fund, have started to involve children and young people as partners in research affecting them (West, 1995). More relevantly for this paper, there is now a small, but growing body of work on ways of involving disabled children and young people in research studies (see, for example, Children and Society, 1996).

The Joseph Rowntree Foundation, in embarking on its Disabled Children and Young People's Programme, decided that it would, so far as possible, ensure that the principles embodied in its Disability Programme (whereby disabled people should be involved as partners in all stages of the research process) should be extended to research and development projects affecting disabled children and young people. Our expectation is that disabled children and young adults will be active participants in all projects concerning them, though we recognise that the involvement of some children, including those with profound and multiple impairments and those who do not communicate with speech or conventional signs will pose particular challenges. Involving disabled children in projects means paying careful attention to safeguards and strategies to maximise their participation and well-being. To facilitate this, we have drawn together resources, issues and strategies for guidance. What follows is a brief summary of key roles that disabled children and young people can play as partners in projects drawn from the guide by Ward (1997b).

PARTICIPATING IN RESEARCH

The first – and most basic step – is to recognise disabled children and young people as appropriate respondents in research which is about their lives. This involves both careful attention to issues of meaningful consent (see especially Alderson, 1995) and also to appropriate and imaginative techniques for working with children who may not read or speak (see Beresford, 1997 for a valuable review of the literature in this area). Encouraging participation in research, means paying attention to the right of disabled and young people not to participate or to change their minds about doing so. It involves the preparation of accessible, illustrated leaflets or material in other forms, which will give them some idea of what involvement will mean. For the researcher it requires adequate preparation, proper attention to relevant approaches and techniques, plus careful thought about how to bring interviews or other research encounters to a close while enabling the young person to express any issues of concern which may have arisen. Strategies for dealing with any distress which might have been aroused; arrangements for appropriate payment of fees where relevant and strategies for feeding back information both to participants and the wider groups whom they might represent are all necessary ingredients for a successful – and ethical – involvement (Ward, 1997b).

PLANNING AND CONSULTANCY

Research projects which may not originate from disabled children and young people themselves will, nonetheless, be greatly strengthened by consultation with them at the planning and subsequent stages. Sarah McCrum and Paul Bernal (1994) in their pamphlet aimed particularly at journalists stress how valuable consulting with children at an early stage of planning research (in their case for articles or programmes) can be:

> 'You could try to find out what issues are particularly important from their perspective (often surprising), what kind of children might take part or be interviewed, where you can find the right children, etc. These are all the same areas you would research for any interview but journalists often only ask adults, even when the subject concerns children....It is important to remember that children, like adults, talk best about subjects they are interested in' (p. 9).

In some places groups of disabled young people already exist and adult researchers (whether disabled or not) need to consult with them to check that any work proposed addresses issues they consider worth pursuing. Partnership can be very productive: the group of disabled young people may know the important issues to address and will have relevant insights and contacts. The other parties to the partnership can bring additional research skills to the process. Obviously, projects conceived and run by disabled young people are particularly important; building in specialised advice and support from others (for example, on research techniques) where this is welcome, may strengthen their endeavour. Experience at The Who Cares? Trust suggests that where young people complain of bad experiences of involvement it often centres on 'not knowing what's going on': involvement at the planning stage should avoid this and make it more likely that participating children and young people are given clear information on their role in the project and proper preparation and training as required.

Disabled children and young people are likely to have different perspectives from those of disabled adults. Research projects undertaken by adults will benefit from employing disabled young people as consultants to advise as the project progresses, with, of course, appropriate payment being made for involvement. Research projects also benefit from the ideas generated by advisory groups. Where projects concerning disabled children and young people are concerned, then it is probably better to set up a separate consultative group of disabled young people focusing on aspects of the project of particular concern to them, rather than having them involved in a larger group where they might feel outnumbered and overwhelmed by professionals and other adults. In some cases, it has become clear that it is more appropriate to involve disabled children and young people as consultants on an individual basis than to bring them together as a group: project workers need to be sensitive to both possibilities.

UNDERTAKING RESEARCH AND PROJECT WORK

The idea of involving young people as interviewers and project workers is still relatively novel. Alderson (1995) reports on the Barnardo's Young Interviewers project and includes copies of materials used together with a report on the young interviewers' experiences and views. Significantly, the young interviewers were uncertain about their competence to undertake the work beforehand but were subsequently confident enough to suggest that in future they should be involved in the interviewer training process!

McCrum and Bernal (1994) also stress the value of letting children have a say at the editing and analysis stage of the project, perhaps looking at early drafts and making comments or even having a fuller involvement. Where disabled children or young people cannot easily read then alternative means of sharing this process, perhaps via a group meeting or through using audio or video tapes, needs to be followed.

DISSEMINATION

Disabled young people also have a useful role to play in suggesting what the key messages from a project are for other disabled children and young people and how these messages can best be got across in terms of both content and of format or medium. They may be able to help with illustrations or by contributing to audio-tape summaries. Clearly it is vital that key findings from projects which are relevant to disabled young people are made available to them in appropriate and accessible ways whether this is via illustrated leaflets, cartoons, audio or video tapes. Some disabled young people may also wish to play a role in contributing to conferences or workshops, as the three young interviewers involved in the Barnardo's project did at the launch of Priscilla Alderson's report. Where disabled children and young people are involved in this way then careful preparation and skills training may need to be provided. The Who Cares? Trust gives useful advice for both journalists and young people in this area (The Who Cares? Trust, 1993).

CONCLUSION: FUNDING FOR CHANGE

The title I chose for this contribution was 'Funding for Change'. I have tried to show how a funding body which is idealistic in its original goals and values, pragmatic in its operational style, can do a good deal to begin to shift the balance of power in disability research and to help change the face of what is seen as acceptable, desirable or feasible within it. Of course, funding bodies like the Foundation have multiple missions, programmes and agendas, of which the movement to a more emancipatory disability research is only one. Inevitably, this means that not all that commentators like Oliver feel should be done, will be. Nonetheless, those changes that are publicly advocated and instituted (like those discussed in this chapter) have the potential to influence both other researchers (through their exposure to the Foundation's expectations) and other funders (as, for example, the National Lottery Charities Board in the research strand of its recent Health, Disability and Care grants round). The unifying characteristic of all the hats I mentioned in my introduction was the desire for positive, practical and empowering change for disabled and other marginalised and disadvantaged people. Debate and dialogue between the disability movement, disabled and non-disabled researchers and funding bodies has a critical, if necessarily sometimes uncomfortable, role to play in moving forward that agenda for change.

REFERENCES

ALDERSON, P. (1995) *Listening to Children: Children, Ethics and Social Research*. Barkingside: Barnardo's.

ATKINSON, D. (1988) 'Research interviews with people with mental handicaps', *Mental Handicap Research*, 1(1): 75-90.

BERESFORD, B. (1997) *Personal Accounts: Involving Disabled Children in Research*. London: The Stationery Office.

BRIGHT, A. (1997) 'Evaluation of information produced by Southwark Inform' in A. Whittaker, ed. *Looking at our services*. London: King's Fund.

Children and Society (1996) 10 (2) (Issue focusing on the ethics and methodology of research with children).

GOLDSMITH, M. (1996) *Hearing the voice of people with dementia: Opportunities and obstacles*. London: Jessica Kingsley.

GYDE, K., HENRY, L., WILLIAMS, C. (1995) *Cracking crime: A learning and resources pack on coping with crime for people with learning difficulties*. Brighton: Pavilion.

HOLMAN, A. and COLLINS, J. (1997) *Funding freedom. A guide to direct payments for people with learning difficulties*. London: Values Into Action.

KINDRED, M. and GOLDSMITH, M. (1997) *Quiz quest on hearing the voice of people with dementia*. University of Stirling: Dementia Services Development Centre.

LANSDOWN, G. (1995) *Taking Part: Children's Participation in Decision Making*. London: Institute for Public Policy Research.

MACADAM, M. and SUTCLIFFE, J. (1996a) 'College and adult education'. *Plain Facts*, No. 6. University of Bristol: Norah Fry Research Centre.

MACADAM, M. and SUTCLIFFE, J. (1996) *Still a chance to learn? A report on the impact of the Further and Higher Education Act 1992 on education for adults with learning difficulties*. Leicester: NIACE.

MARCHANT, R. and PAGE, M. (1993) *Bridging the Gap: Child Protection Work with Children with Multiple Disabilities*. London: NSPCC.

MCCARTHY, M. (1997) *The sexual experiences and sexual abuse of women with learning disabilities in institutional and community settings*. Middlesex University, PhD thesis.

MCCRUM, S. and BERNAL, P. (1994) *Interviewing Children: A Training Pack for Journalists*. Buckfastleigh: Children's Voices.

MINKES, J., TOWNSLEY, R., WESTON, C. and Williams, C. (1995) 'Having a Voice: Involving people with learning difficulties in research', *British Journal of Learning Disabilities*, 23 (3): 94-7.

MORRIS, J. (1993) *Independent lives? Community care and disabled people*. Basingstoke: Macmillan.

NOTTING HILL HOUSING TRUST (1994) *Supported housing tenants' survey 1994.* London: Notting Hill Housing Trust.

OLIVER, M. (1997) 'Emancipatory research: realistic goal or impossible dream?', in C. Barnes and G. Mercer, eds. *Researching Disability.* Leeds: The Disability Press.

PEOPLE FIRST (1994) *Outside but not inside ... yet?.* London: People First.

ROBINSON, C. and SIMONS, K. (1996a) *In Safe Hands: Quality and regulation in adult placements for people with learning difficulties.* Sheffield: University of Sheffield/ *Community Care.*

ROBINSON, C. and SIMONS, K. (1996b) 'Living with another family', *Plain Facts,* No. 2. University of Bristol: Norah Fry Research Centre.

RODGERS, J. (1996) *Healthy lives. How the lives of people with learning difficulties affect their potential for health.* Univeristy of Bristol, PhD thesis.

SIMONS, K. (1994) 'Enabling research: people with learning disabilities'. *Research policy and planning,* 12 (2): 4-5.

TOWNSLEY, R. (1995) 'Avon Calling', *Community Care,* Jan. 12-18, pp 26-7.

TOWNSLEY, R. and GYDE, K. (1997) *Writing Plain Facts.* York: Joseph Rowntree Foundation.

TOWNSLEY, R., HOWARTH, J., LE GRYS, P. and MACADAM M. (1997) *Getting involved in choosing staff.* Brighton: Pavilion Publishing/Joseph Rowntree Foundation.

TOWNSLEY, R. and MACADAM, M. (1996) 'Choosing staff', *Plain Facts,* issue 7. University of Bristol: Norah Fry Research Centre.

WARD, L. (1997a) 'Practising partnership: involving people with intellectual disabilities in research' in M. Bach and M. Rioux, (eds.) *Disability discourse: research public policy and human rights.* North York, Ontario: Roeher Institute.

WARD, L. (1997b) *Seen and Heard: involving disabled children and young people in research and development projects.* York: York Publishing.

WEST, A. (1995) *You're on your own: Young people's research on leaving care.* London: Save the Children.

WHITTAKER, A. (1997) *Looking at our services. Service evaluation by people with learning difficulties.* London: King's Fund.

WHITTAKER, A., GARDNER, S. and KERSHAW, J. (1991) *Service evaluation by people with learning difficulties.* London: King's Fund Centre.

THE WHO CARES? TRUST (1993) *Code of Practice for Media Representatives and Young People Under 18 In or Ex-care.* London: The Who Cares? Trust.

WILLIAMS, C. (1995) *Invisible victims: crime and abuse against people with learning difficulties.* London: Jessica Kingsley.

ZARB, G. and NADASH, P. (1994) *Cashing in on independence.* Derby: BCODP.

CHAPTER 4

Researching Disabling Barriers

Gerry Zarb

INTRODUCTION

This chapter provides a critical examination of research activities based on the social model of disability and, in particular, our current research on the definition and measurement of disabling barriers – the *Measuring Disablement in Society*[1] project – which is being carried out by the Policy Studies Institute (PSI) in association with the Disability Research Unit at the University of Leeds.

The project is intended to provide a model for undertaking large-scale participatory research based on the social model of disability. In practice there has been a number of significant problems in meeting this objective. Some of these problems have resulted from factors which it would have been all but impossible to predict. At the same time, some of the obstacles – particularly those relating to the structures for supporting the active participation of disabled people in the research – result from contradictions in both the social and material relations of research production and, as such, provide a salutary reminder that there is still a long way to go before the transformative potential of this kind of research can be fully realised. Nevertheless, there is still much encouragement to be drawn from the experience and important lessons to be learnt for the future development of disability research.

1 The Measuring Disablement in Society project is funded by the Economic and Social Research Council (Grant award ref: R000235360)

DEFINING THE GOALS FOR DISABILITY RESEARCH

Before describing the details of our research, and the practical issues which we have had to address, I would first like to outline some of the guiding principles which underpin both how we have tried to engage in the research and, most importantly, what we are trying to achieve.

The research we are currently engaged in is essentially concerned with investigating institutional social and economic structures and the extent to which these structures contribute to the specific forms of exclusion experienced by disabled people. However it is worth remembering that, as with any form of social activity, research does not operate outside of such institutional structures but is in fact deeply implicated in their construction. It is important therefore to try and retain a critical awareness about how our work can either contribute to or challenge the particular forms of exclusion we are researching. This in turn points to the important distinction between what have been termed the social and material relations of research production. As I have argued previously (Zarb, 1992), while researchers may have a degree of choice over how they engage with disabled people as part of their research activities (i.e. the social relations of research production), the extent to which either party can be said to be directing the overall research enterprise is constrained by the parameters set by funding institutions and policy makers who control the resources which enable them to undertake research in the first place:

> 'A critical appraisal of our research over the last few years indicates a clear relationship between the level of participation of disabled people in decision making about the research, the extent of consultation during and after the research, and who instigated and funded the research (i.e. disabled people or traditional funding institutions). In other words, the material relations of research production can be demonstrated as constraining the social relations of research production. This in turn has influenced how the objectives of the different projects were defined and operationalised, the kinds of questions we asked, and what happened to the products of the research – including the crucial question of whether or not there were any practical benefits to disabled people' (Zarb, 1992, p.129)

The question of whether or not research brings any practical benefits to disabled people points to one of the other guiding principles underpinning the development of the *Measuring Disablement* research project. A key objective for the research has been to develop methodologies which would enable us to identify and quantify disabling barriers. This was in part motivated by a need to address the conceptual and methodological criticisms of existing social model research from within the academic and research communities. In particular, the criticism that research based on the social model of disability has failed to provide 'a thought through alternative research strategy, or an adequate approach to the diverse views and experiences of disabled people in different contexts' (Bury, 1996). While I would have a great deal of difficulty accepting the charge that the social model lacks conceptual clarity, the arguments relating to the perceived under-development of empirical research tools consistent with the social model do seem to have a certain justification. However it is important to recognise that this situation is itself largely the product of existing material relations of research production as, prior to the *Measuring Disablement* project, the vast majority of funding for large-scale primary research had been devoted to work based on the individual model of disability, thus denying researchers the opportunity to redress the perceived imbalance in the empirical knowledge base supporting these two approaches.

The development of methodologies to redress this imbalance is of more than academic interest however. As noted earlier, our overriding objective was to provide research tools which could lead to clearer identification of disabling barriers, thereby contributing to the process of highlighting the particular forms of exclusion they help to create and maintain. At the same time, any attempt to challenge the criticisms levelled at social model research by seeking to develop greater methodological rigour is a relatively 'risky' enterprise in that the distinctions between competing research paradigms can sometimes appear blurred. Great care is needed therefore to ensure that the orientation of the research to disabled people's exclusion is made explicit from the outset. This is particularly important in the context of expectations about how the products of the research are used and the extent to which our research activities could be said to have any transformative or emancipatory potential.

A crucial but often poorly understood distinction between participatory and emancipatory research is that the former simply involves disabled people in research, while the latter means that the research is actually controlled by them as part of a broader process of empowerment (Zarb, 1992). The active participation of disabled people is therefore a necessary but not a sufficient condition for emancipatory research. Unless disabled people themselves are actively involved in determining the aims, methods and uses of the research then, clearly, it could not lay any claim to having any transformative potential. In this respect I certainly agree with Mike Oliver's argument that the participatory approach does not really go any further than allowing previously excluded groups to participate in the research 'game' whereas emancipatory research is concerned with 'conceptualising and creating a different game, where no one is excluded in the first place' (Oliver, 1997).

My main purpose in drawing the distinction between participatory and emancipatory research however was to offer a corrective to the idea that research carried out within existing material relations of research production could possibly contribute directly to any transformative action with respect to disabled people's position in society. I also wanted to emphasise that – even within these constraints – we are still able to exercise some meaningful choices about how we work with disabled people. In other words, we are still able to exercise some control over the social relations of research production. While accepting that this situation does not fundamentally alter existing power structures, it need not lead us to a completely negative conclusion about the value of the social relations we create or, for that matter, about what the products of our research can achieve.

WHAT CAN DISABILITY RESEARCH ACHIEVE?

As I have already suggested, disability research can only be said to be transformative to the extent that disabled people (and other groups or organisations with an interest in challenging social and material exclusion) are able to use such research as an aid to bringing about changes in the status quo. Indeed, as Barton (1996) has argued, this is (or should be) the litmus test for the whole sociological enterprise and is not in any way the exclusive concern of either disabled people or disability research.

Following the publication of the special issue of *Disability and Society* in 1992, there has been an ongoing debate about the nature of participatory and emancipatory research and some commentators have – quite rightly – continued to question whether any disability research to date could be said to have passed the test of contributing to the empowerment of disabled people (see chapter 2 by Mike Oliver in this volume). However, while sharing in much of this scepticism, I do not believe that the situation is entirely negative. Indeed, I would go further than this and argue that there are practical examples of research which has, and will continue to, contribute to the process of emancipation among both particular groups, and among disabled people as a whole.

The fact that these are still vastly outnumbered by research projects which have at best done nothing to contribute to the process of empowerment and, at worst, have often helped to shore up disablist social structures should not distract our attention from the transformative potential of the few exceptions to this rule. Similarly, while none of these examples are without their contradictions and limitations, this does not mean that they should be rejected out of hand. Emancipation is not an event or series of events with a fixed beginning and end. Rather, it is an ongoing dialectical process of growth and development which, as the history of the disabled people's movement itself illustrates, is essentially characterised by conflict and resolution. It should not be surprising, therefore, that disability research is also characterised by contradictions which remain to be fully resolved.

The most important example of research which has contributed to the empowerment of disabled people is probably the work on disability and discrimination carried out by Colin Barnes for the British Council of Disabled People (BCODP) (Barnes, 1991). The subtitle for this research was 'the case for anti-discrimination legislation', reflecting one of the principal aims of the research which was to help bring about the introduction of civil rights for disabled people. While the disabled people's movement has not yet succeeded in its aim of securing comprehensive civil rights, it is undoubtedly the case that the evidence compiled by this research has provided a bedrock on which to base the campaign for achieving this goal and will continue to do so as the history of the campaign for civil rights unfolds. As Rachel Hurst (1995) has pointed out, the BCODP commissioned research on disability discrimination has been a major influence, not only in terms of reformulating disability as a rights issue, but also in terms of shaping the agenda for disability research:

'Within this country I would like to say that I think the disability movement has played a major role in the whole battle, this whole struggle at the international level, partly because we have been so marginalised here. As a result we have turned ourselves into thinkers and articulators and that articulation and that thinking about our oppression have been very useful tools. The book that BCODP[2] published in 1991 on disabled people and discrimination in the UK has been the basis for people's thought throughout Europe and in fact there is now going to be a research study throughout Europe based on the findings in that book. It is very important' (Hurst, 1995: 94-5).

In practical terms, one of the key contributions of the research was to refute the arguments that disabled people do not experience structural discrimination. As Richard Wood has pointed out, the research also helped to support a series of civil rights bills in the UK parliament and, despite the fact that none of these were successful, the evidence it presented has nevertheless been of fundamental importance in maintaining the disability rights campaign (Wood, 1996). Similarly, our current research on disabling barriers – which builds on this earlier work – is developing practical tools for measuring the extent of particular sources of discrimination which are intended for disabled people and others to use in their own efforts to monitor and challenge such exclusion. As noted in the extract from Rachel Hurst, the BCODP research on discrimination has also had a similar influence on other disability research projects which may, in turn, contribute to the ongoing struggles for comprehensive civil and human rights legislation, both nationally and internationally.

There have, in addition, been recent examples of research which has contributed directly to specific changes in policy or practice. More generally, there have been research projects which have contributed to making visible the experiences of particular groups of disabled people, thereby directly challenging the particular forms of exclusion and marginalisation which they face.[3] An example of the former was the work on direct payments which PSI carried out on behalf of BCODP (Zarb and Nadash, 1994) which effectively demonstrated the validity of the independent living movement's claims that direct payments were a more cost-effective solution to meeting disabled people's personal assistance needs than dependency creating services. As John Evans and Frances Hasler (1996) have pointed out, the research commissioned by BCODP has made a major contribution to the campaign for legislation to bring direct payments into the mainstream of social policy:

2 Barnes (1991)

3 See for example Shakespeare et al (1996) and Vernon (1997)

'Our research was the first study to combine the issues of cost and quality. It showed that on both counts direct payments are preferable, both cheaper and better. Information from our research was used by our allies in persuading the politicians to bring in direct payments. ... Interestingly enough, a week before the BCODP/PSI launch of the Direct Payment research findings, the Minister of Health announced that it was the Government's intention to bring about Direct Payments legislation in the next parliamentary year. We were ecstatic! After five years of campaigning vigorously, we had achieved the beginning of our main goal. We were more than pleased that the research and the lobbying had the impact that we were hoping for' (Evans and Hasler, 1996)

A key feature of the particular examples noted above is that they were either commissioned directly by accountable organisations controlled by disabled people (i.e. BCODP) or, as with our current research on *Measuring Disablement in Society*, explicitly influenced by disabled people's agenda on the important issues which research should be addressing. Another important feature which they share is the active involvement of disabled people in both defining and carrying out the research. Colin Barnes' research on disability discrimination for example was one of the first of many projects carried out by the Disability Research Unit at Leeds. Similarly, the research proposal which led to the work on direct payments was drawn up by members of BCODP's Independent Living Committee prior to the research being commissioned, while nearly all of the interviewing for the project was carried out by disabled people who were themselves personal assistance users. Disabled people have also been actively involved in both the design and execution of our current work on disabling barriers.

ABOUT THE *MEASURING DISABLEMENT IN SOCIETY* RESEARCH

The *Measuring Disablement in Society* research project was started in summer 1994 and is now due to be completed by the end of 1997. The project is intended to provide empirical evidence on the physical, social and economic barriers faced by disabled people and attempts to demonstrate how such barriers can be measured. In contrast to research based on the individual model of disability, the study is evaluating key areas of social life and organisation in terms of the degree of disablement (i.e. exclusion) they create.

In practical terms, the project is essentially a methodological one. As noted earlier, one of the main criticisms levelled against social model research has been that it has lacked fully developed methodologies which would allow some of the primary propositions contained in the model to be subjected to empirical analysis. By attempting to at least make a start on developing such methodologies it is hoped that the research will help to demonstrate that it is possible to carry out sound 'objective' and empirical research within the framework of the social model of disability.

All of the data we are collecting is clearly focused on measuring deficits in society rather than in individuals, which is of course the primary focus for research based on the individual model of disability (Zarb, 1995a). So, for example, rather than asking questions like how far individuals with mobility impairments can walk unaided, we have carried out a national survey designed to measure how much of the existing rail and bus network is accessible to people with different types of impairments. Similarly, we are carrying out empirical analysis on the provision of accessible housing and the barriers to disabled people's access to public spaces and local amenities. We have also done work on developing tools for measuring the degree to which disabled people are able to influence local planning in areas such as the provision of social services and town planning. We are currently (summer 1997) carrying out an interview survey on disabled people's objective experiences of different forms of disablement such as educational disability, employment disability, information disability and so on, while the final part of the project will be focused on quantitative analysis of social and economic exclusion at national and regional levels.

However, this emphasis on the objective and measurable dimensions of social exclusion may, in itself, leave the project open to the counter-criticism that the research ignores the subjective or experiential aspects of discrimination. Honesty requires an admission that this was not considered to be a major concern at the outset. However, recent debates about the social model of disability among disabled people and researchers do raise important questions about the extent to which our emphasis on structural issues might disguise and/or distort these experiential dimensions of disablement. Indeed, this issue has been the subject of debate with some of the organisations of disabled people who have been closely involved in the project's development and this has resulted in modifications being made to certain aspects of the research methodology. The parts of the research dealing with access barriers, for example, have undergone considerable modification from the design originally planned. While the original focus was on attempting to quantify particular physical features of buildings and places, this has now been supplemented by an experiential design which focuses on the ways in which disabled people actually use buildings and public spaces in the course of carrying out their day-to-day activities.

HOW THE PROJECT HAS BEEN CARRIED OUT

The first six months of the project were taken up with wide-ranging consultation between the researchers and numerous local and regional organisations of disabled people, government departments and other groups with an interest in different types of disabling barriers. While this process has, to a certain extent, been on-going, the main wave of consultation was used to inform the methodological design of the project and to identify ways of defining and measuring the different types of disabling barriers to be covered by the research. These initial plans are subsequently being refined in consultation with local organisations of disabled people and other organisations in the two case study areas in which the main stage of field work is located.

We also organised a major two-day conference on the theme of 'Removing Disabling Barriers' which was held at the Policy Studies Institute in September 1994. Papers presented at the conference – mostly by leading disabled academics and activists – drew together the evidence on the extent and causes of discrimination and disadvantage faced by disabled people and examined the policy options for removing the barriers to disabled people's participation in social and economic life (Zarb, 1995b). The conference has also made a very useful input into the development of the project and, perhaps more importantly, provided an important platform for generating interest in the ideas on which it was originally based. The fact that the conference was held at a time when the campaign for civil rights legislation was in full-swing certainly added an edge to the proceedings. The energy generated by participants during those two days probably did more to contribute to the empowerment of disabled people than anything else the project has done since.

The research team has also been working with local authorities and local organisations of disabled people in two case study areas – Manchester and Leicester – where the second stage of the research is located. Local disabled people are also being recruited to carry out some of the fieldwork in these areas, including the access surveys mentioned earlier. This part of the research involves a more detailed investigation of barriers at a local level and provides an opportunity to develop and test different ways of measuring levels of inclusion and exclusion which, hopefully, local authorities and local disability organisations might be able to adapt for their own use after the project has finished. Consultation with local organisations of disabled people has been undertaken at each stage and will continue up to and including the production of the final set of findings from the research.

BARRIERS TO DEVELOPING INCLUSIVE RESEARCH PRACTICE

As discussed earlier, it has always been the intention that disabled people should be actively and closely involved with both the design and execution of the project. In practice this involvement has taken a variety of forms including the recruitment of disabled researchers, the involvement of local organisations of disabled people as paid consultants to the project, and the canvassing of comments on our proposed research plans from a number of local and regional organisations in both the case study areas and elsewhere. In terms of the scale of disabled people's involvement, this aspect of the project has been relatively successful. However, there have also been some significant practical problems along the way which have created obstacles to disabled people being as fully involved as we had intended.

Three main areas of difficulty have been encountered: the employment of disabled researchers; the resources required to facilitate the maximum involvement of local disabled people; and conflicts between the need for such involvement and the institutional constraints posed by the material relations of research production.

Turning first to the issue of employing disabled researchers. In one of the keynote presentations at the national conference held to mark the end of the 1991-92 Disability Research seminar series, Vic Finkelstein outlined an agenda for change in the way research is carried out. One of the key issues highlighted in his presentation related to the active involvement of disabled people through their employment and development as researchers. This is not only important in terms of utilising disabled people's experience and expertise to inform the content of research, but also in terms of directly challenging social and economic exclusion:

'...as long as disabled people avoid, or are discouraged from, participation in research into their own affairs they will remain passive and dependent upon others. This means that the "subjectivity" of disabled people should be regarded as an "objective" asset, to be cultivated in the research setting' (Finkelstein, 1992)

This was certainly one of the guiding principles informing the organisation of the *Measuring Disablement* research. In addition to involving local organisations of disabled people in the project's development, we were also keen that new researchers recruited to work on the study should be disabled people. Indeed at the outset, both research posts which we needed to fill were advertised on the basis that priority would be given to disabled applicants and this intention had also been specified in the original funding application made to the Economic and Social Research Council (ESRC). In taking this step we were aware that, as a result of the limited opportunities available to disabled people wishing to develop research careers, we were not certain to receive a large number of applications from people able to offer both a range of practical research experience and a detailed understanding of the application of the social model to research on social and material exclusion. While the former obviously offers practical benefits, this can – as Vic Finkelstein suggests – be developed through training and on-the-job experience. Consequently, we were much more concerned to ensure that researchers employed to work on the project were able to demonstrate an awareness of some of the fundamental research issues around disabling barriers.

However, in practice, we soon found that there were considerable obstacles to achieving this seemingly straightforward objective. The problems started more or less straightaway as the first round of recruitment failed to produce any applications at all from disabled researchers. Consequently, the post had to be re-advertised, with the result that the start of the project was delayed for three months. The fact that we were initially unable to shortlist any disabled applicants also led to questions being raised within the Institute about whether or not we should be insisting on the post being filled by a disabled researcher. It was suggested that we needed to be sure that this would offer a particular kind of expertise which we could not have accessed by other means.

Other questions were raised – both on that occasion and in subsequent recruitment rounds – about the potential difficulty in managing the tensions between the 'subjective' and/or 'political' dimensions of disabled researchers experiences and the 'objectivity' of the research – particularly if they were, or had been, directly involved in the disability movement. This was not so much an internal concern but, rather, reflected our awareness of how the organisation and direction of the project might be viewed by those seeking to detract from the validity of social model research. As Finkelstein (1992) has argued, disabled people who become involved in this kind of work:

> '...often do so as a result of personal experience and this brings the subjective element out into the open. This subjectivity is immediately identified as a danger (while the able-bodied subjectivity goes unrecognised) and the applicant for the job can then be regarded as unsuitable' (Finkelstein, 1992)

While we were of course aware of the potential tensions in the relationship which a politically conscious disabled researcher might have to the research, it was understood that this was, in a sense, 'part of the deal'. Indeed, given that we were actively seeking researchers with an appropriate level of understanding of issues around social and material exclusion it would have been unrealistic to expect anything else. Rather, this subjectivity can be regarded as an asset in the context of disability research. This does not mean that any tensions and contradictions which do arise should be swept under the carpet, nor that we never have to face some difficult choices about the positions we adopt in a public setting. However, the primary aim in managing this relationship has always been simply to try and ensure that the subjective consciousness which disabled researchers bring to the project remains analytically focused.

The main difficulties in practice arise when we engage with the external world as there are always those who seek to challenge the validity of research which is suspected of diverging from the canons of 'scientific objectivity'. Our main 'weapon' in trying to deal with this kind of opposition has been to focus on the methodological rigour of the research through the adaptation of conventional research methods and through development of alternative methodologies informed by the social model. However, there is a sense in which this approach can be interpreted as a subordination of disability research to the ideological version of 'objectivity'. Further, while we did already have some awareness of this potential contradiction at the outset, it is certainly the case that the involvement of disabled researchers in the project has contributed to a heightened consciousness of the compromises which this involves. As a result there have been occasions when, because of the questions raised by disabled researchers, certain aspects of the project's methodology have been re-examined and/or altered in an attempt to make them more experientially grounded. The fact remains however that the project is still essentially seeking to meet head-on the methodological criticisms of social model research on the grounds that this is the best way to refute them. Only time will tell if this pragmatism has been successful and whether the compromises which have had to be made along the way have been worthwhile.

The second main area of difficulty associated with recruiting disabled researchers to work on the project relates to the organisation of the research and the structural barriers to accommodating the individual needs of the researchers involved. For two of the three disabled researchers who have worked on the project, this was either their first job since becoming disabled, or their first after an extended period out of employment. In both cases, therefore, the individuals concerned viewed their employment as 'experimental' in the sense that neither they nor the Institute could be sure either about how they would cope with the demands of the job, or exactly what accommodations might need to be made in terms of working arrangements. In the event, these turned out to be quite substantial.

For example, all of the disabled researchers recruited to work on the project requested, either at the outset, or not long after joining the project that they work on a part-time basis and/or work mostly from home. Although this is not a major problem in itself, it did require a fair amount of re-organisation in terms of team working, as well as the arrangements which needed to be made in order to try and avoid researchers becoming isolated from their colleagues. The restrictions on availability, combined with the considerable difficulties which two of the three researchers experienced with trying to use inaccessible transport systems, also meant that fieldwork (e.g. meetings with local organisations of disabled people, research interviews and so on) often needed to be re-allocated to other members of the research team or, in some instances, involved extra expenditure on providing accessible overnight accommodation so that the researchers did not have to undertake long journeys all on the same day.

All of these employment related issues were of course largely under our own control in the sense that, financial considerations aside, we were able to exercise choice over the accommodations which needed to be made. However, on this particular project we have also had to deal with the consequences of unforeseen problems relating to extended periods of sick leave and the impact which certain aspects of the work (particularly travel) have had on the researchers involved. While it would be inappropriate to go into any detail about the personal circumstances involved, it is the case that for reasons relating to either impairment or sickness, all three researchers found it necessary to leave the project after less than a year in post. It is also the case that the difficulties faced by these workers were added to by the very long delays in obtaining suitable equipment such as an adapted workstation, voice controlled computer software, and an electric wheelchair through the Access to Work scheme. (In fact, some of this equipment only arrived after the researcher concerned had already left!) The delays created by the necessity of readvertising the post each time, and the work lost due to ill-health, were detrimental to the project.

Statistically, the chances of three consecutive post-holders having to leave their jobs in this way must be viewed as pretty remote. We know from our contacts that other organisations employing disabled workers have had nothing approaching this level of sickness and staff turnover. To say that both the project and the workers involved have been unlucky would therefore be something of an understatement. The main purpose for recounting this sorry tale, however, is to examine the practical consequences which such eventualities have had for the project and, in particular, what our experiences can tell us about the social and material relations of research production.

The first point to note is that any research organisation faced with this set of circumstances will have to deal with some difficult choices about how to respond and about the extent to which they are able to support the researchers involved. I would like to think that we have been as flexible as possible in terms of trying to enable the individuals concerned to carry on working by making changes to working arrangements, accommodating periods of reduced productivity and – in one case – being prepared to hold the job open indefinitely rather than looking to terminate the contract after six months sick leave (as often happens elsewhere). In one sense these were not difficult choices as it was of course in our own interests to try to retain the services of able and talented researchers who we had been keen to recruit in the first place. At the same time, we were also aware of the practical difficulties this can create in terms of keeping the project on schedule (which we have failed to do) and the negative impact on the project's financial resources (the equivalent of at least 60 working days were lost as a result of these problems).

The most significant consequences of these staffing problems however were those relating to the relationship between ourselves and other organisations involved with the research, particularly the project's funders.

First, the protracted delays in progressing the research have had a negative impact on relationships between the research team and some (but, fortunately, not all) of the local organisations of disabled people with whom we have been working. Not surprisingly, the fact that we have not been able to deliver all that was promised from the research has meant that the considerable enthusiasm about the project which they expressed at the outset has gradually been replaced by varying degrees of cynicism, frustration and apathy. While it is to their great credit that the organisations concerned have not abandoned the project altogether, a considerable amount of effort is having to be spent on repairing this damage so that we can move forward together towards bringing the research to a satisfactory conclusion.

Second, the delays resulting from long-term staffing problems on the project have had very serious consequences for our relations with the organisation funding this research. As noted earlier, we have done our best to accommodate an unusual and unfortunate set of circumstances. However, the impact which this has on a research organisation's ability to cope with this kind of situation is obviously affected by the existing material relations of research production. As Barnes (1996) has pointed out, some disabled workers (particularly if they have 'unpredictable' or intermittent impairments) are always likely to experience a need for 'a more flexible and less demanding work schedule' from time to time and that this needs to be taken into account by funders:

> 'Clearly, if we are serious about encouraging disabled people to enter the research field ...... then these concerns must be accounted for in all future research proposals and research agendas. Moreover, funding agencies must also recognise that these are legitimate considerations and they must be encouraged not to discriminate against research organisations and researchers who adopt such a policy when awarding research contracts' (Barnes, 1996).

Unfortunately, in this particular case, the research funding body has not been able to accommodate the difficulties we have experienced as the regulations covering the funding for this project include specific and strictly enforced sanctions against failure to complete projects within the agreed timescale. This has resulted in the balance of the funding for the research being withheld. Together with the resources which we have already lost through extended periods of sick leave, this has created a shortfall in excess of £20,000. Commitment to the project is such that some members of the research team have volunteered to take unpaid leave in order to finish the work on the project. This will still leave some funds to be found from PSI's reserves. This has also meant that we have had to scale down some aspects of the consultation process, thereby reducing the extent of disabled people's involvement in the final stages of the research.

Again, this is in some ways an atypical situation. Nevertheless, our experience does also highlight some wider issues relating to the economics of doing disability research as some of the problems we have encountered are clearly endemic to the way in which the material relations of research production are organised.

The intense competition for research funding over recent years has led to many elements of research budgets being 'squeezed' in order to meet the increasing demands for 'value for money' from sponsors. There are a number of negative consequences of this trend which, as Colin Barnes has pointed out:

> 'has important and worrying implications for those of us trying to develop a more emancipatory research agenda... particularly with reference to disabled researchers' (Barnes, 1996).

This has certainly been the case with the *Measuring Disablement* research as several items of expenditure relating to both the employment of disabled researchers (e.g. expenses for facilitation and/or personal assistance), and the involvement of organisations of disabled people in the research (e.g. consultation fees) were declined at the time the research grant was awarded on the grounds that these were 'exceptional items' which the funding body was unable to support. Further, while a proportion of this additional expenditure could be offset by support offered though the Employment Service Access to Work scheme, in practice, this only applied to certain items of equipment and a partial contribution to travel expenses which has resulted in the costs having to be met from our own resources.

Similar comments apply to the costs of facilitating the involvement of local disabled people in the two case study areas. Again, some of these expenses – particularly consultation fees for the local organisation of disabled people advising the project on the design of the research – had to be met from our own resources by transferring funds which should have been used to pay for our own research time. In one case there have been additional expenses associated with the fact that many members of the local organisation of disabled people are Asian and require translation and interpreting services to facilitate their participation. Fortunately, these costs have subsequently been met by additional funding from the City Council concerned (Leicester). Altogether, the costs of facilitating the involvement of local disabled people in the two case study areas have amounted to around £10,000 yet none of these items was considered eligible for funding through the research grant mechanism.

CONCLUSIONS

Even without the additional staffing problems which have dogged the project all the way through, it is clear that the material relations of research production are far from ideal in terms of supporting the model of participatory research which we have been trying to follow. Nevertheless, I hope that the experience of the *Measuring Disablement* project, and other research projects based on similar principles, has demonstrated at least some of the possibilities for progressing the development of participatory research – despite the obstacles which exist. Whether or not such research can deliver anything beyond this in terms of contributing to the transformative process required by the emancipatory paradigm remains an open question. However, this is really a question which only disabled people themselves can answer and one which, ultimately, depends on the uses (if any) they and others find for the products of research. I remain optimistic that at least some of the products of our research will – eventually – pass this test but, as ever, only time will tell.

REFERENCES

BARNES, C. (1991) *Disabled People in Britain and Discrimination: A Case for Anti-discrimination Legislation*. London: Hurst and Co/BCODP.

BARNES, C. (1996) 'Observations on the economics of doing disability research', Paper presented at the Sociology and Disability seminar, Weetwood Hall, Leeds, 5 December 1996.

BARTON, L. (1996) 'Sociology and Disability: some emerging issues', in L. Barton, ed. *Disability and Society: Emerging Issues and Insights*. London: Longman.

BURY, M. (1996) 'Defining and Researching Disability: challenges and responses', in C. Barnes and G. Mercer, *Exploring the Divide: Illness and Disability*. Leeds: The Disability Press.

EVANS, J. and HASLER, F. (1996) 'Direct Payments Campaign in the UK', Paper presented at the European Network on Independent Living Seminar, Stockholm, 9-11 June 1996.

FINKELSTEIN, V. (1992) 'Setting Future Agendas', Keynote address presented at the Disability Research National Conference, Kensington, London, 1 June 1992.

HURST, R. (1995) 'International Perspectives and Solutions', in Zarb, G. ed., *Removing Disabling Barriers*. London: Policy Studies Institute.

OLIVER, M. (1997) 'Emancipatory Research: Realistic Goal or Impossible Dream?', in C. Barnes and G. Mercer, eds. *Doing Disability Research*. Leeds: The Disability Press., ch. 2.

SHAKESPEARE, T., GILLESPIE-SELLS, K. and DAVIES, D. (1996) *The Sexual Politics of Disability*. London: Cassell.

VERNON, A. (1997) 'Deafness, Disability and Multiple Oppression', in M. Corker and G. Zarb, eds. *Deafness and Disability: towards a new understanding*. London: PSI/Deafsearch.

WOOD, R. (1996) 'Have they run out of steam?', *Disability Now*, April 1996, p.12.

ZARB, G. (1992) 'On the Road to Damascus: First Steps Towards Changing the relations of Disability Research Production', *Disability, Handicap and Society*, Vol 7 (2): 125-38.

ZARB, G. (1995a) 'Modelling the Social Model of Disability', *Critical Public Health*, Vol 6 (2): 21-29.

ZARB, G., ed. (1995b) *Removing Disabling Barriers*. London: Policy Studies Institute.

ZARB, G. and NADASH, P. (1994) *Cashing In on Independence: Comparing the Costs and Benefits of Cash and Services*. Derby: BCODP/PSI.

CHAPTER 5

Psychiatric System Survivors and Emancipatory research: Issues, overlaps and differences

Peter Beresford and Jan Wallcraft

To approach emancipatory research in the survivors' movement, it is helpful first to have an understanding of the relation of the movement to disability and the disabled people's movement, as well as an understanding of the survivors' movement itself and of the issues facing survivors. We begin with the relation between survivors and disability and the disabled people's movement.

THE SAME BUT DIFFERENT

The relations between survivors and disability and between the survivors' and disabled people's movements are complex and there is little agreement about them. For example, there was only one mention of survivors in Jane Campbell and Mike Oliver's major examination of disability politics and the only organisation referred to is an organisation *for* mental health service users (Campbell and Oliver, 1996). Jenny Morris's exploration of feminism and disability on the other hand, included a chapter by a woman survivor, highlighting the links with disability and the disabled people's movement (McNamara, 1996). Some disabled people do not see survivors as disabled, because they do not have an impairment or their situation may not be permanent, while others do. Some survivors do not see themselves as disabled because they associate disability with the medicalisation of their distress. There are also fears and anxieties among survivors and disabled people about being associated with the negatives linked with the other group.

There are also important overlaps between the two groups. Some survivors also have physical or sensory impairments, often related to the chemical and other damaging 'treatments' like ECT, which they have experienced. Some people with impairments and with learning difficulties also have experience as survivors which may be linked with the way they have been treated as disabled people.

There are many similarities in how disabled people and survivors are treated in society. Both have their experience subjected to medical interpretation and 'treatment'. Both face social oppression and discrimination. As a result, both face disproportionate problems of poverty, unemployment, social and economic insecurity. Many survivors are included as 'disabled people' in the medical definitions upon which eligibility to disability benefits and services is based. Survivors are also included in the medically-based Disability Discrimination Act and some survivors are eligible to run their own personal assistance schemes under the Direct Payments Act.

There are also links and overlaps between the two movements. Some people involved in the survivors' movement are also involved in the disabled people's movement. Survivors were involved in the campaign for civil rights legislation. The British Council of Disabled People struggled successfully alongside Survivors Speak Out to gain the inclusion of survivors in direct payment legislation (Beresford, Gifford and Harrison, 1996).

THE PHILOSOPHY OF THE SURVIVORS' MOVEMENT

The survivors' and disabled people's movements are very different, yet also have important similarities. So far, most emphasis has been placed on the differences. Yet there is one difference which it is important to explore. This concerns the philosophies of the two movements.

The social model of disability, developed by the disabled people's movement, has provided a dynamic and developing conceptual framework which has been both liberating for individual disabled people and a basis for coherent and effective collective action and strategies. It underpins the commitment of the disabled people's movement to civil and human rights, its stress on self-organisation and the goals of independent living, social inclusion and anti-discrimination. It has also provided a framework for the emancipatory research of the disabled people's movement as well as being a subject of such research.

The survivors' movement does not have an equivalent of the social model. While some survivors have found the social model of disability helpful because of its stress on social oppression and discrimination, others reject it for themselves, because they do not see themselves as having any kind of impairment. They interpret their madness or distress in terms of different understanding, experience or perceptions, rather than as an impairment. The social model of disability, therefore, cannot simply be transposed to the survivors' movement, although some disabled commentators, in an effort to be inclusive, have done this.

The survivors' movement therefore does not have a clear philosophy of its own. This has long been seen by many of its members as one of its strengths and attractions. It has had the appeal of being a broad church, where people of very different experience, background, education and politics, could co-exist. Survivors Speak Out, for example, includes people who are opposed to demonstrations and direct action, as well as others who take part in them, both as survivors and as disabled people. There has been no pressure to conform to a particular belief system.

This does not mean that the movement is not informed by values and ideals. Where there has been a strong sense of agreement is that survivors should be treated with respect and have the right to speak for themselves. Involvement in the movement brings with it a strong sense of self-worth and shared experience and understanding. Survivors know that in the movement, psychiatric judgements on and interpretations of them do not rule. In this sense there is a challenge to the dominant ideology, but so far it has not developed into a shared alternative analysis and vision of distress.

It is not clear why the movement has developed in this way. It may be because of survivors' fears of replacing one rigid belief system, embodied in the medicalisation of madness and distress by the psychiatric system, with another, or of dividing rather than uniting survivors. One reason, which Peter Campbell identifies, is the concern about further reducing survivors' chances of gaining 'a decent hearing for their proposals' (Campbell, 1996a: 221). Thus while some founding members of the survivors' movement were either in contact with or sympathetic to the anti-psychiatry movement of the 1960s and 1970s, this should not be taken to mean that the movement is particularly informed by or reflects an anti-psychiatry position. Furthermore as Peter Campbell says:

> ' "Anti-psychiatry" has become a slogan that is routinely used by traditional mental health workers to denigrate and dismiss ideas that threaten their expert world-view and status' (Campbell, 1996a: 221).

The power of the psychiatric establishment and its influence on broader social values and understanding cannot be overstated. It has had a profound effect on the identity of survivors/mental health service users. While part of the dominant message about mental distress is that 'it can happen to anyone', the powerful subtext is that to use or have used mental health services or to experience mental distress is to have a fundamentally spoiled identity. This has many expressions at both individual and collective levels. It means that many mental health service users find it very difficult if not impossible to feel proud of who they are and do not see their situation as comparable with that of people with impairments. For them, this might seem almost like another manifestation of their madness. They can certainly expect it to be interpreted as such by the psychiatric system.

This expectation also means that many activists feel closely circumscribed in what they can do. They expect their views and analysis to be dismissed and attacked as extreme and symptomatic of their defective understanding, reason and intellect. Similarly, many fear that if they take direct action along the innovatory lines of the disabled people's movement, this will be seen as further evidence of their irrationality and madness and receive an aggressive and regulatory response.

Thus the survivors' movement's lack of a distinct and coherent philosophy may be traced to its desire to be inclusive and minimise conflict within, as well as a concern to limit attack from outside. We can also add to this the difficulties which the movement has had developing a philosophy because of the practical problems of very limited resources and restricted opportunities for survivors to get together to develop their thinking collectively. However the hole created by this lack of agreed and coherent philosophy has not remained unfilled. Instead at least two sets of ideas from the dominant ideology have moved in to occupy the space. These are the concepts of mental illness and consumerism. Both have important implications for the survivors' movement and research associated with it and both have added to the uncertainty and ambiguity of its thinking and activities.

Some members of the survivors' movement, including the authors, reject a medical model of madness and distress. They see it as intellectually unsustainable and deeply damaging to the people to whom it is attached. It is the equivalent of the individual medicalised model of disability. They reject the ideology of *mental illness*, as inextricably associated with pathology and inconsistent with securing the rights and needs of people experiencing madness or distress. The construct of 'mental illness' is a part of a modernist project which devalues the diversity of human experience and perceptions and is preoccupied with analysis, eradication, physicality and mechanical and chemical constraint, rather than understanding, empathy, support and an holistic approach to the body and self.

For many other members of the movement and many more users of mental health services generally, however, the idea of 'mental illness' is internalised. This is as a result of their broader socialisation and passage through the psychiatric system. It is also likely to be the only analytical framework with which they are familiar for understanding their situation, feelings and perceptions. The survivors' movement, including organisations like Survivors Speak Out, aware that its membership includes both people who reject and accept a medical model, has not adopted a clear position on the issue, to enable the two groups to continue in broad alliance.

The second key concept which has entered the survivors' movement is that of *consumerism*. Consumerism has emerged as a key idea in current health and welfare because of the broader shift to the political right and to the private market in the UK and its association with a new interest in 'consumer choice', 'user involvement' and 'needs-led' services. This interest in the individual service user as 'customer' and 'consumer' undoubtedly served as a major impetus and legitimation for the UK mental health service users/survivors' movement. Certainly survivors involved in developing the movement saw it as an opportunity to be used. Comparing mental health service users' and disabled people's groups, Marian Barnes and Polly Shardlow, distinguish between the strategies of the former which they see as based on 'consumerism' and of the latter, based on 'citizenship (Barnes and Shardlow, 1996a). But this raises a key point about the survivors' movement's use of consumerist ideas and rhetoric. These have frequently been adopted uncritically as symbols of a new determination to speak and act for themselves by individuals and groups who are not necessarily familiar with their ideological associations. It may be not be helpful or advisable to take their use at face value.

The indebtedness of the survivors' movement for what philosophy it has to exterior, dominant institutions and ideologies, is not only the result of its limited development of its own philosophy. It is also closely related to the nature of its relation with the mental health service system. The UK disabled people's movement has largely developed independently of disability professionals and the disability service system. It has placed an emphasis on developing organisations of disabled people and challenging the traditional dominance of organisations for disabled people. In the US, there is a strong tradition of separatism in the survivors' movement, most notably reflected in the work of Judi Chamberlin and her pioneering book, *On Our Own* (Chamberlin, 1988). But there is also another wing to the US movement which is more closely associated with the mental health system and dominant values.

THE SURVIVORS' MOVEMENT AND THE MENTAL HEALTH SYSTEM

In the UK, the survivors' movement has been closely linked with the mental health service system in two important ways. First, many of its activities have been based in the system; establishing self-advocacy groups and patients' councils within services and seeking to reform the service system. Second, much of its work has been undertaken in close association with professional 'allies' and through organisations *for* mental health service users. The dominant way of working has been co-operation rather than separatism. The organisations with which it has worked, many of which have been involved in service provision, as well as in campaigning, advocacy and research, have generally rested on a medical model of madness and distress. Conventional fudges, which some have adopted, like MIND's, talking about 'mental health' and 'people with mental health problems', rather than 'mental illness' do not separate it from the psychiatric system, nor offer either an intellectual or political way forward.

The survivors' movement's relation with the service system and these organisations is complex and ambiguous. It is linked with the movement's continuing reliance on these organisations for funding, employment and legitimation. To maintain relationships with them, therefore, there have been strong pressures to fudge the movement's philosophy, for both individual activists as well as the movement more generally.

The reading which we offer here of the development of the survivor's movement is one which highlights caution, collaboration and a desire to minimise conflict. What has been the result? This seems to be a movement which is fragmented, vulnerable and, as we have said, without a clear and agreed philosophical base. While, for example, the disabled people's movement has established one national umbrella organisation controlled by disabled people and their organisations, in the survivors' movement, there are several, including Survivors Speak Out, the United Kingdom Advocacy Network and MindLink. MindLink, which is perhaps the best resourced of the three, is linked with an organisation for mental health service users that is regarded with increasing caution by many members of the survivors' movement (Anonymous, 1996).

Money and resources are still concentrated in organisations for rather than controlled by survivors. For example, MIND has received £1 million to distribute as the MIND Millennium Award Scheme and the Mental Health Foundation, another organisation for mental health service users, has received a lottery grant of more than £500,000 to undertake a user-led research study of alternative and complementary treatments. Meanwhile Survivors Speak Out has very limited funding and one part-time worker. Much of the research undertaken by survivors has been carried out under the auspices of non user-led organisations, raising issues of ownership and control.

When the disabled people's movement sought civil rights legislation, it produced its own detailed study as a basis for its own campaigning (Barnes, 1991). MIND, the organisation for mental health service users, published a short pamphlet as the basis for its anti-discrimination campaign, jointly written by a survivor and its head of media relations (Read and Baker, 1996). Another research study by a survivor, Diana Rose, highlighted the discrimination mental health service users could expect 'in the community', but again it was produced within a non-user led organisation (Rose 1996).

Despite the efforts of the survivors' movement to collaborate, significant divisions remain. For instance, a new Open University Course *Mental health and distress: perspectives and practice* is linked with an anthology of writings by people who have experienced mental distress (Read and Reynolds, 1996), and a reader 'by acknowledged experts in the mental health field', which is described as 'challenging traditional understandings of mental health, emphasising the perspective of mental health service users' (cover blurb). Yet only one of its 53 contributors writes from the perspective of the survivors' movement (Heller, Reynolds, Gomm, Muston and Pattison, 1996). As far as the dominant debate is concerned, survivors and the survivors' movement still seem to be seen primarily as a source of experiential data, rather than creators of our own analysis and theory.

FROM INVOLVEMENT TO EXCLUSION

Two related developments are currently causing some members of the survivors' movement to take stock of their position and the future of the movement. These are first, their participation in service system initiatives for consultation and 'user-involvement', and second, the increasing association of mental health service users with dangerousness and violence. We begin with the first of these.

Survivors have invested a lot of time, effort, emotional energy, commitment and trust in agency-led schemes for user-involvement. This has also been linked with the movement's particular focus on reforming the service system and working in partnership with professionals. In recent times, however, there has been a growing sense of disillusion with this reactive strategy, particularly among experienced members of the movement and concerns that it may actually be adding to survivors' disempowerment. While, of course there have been exceptions, in general the results seem to have been very limited. In this, survivors' experience has been similar to that of the disabled people's movement (Bewley and Glendinning 1994). However a difference between the two movements has been the extent of survivors' investment in such activities. The disabled people's movement has devoted much more of its energy and resources to its own broader campaigns independent of the service system, for example for civil and human rights, accessible 'public' transport and challenging the traditional imagery and activities of charities for disabled people. One expression of the survivors' movement's rising dissatisfaction with conventional initiatives for 'user-involvement', is a growing interest in increasing the control which individual survivors have in their contact with the psychiatric system (e.g. Leader, 1995).

The increasing association of mental health service users with violence and dangerousness has, like the introduction of schemes for user-involvement, been closely associated with the 1990s community care reforms. While the catalogue of tragedies, murders and suicides associated with mental health service users, particularly people labelled as schizophrenic, have been linked in official enquiries with the failure to provide adequate and appropriate support, its political and media presentation has been in terms of the threat from service users. They are represented as threatening, irrational and unpredictable. There has been an increasing emphasis on them as 'other'. The dominant media image has been of staring black faces and headlines like: 'Nightmare In the Community' (Palmer 1997).

While the tragedies have been linked less with people discharged from longstay institutions than with 'revolving door patients' left unsupported, the dominant pressure group and media demand has been for the reinstitutionalisation of 'mental patients'. There has been cross-party political consensus that more restrictions should be imposed on mental health service users. Labour spokespersons are as likely as Conservatives to say that:

> 'there must be proper supervision... We need a new Mental Health Act that provides proper powers for the care of seriously ill people' (Jowell, 1997).

As well as demands for the reincarceration of mental health service users, they are now subject to new restrictions in their own homes. The demonisation of mental health service users and the emphasis on their 'otherness', has also meant a shift of resources from supporting people in distress to regulating people stereotyped as a public or political threat. Survivors' organisations have been able to play very little part in this discussion.

The political and social climate for both survivors and the survivors' movement has if anything deteriorated during the 1990s. As Peter Campbell has said:

> 'Outside the mental health services and despite the good work of user/survivor action groups, current or former mental health service users are held in little higher regard now than they were in 1983 (the year of the Mental Health Act). Arguably, they are now more likely to be seen as dangerous and inferior' (Campbell, 1996a: 224).

THE DENIAL OF SURVIVORS' RIGHTS

This leads us to another important distinction to draw between the situation of survivors and disabled people. The disabled people's movement has campaigned against the arbitrary abuse of disabled people's human and civil rights. The restriction of survivors' rights, however, is *enshrined in law* as part of the provisions established to maintain and 'treat' them. Denial of rights is not presented as an aberration in the treatment of survivors, but as necessary and legitimate. While the public debate about disabled people has increasingly been about the need for their inclusion in society, that about survivors has been about the need to *exclude* them.

While the survivors' movement would not disagree that survivors may sometimes need security and asylum to safeguard both their own rights and those of other people, they would draw a clear distinction between this and the way in which they are actually treated by the psychiatric and criminal justice system, where their rights are routinely restricted and dangerous treatment imposed forcibly and routinely without adequate safeguards or redress. Much less attention has been paid to the mental health service users who have died within the psychiatric system in worrying circumstances than to the smaller number who have harmed others.

THE CONTEXT OF SURVIVORS' RESEARCH

It may be helpful at this point to sum up the context of emancipatory research in the survivors' movement. It is a context of:

- the dominance of organisations for survivors and survivors' unequal relationship with them;
- a political, media and social climate which is increasingly hostile to survivors;

- the continuing dominance of the psychiatric profession and system;
- the association of distress with spoiled identity and defective understanding; and
- the survivor movement's lack of a coherent and agreed philosophy.

Despite these difficulties, indeed in some cases, perhaps because of them, there has been a significant development of emancipatory research in the survivors' movement. It has not always been conceived of as 'emancipatory' research. It has also been understood as 'user-led' research, with an emphasis on survivors themselves undertaking research. But while it has its distinct identity and history and has developed separately, it also has much in common with the emancipatory research of the disabled people's movement. There have also been research collaborations with different movements, including the disabled people's movement, like, for example, the research project led by Viv Lindow analysing the National User Involvement Project (Lindow, 1996). Undertaking emancipatory research has been part of the survivors' movement's project of survivors speaking and acting for themselves; improving their lives and liberating themselves from an oppressive psychiatric system; of changing and equalising relationships between research and research subjects, and developing survivors' own knowledge collectively.

It has also represented a revulsion from traditional research on survivors, not least medicalised and drug company research which objectified and pathologised mental health service users. Mike Lawson, founding member of Surviors Speak Out talked of invasive research which was 'psychiatric pornography' (Lawson, 1988). More recently Ann Davis has referred to the way in which mental health research continues to 'use' mental health service users (Davis, 1992). For many mental health service users, the researcher has represented another psychiatric professional with power over them (Wallcraft, 1997).

More subtle processes of restructuring and incorporation are still taking place in mainstream research on survivors. For example, Ann Rogers and David Pilgrim, in their study of a service users' organisations imposed their own interpretations on their activities and their own conceptualisation of the movement as a 'new social movement' (Rogers and Pilgrim, 1991). Marian Barnes and Polly Shardlow in their examination of survivors/mental health service users' own perceptions of their identity, pre-empted their conceptualisation by defining them as 'people with mental health problems' and 'mental health user groups' (Barnes and Shardlow, 1996b).

Emancipatory research associated with the survivors' movement has developed in different ways and from different bases. These include:

1. Survivors acting as paid and unpaid consultants and researchers for non-statutory and statutory mental health organisations

The Sainsbury Centre for Mental Health developed a long-term co-research relationship with a group of psychiatric service users. The group acted as consultants to research into community mental health services, produced their own report and then three members carried out a user evaluation of a case management project. The Centre provided support in designing and undertaking the project and published the final report, while the user-researchers maintained final editorial control. In their report, they set out their case for user-led research:

> 'It was strongly believed that users, who can demonstrate their common experience with other users, could get at the truth much better because they could persuade others of their independence from the service...In particular the issue of independence from the service provider is very difficult for non-user researchers. Their background, presentation and links with service agencies make it difficult for users to believe that their views will not get back to those who provide the service directly. They then fear that their service might be withdrawn or that they will be made to suffer for their criticism...The perceptions that (user-led research) seeks are those that users would want to tell each other, not what they have been told is good for them' (Beeforth, Conlan and Graley, 1994: 4).

A second example is the Mental Health Task Force User Group made up of nine current and former mental health service users representing the three main user organisations in England, which was commissioned to carry out 'consumer satisfaction research'. The Mental Health Task Force was an executive group set up for two years by the Department of Health to investigate the closure of large psychiatric hospitals and the transfer of services 'to the community'. A small working group of the user group, of whom one of the present authors was a member (JW), identified a set of rights and principles on which mental health service users wanted services to be based, for local application, based on research with local and national user organisations and agreed by service users more widely (Mental Health Task Force User Group, 1994).

2. Research produced by conferences of service users

An example of this approach, which has frequently been used in survivor-led research, is the report and manifesto which resulted from the 1992 Mid-Glamorgan Mental Health Service Users' Conference. This called for major changes in services to provide the services which mental health service users wanted, for example, crisis support services, in which they had more control; as well as restrictions on 'treatment' which people experienced as oppressive, including the use of ECT, major and minor tranquillisers and negative staff attitudes. One of the key issues raised was discrimination against women in the psychiatric system:

> 'Doctors (often men) contribute to why women feel bad by assuming or implying that a woman's problem or distress has physical causes, such as her appearance, hormones or PMT.

> Male doctors don't or can't listen, so they prescribe drugs.

> Once you have been labelled "mentally ill", doctors use it as an excuse not to have to listen to you.

> Many of the women who attended the conference had had ECT. They had been told things like, "It will help you to forget the past" – if they had been told anything at all. Women were not told about the side-effects of ECT' (Mid-Glamorgan Association of Voluntary Organisations, 1992: 51-2).

3. Funded research by survivors

An important example of such funded research is Mary O'Hagan's report of her study visits, supported by a Churchill Fellowship, visiting survivor organisations in the US, UK and the Netherlands. Her work was aimed primarily for a readership of psychiatric survivors. She made her personal and ideological position clear and offered her research as a contribution to the movement for survivor-led services, warning against the danger of 'mimicking' existing services, social relations and structures. She talked about the need for the survivor movement to link experience with ideology and ideology with practice, saying:

> 'Looking back, this report is the working and reworking of two themes. The first theme can be condensed into the word "meaning". What is the meaning of our

madness? How does this meaning contribute to the ideology of our movement? The second theme is "management". How do we manage our activities so they will truly reflect our ideology' (O'Hagan, 1994: 95).

4. Unfunded research by survivors

An important example of such unfunded research is a survey of 85 mental health service users, at home and in hospital, undertaken by Janet Cresswell, a long-term patient in Broadmoor special hospital. Half her sample talked of the negative effects of treatment, like addiction to tranquillisers:

> 'Further problems to the ones for which help was originally sought were experienced by over half the users. The suffering of many users under the heading of "medical treatment" is an indictment of the medical profession' (Cresswell, 1993).

Survivor-led research challenges psychiatric orthodoxy which has traditionally emphasised professional boundaries, scientific objectivity, technological solutions to emotional problems, treatments with quick 'results', standardisation of diagnosis and treatment, clinical settings and the central role of the medically trained psychiatrist. Some of the ways in which survivor research challenges the medical paradigm, either subtly or overtly are that:

- the concept of 'crisis' or distress is often preferred to the concept of 'mental illness';
- social or spiritual models of understanding distress are proposed rather than medical ones;
- hearing voices and other devalued perceptions and experiences are seen as phenomena with a number of possible explanations, rather than as a prime symptom of 'psychotic illness' (Romme and Escher, 1993);
- psychiatric treatments are sometimes described as abuse or torture, rather than medical treatment; and
- medical concepts and language and psychiatric labels are often regarded as damaging, stigmatising, unhelpful and inappropriate.

CHANGING THE SYSTEM

As we have seen, much survivor research has focused on the service system and people's experience of it and has frequently been based within the system itself. It includes evaluation of services as well as surveys of service users' views. (e.g. Wallcraft, 1993; North East Essex Service User Development Group, 1993). But such emancipatory research seeking to bringing about change in the service system frequently runs into major difficulties. There are problems of restricted access and dissemination and of massive resistance to making change when its findings are negative and uncomfortable for service providers, as frequently they are. Mary Nettle (1996) has reported just such an experience in detail. But this draws us to one of the key dilemmas facing the survivors' movement and survivor-led research. The psychiatric service system is unpromising ground for reform, but many survivors are *held within it*. It cannot be ignored. Louise Pembroke, of Survivors Speak Out, has talked of some of the continuing dilemmas and contradictions which this poses for survivors as both activists and researchers:

'I want to make things better for people in the psychiatric system but I also want to demolish it. There are dangers in collaboration, but there are positive things too, like patients' councils where we can at least help people gain their voice before leaving the bin' (quoted in Croft and Beresford, 1991: 72).

Sharp differences between survivor-led research and that carried out by mental health professionals are often revealed in the choice of starting point, subject matter and perspective. While psychiatric researchers generally evaluate existing orthodox psychiatric interventions from an assumption that mental illness can be clinically defined, survivor-led research often treats the concept of mental illness as open to question. While the findings of orthodox research generally point to incremental changes within the existing paradigm, user-led research posits more radical shifts of control, rights, knowledge and resources to service users and their organisations. It indicates the need to replace the dominant biochemical and genetic research paradigms, with more open, equal and holistic approaches. This has led to an increasing interest in and focus on *alternatives*, to both existing ideas and services.

SURVIVOR RESEARCH ON ALTERNATIVES

Emancipatory research in the survivors' movement is most developed where it focuses on alternatives. This extends to exploring alternative therapies, systems of support and interpretations and analysis of people's experience and perceptions. It will be helpful to examine some of the key examples of such survivor-led enquiry. First is the work on eating distress and self-harm in which Louise Pembroke has been centrally involved. Here we see the reconceptualisation of two key expressions of distress. In both cases, the process of enquiry is one which begins with developing and exchanging people's first hand accounts of their experience, extending survivors' own knowledge, challenging traditional paradigms and value judgements and developing new interpretations and new language. We move from 'eating disorder' to eating distress; from 'self-mutilation', 'self-destructive' and 'para-suicidal' behaviour to self-harm. It is a process which leads to and is directly connected with action and change, through bringing people together, setting up networks and organisations and working for change, both through collaboration with the service system and through pressing for change through collective action (Pembroke, 1992; 1995).

In the discussion of eating distress, for example, there are personal insights into the social pressures which lead to eating problems; how it feels to have an eating problem and the frequent insensitivity of psychiatric services to the realities of people's lives and emotions. As one woman said:

> 'Whatever way I expressed my distress or dissent it was declared invalid, stupid or sick. The so-called eating disorder label is an inadequate explanation of the very complex reactions and feelings I experience. Indeed for me it is a simplification of an expression of distress which clearly demonstrates the need for cultural and social change... I feel that people labelled as mentally ill experience and express feelings the majority do not allow or open themselves to...What I am is a woman who discovered at an early age that a woman's worth in our society is based upon her appearance' (Pembroke, 1992:19).

Another expression of this development in survivor research is Vivien Lindow's Joseph Rowntree Foundation supported study of self-help alternatives to mental health services. Against the odds of inadequate funding and support, the survivors' movement is beginning to develop alternatives to existing services, from asylums and sanctuaries, advice and counselling services and personal assistance schemes, to training courses, employment schemes and complementary therapies, as well as offering their own visions of the kind of support they want (Campbell, 1996b; Read, 1996). Vivien Lindow explores some of the initiatives that have already emerged in the UK and elsewhere and identifies the ideas and principles underpinning them as a basis for future development of user-led alternatives and the increased commissioning of such schemes (Lindow, 1994a; 1994b).

Another survivor, Brenda Alexander, carried out a small-scale study of survivors' experience of alternative therapies, particularly aromatherapy. She concluded:

> 'The abuse of power personified in the control and management of some individuals coping with a "disorientated" mind and body are only reinforcing low esteem and adding to their problems. A continuing partnership between professionals and users on a more holistic, informed choice and consent basis is indicated by my research. The "medication culture" must be re-evaluated in the nineties' (Alexander, 1993).

TOWARDS A SOCIAL MODEL OF MADNESS AND DISTRESS

Survivors' interest in alternatives and their emancipatory research exploring it, point to some of the most hopeful ways forward both for the movement and for individual mental health service users. There seems to be some truth in the generalisation that the social model of disability has provided a helpful framework giving purpose and direction to the emancipatory research emerging from the disabled people's movement. In the survivors' movement, the developments seem to be the other way round. The growing body of emancipatory research being undertaken by survivors is beginning to point to a clearer philosophical basis for the movement. There is a growing recognition from within that the movement needs to develop its own philosophy. In a recent history of the UK survivors' movement, Peter Campbell, one of the movement's founding members concludes:

> 'One of the major challenges of the next few years may be to find a coherent overall philosophy that can integrate a clearer range of focuses' (Campbell, 1996a: 224).

The nature of such a philosophy is beginning to be clearer, although as yet there is no clear consensus about it (Beresford, 1997). We can expect such a philosophy to be based on a social model of madness and distress. The issues that this is likely to highlight include:

- the social causes of our madness and distress;
- the medicalisation of our experience and distress;
- the destructive and discriminatory response to it from both psychiatry and broader society;
- the need for a social response to the distress and disablement which survivors experience, addressing the social origins and relations of their distress, instead of being restricted to people's individual difficulties; and
- the need for survivor-led alternatives to prevent distress and offer appropriate support for survivors (Beresford, Gifford and Harrison, 1996).

Emancipatory research by survivors will have a key role to play in both exploring these issues and in developing and disseminating such a social model of madness and distress.

REFERENCES

ALEXANDER, B. (1993) *The Place of Complementary Therapies In Mental Health: A user's experiences and views.* Nottingham: Nottingham Advocacy Group.

ANONYMOUS (1996) 'After Fifty Years of Caring – Does MIND have a role', *Asylum: a magazine for democratic psychiatry,* 9 (4): 25-30.

BARNES, C. (1991) *Disabled People in Britain and Discrimination.* London: Hurst and Co/BCODP.

BARNES, M. and SHARDLOW, P. (1996a), 'Effective Consumers and Active Citizens: Strategies for users' influence on service and beyond', *Research Policy and Planning,* 14 (1): 3-38.

BARNES, M. and SHARDLOW, P. (1996b) 'Identity Crisis: Mental health user groups and the "problem of identity"', in C. Barnes and G. Mercer, eds., *Exploring the Divide: Illness and Disability.* Leeds: The Disability Press.

BEEFORTH, M., CONLAN, E. and GRALEY, R. (1994) *Have We Got Views For You: User evaluation of case management.* London: Sainsbury Centre for Mental Health.

BERESFORD, P. (1997) 'New Movements, New Politics: Making participation possible', in T. Jordan and A. Lent, eds, *Storming The Millennium: The new politics of change.* London: Lawrence and Wishart.

BERESFORD, P., GIFFORD, G. and HARRISON, C. (1996) 'What Has Disability Got To Do With Psychiatric Survivors?', in J. Read and J. Reynolds, eds, *Speaking Our Minds: An anthology.* Basingstoke: Macmillan.

BEWLEY, C. and GLENDINNING, C. (1994) *Involving Disabled People In Community Care Planning,* York: Joseph Rowntree Foundation.

CAMPBELL, J. and OLIVER, M., (1996) *Disability Politics: Understanding our past, changing our future.* London: Routledge.

CAMPBELL, P. (1996a) 'The History Of The User Movement in the United Kingdom', in T. Heller, J. Reynolds, R. Gomm, R. Muston and S. Pattison, eds. *Mental Health Matters: A Reader.* Basingstoke: Macmillan.

CAMPBELL, P. (1996b) 'What We Want From Crisis Services' in J. Read and J. Reynolds, eds, *Speaking Our Minds: An anthology of personal experiences of mental distress and its consequences.* Basingstoke: Macmillan.

CHAMBERLIN, J. (1988) *On Our Own: User controlled alternatives to the mental health system.* London: MIND.

CRESSWELL, J. (1993) 'Users' Report On Psychiatric Services', *Asylum,* 23, 7(2).

CROFT, S. and BERESFORD, P. (1991) 'User Views', *Changes: An International Journal of Psychology and Psychotherapy,* March, 9 (1): 71-72.

CROW, L. (1996) 'Including All Our Lives: Renewing the social model of disability', in J. Morris, ed., *Encounters With Strangers: Feminism and disability.* London: The Women's Press, pp 206-226.

DAVIS, A. (1992) 'Who Needs User Research?: Service users as research subjects or participants; implications for user involvement in service contracting', in M. Barnes and G. Wistow, eds. *Researching User Involvement.* Leeds: The Nuffield Institute for Health Studies, University of Leeds.

HELLER, T., REYNOLDS, G., GOMM, R., MUSTON, R. and PATTISON, S., eds. (1996) *Mental Health Matters: A reader.* Basingstoke: Macmillan.

JOWELL, T. (1997) 'Experts Say Care Crisis is A National Scandal', *The Mirror,* April 22, p.6.

LAWSON, M. (1988) 'The Involvement of Users In Research', Mental Health Researchers' Network Seminar, London, 12 February.

LEADER, A. (1995) *Direct Power: A resource pack for people who want to develop their own care plans and support networks.* Brighton, The Community Support Network, Brixton Community Sanctuary, Pavilion Publishing (Brighton) Ltd and MIND.

LINDOW, V. (1994a) *Self-Help Alternatives To Mental Health Services.* London: MIND.

LINDOW, V. (1994b) *Purchasing Mental Health Services: Self-help alternatives.* London: MIND.

LINDOW, V. (1996) *User Involvement: Community service users as consultants and trainers.* Department of Health, National Health Service Executive Community Care Branch, West Yorkshire.

McNAMARA, J. (1996) 'Out of Order: Madness is a feminist and disability issue' in J. Morris, ed. *Encounters With Strangers: Feminism and Disability.* London: The Women's Press.

MENTAL HEALTH TASK FORCE USER GROUP (1994) *Guidelines For A Local Charter For Users Of Mental Health Services.* Leeds: National Health Service Management Executive.

MID-GLAMORGAN ASSOCIATION OF VOLUNTARY ORGANISATIONS (1992) *Moving Together: Working Together.* Mid-Glamorgan Association of Voluntary Organisations, unpublished report, Mid-Glamorgan.

MORRIS, J. (1996a) *Encounters With Strangers: Feminism and Disability.* London: The Women's Press.

NETTLE, M. (1996) 'Listening In The Asylum', in J. Read and J. Reynolds, eds., (1996) *Speaking Our Minds: An anthology.* Basingstoke: Macmillan.

NORTH EAST ESSEX SERVICE USER DEVELOPMENT GROUP (1993) *Are You Listening?* Essex: Essex Social Services Department.

O'HAGAN, M. (1994) *Stopovers On My Way Home From Mars.* London: Survivors Speak Out.

PALMER, J. (1997) 'Mental Health: Nightmare in the community', *The Mirror*, 22 April, pp 6-7.

PEMBROKE, L.R., ed. (1992) *Eating Distress: Perspectives from personal experience*, London: Survivors Speak Out.

PEMBROKE, L.R., ed. (1994) *Self-Harm: Perspectives from personal experience.* London: Survivors Speak Out.

READ, J. (1996) 'What We Want From Mental Health Services', in J. Read and J. Reynolds, eds., *Speaking Our Minds: An anthology of personal experiences of mental distress and its consequences.* Basingstoke: Macmillan.

READ, J. and BAKER, S. (1996) *Not Just Sticks and Stones: A survey of the stigma, taboos and discrimination experienced by people with mental health problems.* November, London: MIND.

READ, J. and REYNOLDS, J., eds. (1996) *Speaking Our Minds: An anthology.* Basingstoke: Macmillan.

ROGERS, A. and PILGRIM, D. (1991) 'Pulling Down Churches: Accounting for the British mental health users movement', *Sociology of Health and Illness*, 13(2), 129-48.

ROMME, M. and ESCHER, S., eds. (1993) *Accepting Voices.* London: MIND.

ROSE, D. (1996) *Living in the Community*, London: Sainsbury Centre for Mental Health.

WALLCRAFT, J. (1993) 'Self-Advocacy In 1992', *Open MIND*, 61, February/March, p.7.

WALLCRAFT, J. (1997 forthcoming) 'Survivor-Led Research In Human Services: Challenging the dominant medical paradigm', in S. Baldwin and P. Barker, eds., *Needs Assessment and Community Care*. London: Butterworth Heinemann.

CHAPTER 6

Who's Research?: A personal audit

Mark Priestley

INTRODUCTION

This chapter is based on my experience of 'doing' disability research in collaboration with the Derbyshire Coalition of Disabled People (DCDP) and Derbyshire Centre for Integrated Living (DCIL). I do not propose to discuss the organisations themselves in detail here. Suffice to say that DCDP was the first formal 'Coalition' of its kind in Britain and DCIL the first centre for independent/integrated living (Davis & Mullender, 1993, offer an excellent account of these developments). The project itself provided an empirical basis for my PhD thesis, a case study of quality issues in community care purchasing (Priestley, 1997). However, it also raised many fundamental issues about the very act of doing disability research.

The act of researching disability has become increasingly problematised as disabled people have begun to examine more critically the relationship between themselves and the researchers who have studied their situation. Such critiques have led to the development of an alternative 'emancipatory' paradigm for disability research which has much in common with feminist, anti-racist and anti-imperialist research methods. The key features of this model include a redefinition of the social relations of research production, a rebuttal of positivist and interpretative claims to 'objectivity' and assertions about the political position of the researcher (see Stone & Priestley, 1996).

With this in mind I was aware that the established social relations of research production give rise to inequalities of power between researcher and researched. One of the major challenges for me was then to redress the balance of 'vulnerability' in this process (see Stanley & Wise, 1983: 206). I wanted to find out whether it would be possible to produce an academically credible piece of disability research simply by placing my skills 'at the disposal' of the research participants (Barnes, 1992: 122). I wanted to see how far the research production process could be collectivised amongst its participants. I wanted to establish whether the radical agenda of emancipatory research could be realised in any meaningful way. In order to show what happened I will begin with the theory and then examine the practicalities of 'doing' the research.

THE POLITICAL POSITION OF THE RESEARCHER

Abberley (1987) argues that the sociology of disability has remained 'theoretically backward' because it:

> 'reproduces in the study of disability parallel deficiencies to those found in what is now seen by many as racist and sexist sociology' (p.5).

These deficiencies are evident in the fact that the dominant discourses of disability research have tended to reproduce two sets of disabling social relations – first, between people who 'do' research and people who are 'being' researched and secondly, between disabled people and non-disabled people in the wider world. Thus, I believe that it is inappropriate for researchers to consider disability research production as an activity discrete from its social context.

Abberley (1987: 141), describes how disabled people have been treated predominantly as 'passive research subjects'. This has been true not only of large-scale quantitative surveys (such as those carried out by the Office of Population Censuses and Surveys – OPCS – in 1985) but also in approaches to research interviewing which accept rather than challenge the disempowerment of disabled research subjects – a tendency well-documented within the feminist research literature (see Oakley, 1981). In so doing, such research may easily reinforce existing feelings of passivity or exclusion amongst its participants.

This objectification (or subjectification) of disabled people through research production has been premised upon the maintenance and reproduction of disabling social relations and discourses within the production process itself (Oliver, 1992: 102). Problematising the social relations of research production brings into question power relationships between the researcher and other participants. This in turn has profound implications for their respective roles in the research production process.

In seeking to expose and redefine oppressive social relations in the wider world, new social movements (including the disabled people's movement) have *de facto* challenged many of the mores of social research. In this respect, feminist critiques of 'objectivity' have been among the most significant (Smith, 1988; Stanley, 1990). Similarly, claims to objectivity by disability researchers have been increasingly characterised as methodological collusion with an oppressive discourse which marginalises or subordinates the experience and self-determination of disabled people (Zarb, 1992).

This process was most graphically exposed by Hunt (1981) writing about his experience of being researched as a resident of the Le Court Cheshire Home. Hunt condemned the researchers' self-imposed obsession with 'detachment'. For Hunt, such claims were inherently flawed because they were made within a context of oppression. Similar experiences have led many disabled writers to consider the notion of detached objectivity as a falsely premised, if not inherently oppressive, epistemological standpoint for disability research.

The realist challenge to positivism posed by emancipatory social movements is further accentuated when the subjects of the research are those same social movements. Thus, Touraine (1981: 29) argues that it is difficult for the student of social movements to arrive at an understanding of them other than by identifying with them. Touraine's approach to action research with social movements states openly that the purpose of the research is to 'contribute to the development of social movements' (p. 148) and envisages permanent change in the movement effected by the research. Thus, Touraine concludes (p. 198) that while participant observation can provide 'superficial information', a more productive approach is that of 'committed research'.

TOWARDS A MODEL FOR DISABILITY RESEARCH

Disabled people and disability theorists have responded to the kind of issues I have discussed so far by seeking to formulate new methodologies commensurate with the emancipatory struggles of the disabled people's movement. Such moves have been consolidated in recent years with the articulation of an 'emancipatory' paradigm for disability research (see for example, the 1992 special edition of *Disability, Handicap & Society*, Rioux & Bach's (1994) collection or indeed the contributions in this volume).

In a recent paper with Emma Stone (Stone & Priestley, 1996) we reviewed these developments and identified six core principles which we felt characterised the emancipatory research paradigm as follows:

1. the adoption of a social model of disability as the ontological and epistemological basis for research production;
2. the surrender of falsely-premised claims to objectivity through overt political commitment to the struggles of disabled people for self-emancipation;
3. the willingness only to undertake research where it will be of some practical benefit to the self-empowerment of disabled people and/or the removal of disabling barriers;
4. the devolution of control over research production to ensure full accountability to disabled people and their organisations;
5. the ability to give voice to the personal whilst endeavouring to collectivise the commonality of disabling experiences and barriers; and
6. the willingness to adopt a plurality of methods for data collection and analysis in response to the changing needs of disabled people.

In presenting these arguments, it was important for us to consider how we might address the social relations of our own research production *vis-à-vis* the disabled people with whom we sought to work. At the same time, we found it necessary to satisfy academic peers and examiners. For better or worse it is the academy, rather than disabled people at the grass roots, who pass judgement on a submitted thesis! It was often hard to conceive how this balancing act might be successfully achieved, to which end we prioritised those aspects of the emancipatory model which we saw as mitigating the potential 'tug-of-war' between academic-self and political-self. In problematising our role as non-disabled researchers we highlighted four areas where we anticipated methodological difficulties, namely:

1. the contradiction between surrendering control and maintaining integrity;

2. the tension between accepting our expertise *as researchers* whilst accepting disabled people's expertise *as knowers*;

3. the problem of collectivising analysis within a social model where that model is not necessarily part of the participants' own understanding of disability; and

4. a recognition that positive outcomes in individual lives need not be the sole criterion of 'good research' where a real contribution can be made in a wider context.

I have suggested (after Oliver and others) that the emancipatory research paradigm challenges the established social relations of research production. Thus, disabled writers have argued that the researcher needs to engage directly in the emancipatory struggles of disabled people by laying her/his research skills 'at the disposal of disabled people' (Barnes, 1992: 122), 'for them to use in whatever ways they choose' (Oliver, 1992: 111) and 'turning the researcher into a resource for their new employer' (Ramcharan and Grant, 1994: 237).

Zarb (1992) points out that simply increasing levels of participation does not necessarily challenge or alter the social relations of research production. The emancipatory model requires more. In my view it suggests a collectivisation of ownership over the means of research production and distribution to include all the research participants rather than just the 'researcher'. Since participation is not synonymous with emancipation, it was important for me to consider how I might translate participation into control during the course of my study.

In the remainder of this chapter I will focus on the form and content of my involvement with the research participants in order to show how we worked out this dialectic in practice. I have chosen to adopt a personal and reflexive narrative in order to do this, partly to facilitate the kind of methodological 'vulnerability' mentioned earlier and partly because it is the most direct way of illuminating the processes involved in 'doing' disability research.

SETTING UP THE PROJECT

In the first part of this chapter I have set out the theoretical framework for my approach to disability research in a fairly aspirational way. The study was in this sense driven from the outset by my political and methodological commitment to engage directly with these issues. The purpose of the following discussion is then to illustrate how this framework influenced the way in which I set about the project. In particular I will examine the formulation of an appropriate research agenda, the choice of specific research questions, funding issues, epistemology and control. Later I will deal with the practicalities of data collection, analysis and dissemination.

DETERMINING THE RESEARCH AGENDA

My initial interest in disability research was prompted both by my previous employment as a rehabilitation instructor (with visually impaired people) and by my academic interest in political theory. During the 1980s I had become increasingly aware of inherent contradictions between the ideology of 'care' and 'rehabilitation' within which I was professionally cultured and the ideology of self-empowerment advocated by the emerging disabled people's movement. My increasing exposure to the self-organisation of disabled people at a local level and to work of social model writers such as Vic Finkelstein, Mike Oliver and Jenny Morris served to further illuminate these contradictions.

The opportunity to explore some of these issues in an academic context came in 1993 while I was studying for a Master's degree in Social and Public Policy at the University of Leeds. As a dissertation project, I was able to work closely with the Association of Blind Asians (ABA) in Leeds in order to witness, record and support their struggle to develop new modes of collective welfare provision based on self-advocacy and mutual support (Priestley, 1994b; 1995; 1996a). In particular, I became increasingly interested in determining how the new community care reforms might be exploited by disabled people's organisations in Britain to promote more participatory modes of welfare production.

The ABA study was conducted as far as possible within an emancipatory framework. For example, the research participants were encouraged to exercise a determinant influence over the design, conduct and dissemination of the study. Although this was a small-scale project it did demonstrate that accountability could be effectively widened in the research production process without compromising academic integrity. It was the success of this project above all that shaped my personal agenda for further study and I became increasingly interested in developing further the co-participatory methods which I had adopted.

DEFINING THE QUESTION

Although I was developing my own research agenda, I also wanted to establish whether a credible piece of academic policy research could be conducted within an emancipatory paradigm. If this was to become any sort of reality then co-participation had to begin with the definition of a suitable research question. I wanted if possible to embark on a commitment to the new project without *any* pre-determined research question. Admittedly this is a somewhat unusual and rather vulnerable position for the would-be-researcher and later I would often question the logic of my approach. However, my hope was that by engaging with the participants at the very outset we could work together on defining a research proposal over which they could claim ownership.

At the suggestion of Colin Barnes I wrote, in December 1993, to the then chair of Derbyshire Coalition of Disabled People, Ken Davis, outlining my interests and offering my services for any project that might be useful to the development of the movement. A meeting was arranged between myself, Ken and the research manager at Derbyshire Centre for Integrated Living (Dave Gibbs) during which we discussed the social policy issues facing disabled people's organisations and whether these might form the basis for a PhD. Not surprisingly, implementation of the NHS and Community Care Act earlier that year figured prominently in this discussion.

It was clear that the unfolding purchaser-provider reforms required DCDP and DCIL to re-evaluate their historical relationship with the agencies of the local state. There was much concern that unique support services developed by disabled people in partnership with the local authority might now be threatened by the new contracting criteria. Specifically, it was felt that new criteria for service quality measurement might fail to recognise the 'added value' of an integrated living approach. In view of this it was suggested that I might use my research opportunity to develop an approach to quality measurement which would give due credit to the kind of services developed by the integrated living movement in Britain.

It is important to acknowledge the significance of my organisational affiliation with Leeds University at this stage in the research process. My advances would no doubt have met with rather more scepticism without the backing of Colin Barnes in the Disability Research Unit. The fact that I was being supervised by people publicly committed to social models of disability, with a proven track record of co-participatory research and with directly accountable links to the British Council of Organisations of Disabled People was thus a critical factor in the gatekeeping process. There are few guarantees for disabled people engaging with would-be researchers but it is worth remembering that an institution's track record will invariably be an indicator of likely outcomes.

GETTING FUNDING

Following the initial discussions I set about the task of forming the participants' ideas and concerns into a research proposal. This development was fed back and discussed with DDP/DCIL over a period of two or three months, resulting in agreement on a set of hypotheses and an outline method for the project (based initially on interviews with service users). The proposal was then consolidated into a funding application and submitted as a PhD proposal to the Economic and Social Research Council (ESRC) in May 1994.

It is important to remember that disabled people do not generally control research funding (Zarb, 1992) and proposals which are not within established research paradigms may fail to gain access to limited funding resources. In this context, it is interesting to note that I was persuaded by a member of the faculty to modify the proposal agreed with DCDP/DCIL on the grounds that it might be regarded as too removed from the 'mainstream' (this included removing the word 'emancipatory'). It is impossible to know whether that decision was in the end justified. However, the fact that I felt obliged to make the changes illustrates the way in which academic discourse can generate a self-limiting influence on the radicalism of would-be disability researchers.

To secure funding from a major government research council for a project defined by representatives of disabled people's organisations was in itself a partial vindication of the emancipatory approach. It did at least demonstrate that disabled people (in collaboration with a 'committed' academic institution) could gain access to relatively scarce funding resources. It did not of course provide any guarantees to DCDP/DCIL that I would continue to devolve control over the subsequent use of those resources. The award was after all made to me and not to them. However, as I have already mentioned, there was some security in knowing that I would be supervised by a well-known ally within the Disability Research Unit.

DEVOLVING CONTROL

Having secured funding for the project, the next problem was to determine how control over its production could be devolved to the participants. In August 1994 we discussed the proposal again in order to develop a strategy by which DCDP/DCIL could direct the research. The outcome of this was the suggestion that I could be 'commissioned' (without remuneration) to do 'my' research for DCDP. An initial contract was drawn up and agreed in order to coincide with my registration as a PhD student at the University of Leeds.

In practice, it is fair to say that my contractual obligation to DCDP/DCIL was not evoked by them at any time during the conduct of the research and its primary function had more to do with setting the tone of our relationship rather than governing it. However, it was certainly intended to be much more than a purely symbolic representation of the idea that this research would 'belong' in some way to its primary participants.

In general terms the use of contracts by disabled people's organisations to control researchers seems to me to be a useful one. However, it is relevant to note that, while the transfer of formal control was possible in this case, it might well be incompatible with the contracting criteria of some major research funders. For example, British government research contracts commonly prohibit the researcher from engaging in secondary contracts for the same work. This clearly has implications for the feasibility of using our approach for other projects within the mainstream of academic research.

KNOWLEDGE AND EXPERTISE

Academics working within positivist and interpretative paradigms have often cast themselves in the role of 'expert' or 'knower' – a role which implicitly (and, on occasion, explicitly) maintains that the knowledge and experience of disabled people counts for little (Hunt, 1981; Finkelstein, 1980; Abberley, 1992). Conversely, researchers working within an emancipatory approach have increasingly sought to prioritise that knowledge and experience over and above that of rehabilitation professionals or indeed researchers.

Most criticisms of this approach emanate from outside the radical research community, predominantly in defence of academic research traditions (see

Bury, 1992) although they have also come from 'inside' (see Glucksmann, 1994:151). Kelly *et al.* (1994) develop the debate by acknowledging the positive elements of researchers' expertise:

> 'It is we who have the time, resources and skills to conduct methodical work, to make sense of experience and locate individuals in historic and social contexts' (p. 37).

My initial decision to undertake the study was motivated by my view of disability as a form of social oppression and by my decision to adopt a research agenda defined by the disabled people's movement. The selection of a specific research question was determined by establishing the common ground between my expertise (social policy analysis and research skills) and the knowledge of disabled people's organisations in Derbyshire (derived from service provision and political struggle). The decision on a particular research issue was theirs; the decision to locate it within a broader socio-economic analysis was largely mine.

Later on in the data collection it was important for me to accept that disabled people would be invariably best placed to identify the form and content of disabling barriers in service provision. For the purposes of my study the primary knowers were the people who designed, managed and used DCIL's support services. However, I also had to value knowledge produced by policy makers, other academics and those in the 'caring' professions. Where these knowledges conflicted it was impossible to prioritise one above the other without also considering the relationship between knowledge and power.

CASE STUDY METHODS

Representatives of DCDP and DCIL had selected the topic for my research because it was a pressing organisational issue for them at the time. Thus, it was not surprising that the organisation's own activities frequently coincided with my agenda, providing important and relevant research opportunities. The difficulty for me (as someone hoping to write a PhD) was to forge coherent links between the sometimes disparate opportunities for data collection. I have found it helpful to consider the evolving data collection as a set of three semi-discrete projects guided by the needs and priorities of the research participants. This rationalisation is *post hoc* and, at the time, it is fair to say that I was often unclear where the research was 'going'.

AN ACTION RESEARCH PROJECT ON USER INVOLVEMENT

In July 1994, DCIL's General Council considered a proposal to host a Joint Focus Group project on 'Improving User Participation in Service Monitoring' in collaboration with the Living Options Partnership (LOP). Since this initiative coincided directly with my interests in quality and user controlled services, it was suggested that I could be 'employed' to facilitate the project for DCIL.

DCIL's General Council asked its member organisations to nominate representatives for the group and an initial meeting was convened in November 1994. This meeting was attended by representatives of DCDP, the social services department and two local NHS Trusts. LOP's Network Co-ordinator was also present. At this meeting, each representative was asked to prioritise a user involvement issue in Derbyshire. It was decided that these contributions should form the basis for a series of four workshops to be held at DCIL over a period of several weeks.

The workshops were chaired by me and the representatives invited disabled service users from their organisations to attend. The meetings were tape-recorded and notes were made of the main contributions. The notes and tapes were analysed after each meeting and summaries of the main points were collated. These summaries were copied and circulated to the participants for feedback. After the fourth workshop a summary report and key point checklist was compiled in collaboration with DCIL's research officer. These were circulated to the participants for validation. A final meeting was convened at which the participants discussed the report and decided collectively on its dissemination.

The object of the workshops was twofold. First, we anticipated that each organisation would learn something about the process of user involvement in its own and other agencies. Second, we hoped to produce some draft guidelines for evaluating user participation in purchaser and provider organisations. To this end, the outputs of the project (a short report and an evaluation tool for assessing the quality of user involvement) were widely disseminated among disabled people and service commissioners/providers.

In March 1995 DCIL's General Council formerly adopted the measurement tool as a basis for advocating user involvement in all disability services and agreed to promote the summary report with their constituent organisations at chief executive level. In September 1995 we were able to present a version of the report and recommendations to the Disabled Peoples' International, European Symposium (Gibbs & Priestley, 1996). This prompted much discussion and enabled me to validate the initial work with a wider range of disabled activists. Later, I was able to use the outcomes of the project as the basis for a presentation to an NHS Executive Seminar organised by DCIL in Derby (Priestley, 1996b). This provided an opportunity to disseminate the group's work to a wider constituency of service commissioners and practitioners.

The Living Options project was productive in enabling me to become familiar with current debates about the role of disabled people in Derbyshire's main service provider agencies. It also provided an opportunity for some initial action research addressing the apparent conflict of values between DCIL and its major funders. It was of direct benefit to DCIL in two ways: by making available my time and skills as a facilitator/recorder for the group sessions and by producing a widely disseminated and validated tool for evaluating user involvement in disability services.

A STUDY OF CONTRACTING

Our agreed agenda for research focused attention on the definition and measurement of service quality. However, it was apparent that DCIL perceived the contractual relationship with the local authority as the most immediate barrier to implementing quality services within an integrated living approach. During 1995 we discussed the possibility of using my resources to facilitate further action research with the purchasing authority aimed at resolving some of these conflicts. For this reason it was important to understand as much as possible about the impact of community care implementation on the organisation.

In order to achieve this, DCIL provided me with complete and unrestricted access to their records. I was able to analyse the full text of internal minutes, supporting documents, reports and accounts for the period before and after community care implementation (1991-1996). This enabled me to study in detail the impact of contracting on DCIL's ability to provide participative integrated living services to disabled people in the locality. I was also able to talk at length with DCIL managers about the operational pressures of contracting for services.

Ultimately, there were no tangible outcomes for DCIL from this part of the study. The relationship between DCIL and the social services department was becoming increasingly strained and some of the issues targeted for my research moved onto a more political plane (via DCIL's management committee). In view of this, the opportunities for social services participation in the research design became increasingly limited and it was necessary to re-focus my efforts on the primary research participants.

By this stage I had written up a fairly detailed analysis of DCIL's situation as a draft 'academic' paper but much of the material was politically sensitive and I felt that it would not have been appropriate for me to disseminate my analysis widely at that time. This in itself was a useful lesson, illustrating the potential conflict between 'academic' self and 'committed' self (Stone & Priestley, 1996). To devolve control over the dissemination of research findings to the research participants is to accept that there may well be constraints on the researcher's ability to 'publish'. I am not necessarily advocating the participants' right of 'veto' over research outputs but I do believe that a sincere commitment to collective responsibility requires us to reject our absolute privilege to 'independence'.

AN EVALUATION PROJECT WITH SERVICE USERS

I had discussed for some time with DCIL the most appropriate way of incorporating service user participation into the project. The need for service user input was emphasised as a priority both by DCIL's director and by my academic supervisor. In early 1996 I wrote to DCIL's Personal Support Service Manager asking whether any of the service users might be interested in talking to me and how I might go about this.

On a personal level, I was keen to 'get some interviews' for my PhD; on a methodological level I was concerned (as were DCIL) that there was no point in bothering service users unless this would be relevant and useful to all concerned. There was in fact a delay of some months during which we were unable to clarify how user involvement could be best targeted. However, by early June an opportunity for relevant contact began to present itself.

As the end of the first year of DCIL's contract for the Personal Support Service approached it became evident that there would need to be some evaluation of service quality by the purchasing authority. Managers at DCIL were becoming increasingly concerned that any evaluation conducted by the social services department might be limited in its scope and therefore fail to recognise the 'added value' of an integrated living approach. There was also some concern that it might not be conducted with full user participation.

In view of this situation it was suggested that I might conduct the evaluation as an 'independent' outsider and, in June 1996, DCIL wrote to social services asking for an independent appraisal (to be conducted by me). The social services department declined this offer, preferring to conduct the evaluation themselves. This caused further concern to DCIL, who now felt even more strongly that they needed to 'commission' me for an independent study focused on outcomes for users. By early July, DCIL had identified nine service users as potential participants (some of whom were also participating in the social services review) and DCIL's service manager wrote to each of these people indicating that I would be in touch.

In accordance with the emancipatory research principles outlined earlier, I wanted to maximise participant control over the conduct of the interviews. My plan was to adopt a similar model to Barnes' (1992) 'three stage' strategy for interviewing. Within this approach the first stage would be critical. In particular, I wanted to ensure that the people concerned were able to make informed decisions about their participation before any interviews took place. To this end, I drafted a set of potential interview questions, a statement of good practice and a covering letter. In the letter, I outlined the purpose of the research, my role as a researcher, an explanation of the accompanying documents and a suggested time-scale for the interviews. The statement of good practice gave a concise account of what participants should expect from their contact with me. The list of questions gave a speculative agenda for the interview but provided an opportunity to amend or veto its form and content. These documents were discussed in draft with DCIL, amended, clarified and sent out to the participants at the end of July.

Two people declined to be interviewed (one due to lack of time and one because he had nothing to say other than that DCIL's service was 'excellent'). In consultation with DCIL a schedule of visits was arranged for early August to meet the remaining seven people. The meetings were arranged so as to give the participants several days notice to think about the questions in advance. The interviews themselves were semi-structured and lasted for between forty minutes and an hour and half. Each interview was tape-recorded and typed transcripts were made. The transcripts were reviewed and the major points summarised in note form.

The main points, together with supporting quotes were written up as a draft report and a one page summary. These were circulated back to all the participants (including those who were not interviewed) for comment and amendment. The intention was to encourage the participants to use the interviews not only to give voice to their views and experiences but also to facilitate their greater influence over the development of DCIL's service provision. The final report (Priestley, 1996c) was submitted to DCIL for them to disseminate and the summary was tabled at their September AGM.

ADDITIONAL DATA COLLECTION

In addition to the three 'projects' outlined above I was able to participate in many DCDP/DCIL activities including working parties and discussions directly relevant to the study. During these ongoing contacts the issues raised were fed back to the organisation and discussed. Thus, data from the focus groups, documentation and interviews was supplemented by numerous 'field notes'. Finally, the research data included a wide reading of relevant literature and related studies directed by the changing research priorities of the participants and by my own interests.

Central government data was drawn from legislative documents (Green Papers, White Papers, Bills and Acts); from policy guidance documents (Department of Health circulars etc.) and from Parliamentary debates and Committee Reports. The implementation of the community care reforms during the course of the study produced an enormous amount of such data and it was necessary to prioritise those publications which dealt most directly with the issues raised by participants at DCDP and DCIL. In all, about twenty documents were used directly for detailed content analysis (although a much larger number were consulted as background reading).

It was possible to gain much information about the form and content of the contracting process by a detailed analysis of the general service level agreement and the contract/service specification for the Personal Support Service issued by the County Council. These documents were available in a number of drafts illustrating the changing position of the contracting parties over time. Several attempts were made to engage Derbyshire social services' direct participation in the study at a managerial level but these were unsuccessful and the primary data available from the purchasing authority was therefore limited to textual analysis of a relatively small number of documents.

The operational management of DCIL is made accountable through its Management Committee and General Council. I was able to study the complete minutes of these bodies for the period in question (1991-1996). DCIL's Director and Liaison Group (a working party of key function managers) submit monthly reports to Management Committee on the Centre's activity and strategy. A review of these reports yielded much factual data about the changing nature of DCIL's financial and organisational structure. The management reports, together with various internal papers, also provided important insights into the level of collective consciousness about DCIL's organisational values and mission. This documentary data was supplemented, validated and clarified by ongoing discussions with DCIL's director, research manager and the manager of the Personal Support Service.

The establishment of DCIL arose from the conscious political organisation of disabled people in Derbyshire (through DCDP) in conjunction with the local authority (DCC). This conscious political action and discourse was relatively well recorded in both published and unpublished documentation emanating from all three organisations. It was thus possible to learn much about the historical development of DCIL, its organisational goals and operational dilemmas directly from these accounts. The content analysis of these documents was supplemented by personal discussions and tape-recorded interviews with key informants in DCIL/DCDP who were able to shed additional light on their relevance and accuracy.

In 1993 DCDP produced an historical account of its activity to mark the tenth anniversary of the organisation (Davis & Mullender, 1993) which provided much of the historical background. This account was supplemented by other published accounts emanating from prominent individuals within the Coalition and the wider disabled people's movement. DCDP also publishes a regular newsletter *(Info: the voice of disabled people in Derbyshire)*. An examination of contributions to this periodical provided many additional insights.

As I have illustrated there was a good deal of reciprocity between the data collection and analysis. A large amount of non-uniform qualitative data was collected for the study from a variety of sources. The collection of this data was shaped by the changing priorities of the primary participants, by my shifting analysis of those priorities and by the bureaucratic politics of the organisations involved. Moreover, the analysis was not mine alone. My key informants were also highly analytical and the categories they used to order their actions were necessarily a primary influence on the collection and analysis of data. For this reason it is important to recognise that co-participatory research brings into question the dualist assumption that only the researcher analyses.

SUMMARY AND CONCLUSIONS

In this chapter I have outlined the methodological context for my work with DCDP/DCIL and sought to illustrate the kind of choices which I made. It is important to understand that the project was driven from the outset by my attempts to work within an emancipatory research paradigm. This was not easy nor indeed always possible and the process resulted in some less than ideal compromises (particularly in presenting the research as a coherent PhD thesis). As I have outlined, it was not possible to achieve some of the original action research goals due to considerations of diplomacy and organisational politics. This is undoubtedly the 'price' for conducting such research.

It is important to remember that disabled people are more likely to be concerned with enabling action research outcomes than with the production of 'learned' journal articles or doctoral theses. These publications are of course vital to the career patterns of academic researchers and to the research profiles of university departments. However, as my experience shows, devolving control over dissemination means giving up the 'right' to determine what gets published and how. Ultimately, the most stressful period for me was waiting to find out how DCDP/DCIL would respond to the proposed content of my thesis. It is quite conceivable that if they had expressed major concerns I might have failed to submit on time. However, this is perhaps how it should be when 'the boot is on the other foot'.

In practice, when we finally met in February 1997 to discuss issues of content and dissemination, no such fears were expressed. Indeed, there was much resistance to the idea that emancipatory research should involve a *reversal* of the social relations of research production. Rather, they felt it necessary to stress the importance of a working partnership towards mutually beneficial outcomes. For us the goal became one of *equalising* power rather than devolving it. In the final analysis the responsibility for what I had written could not and should not be devolved to anyone.

DCIL were able to use my research skills to develop, articulate and disseminate aspects of their own thinking in order to influence local policy makers. My involvement as an 'independent' person was felt to be particularly useful in validating this work. They were also able to draw directly on my writing to inform and supplement their own reports. On a very practical level my involvement in data collection, chairing meetings, recording, writing reports, presenting papers and so on enabled DCIL to engage in developmental and advocacy work for which funds would not have otherwise been available.

The research was specifically helpful to the service user participants in helping them to communicate their views and experiences to the service provider and to purchasers. In particular, the research process provided a mechanism for them to think and act collectively where they would not otherwise have been facilitated to do so. It provided the space and resources for them to articulate personal views and opinions which might not have been 'heard' had they expressed them solely as individuals.

It is fair to say that, at the time of writing, the research was more personally empowering to me than to anyone else. I was enabled to learn an enormous amount about the implementation of integrated living services and about the self-empowerment of disabled people. I was enabled to add to my publications list and to write a PhD thesis. I was enabled to generate a modest income for three years and to establish considerable skills and experience for future academic employment. In the final analysis I would not claim to have accomplished a truly 'emancipatory' piece of work but it was certainly fun trying.

REFERENCES

ABBERLEY, P. (1987) 'The Concept of Oppression and the Development of a Social Theory of Disability', *Disability, Handicap & Society*, 2(1):5-19.

ABBERLEY, P. (1992) 'Counting Us Out: a discussion of the OPCS disability surveys', *Disability, Handicap & Society*, 7:139-155.

BARNES, C. (1992) 'Qualitative Research: valuable or irrelevant?', *Disability, Handicap & Society*, 7(2):139-155.

BURY, M. (1992) 'Medical Sociology and Chronic Illness: A comment on the Panel Discussion', *Medical Sociology News*, 18(1): 29-33.

DAVIS, K. and MULLENDER, A. (1993) *Ten Turbulent Years: a review of the work of the Derbyshire Coalition of Disabled People*. Nottingham: Centre for Social Action, School of Social Studies, University of Nottingham.

FINKELSTEIN, V. (1980) *Attitudes and Disabled People: issues for discussion*. New York: World Rehabilitation Fund - monograph 5.

GIBBS, D. and PRIESTLEY, M. (1996) 'The Social Movement and User Involvement', in B.Walker, ed. (1996) *Disability Rights: A Symposium of the European Regions*. Headley, Hampshire: Hampshire Coalition of Disabled People.

GLUCKSMANN, M. (1994) 'The Work of Knowledge and the Knowledge of Women's Work', in M. Maynard and J. Purvis, (1994) *Researching Women's Lives from a Feminist Perspective*. London: Taylor & Francis.

HUNT, P (1981) 'Settling Accounts with the parasite people: a critique of "A Life part" by E. J. Miller and G. V. Gwynn', *Disability Challenge*, 1:37-50.

KELLY, L., BURTON, S. and REGAN, L. (1994) 'Researching Women's Lives or Studying Women's Oppression? Reflections on What Constitutes Feminist Research', in M. Maynard and J. Purvis, eds. (1994) *Researching Women's Lives from a Feminist Perspective*. London: Taylor & Francis Ltd.

OAKLEY, A. (1981) *Subject Women*. London: Fontana.

OLIVER, M. (1992) 'Changing the Social Relations of Research Production?', *Disability, Handicap & Society*, 7(2):101-114.

PRIESTLEY, M. (1994a) 'Blind Prejudice', *Community Care*, 3:28-29.

PRIESTLEY, M. (1994b) *Organising for Change: ABA (Leeds) Research Paper*, Leeds: Association of Blind Asians/Leeds City Council Health Unit.

PRIESTLEY, M. (1995) 'Commonality and Difference in the Movement: an Association of Blind Asians in Leeds', *Disability & Society*, 10:157-169.

PRIESTLEY, M. (1996a) *From Strength to Strength: a report on the recent development of ABA (Leeds) 1995-1996*. Leeds: Association of Blind Asians/Leeds City Council Health Unit.

PRIESTLEY, M. (1996b) *Making Effective Use of User Inputs*, paper presented at the DCIL/NHS Executive Seminar, Midland Hotel, Derby, 23-24 July1996.

PRIESTLEY, M. (1996c) *Perceptions of Quality: user views on DCIL's Personal Support Service*, Ripley: Disability Research Unit, University of Leeds/Derbyshire Centre for Integrated Living.

PRIESTLEY, M. (1997) *Disability, Values and Quality: a case study in Derbyshire*. Leeds: PhD thesis, University of Leeds.

RAMCHARAN, P. and GRANT, G. (1994) 'Setting one agenda for empowering persons with a disadvantage within the research process', in M. Rioux and M. Bach, eds. (1994) *Disability Is Not Measles: New Research Paradigms in Disability*. North York, Ontario: L'Institut Roeher.

RIOUX, M. and BACH, M. (1994) *Disability Is Not Measles: New Paradigms in Disability*. North York, Ontario: L'Institut Roeher.

SMITH, D. (1988) *The Everyday World as Problematic: a feminist sociology*. Milton Keynes: Open University Press.

STANLEY, L. (1990) *Feminist Praxis: Research, Theory and Epistemology in Feminist Sociology*. London: Routledge.

STANLEY, L. and WISE, S. (1983) *Breaking Out: Feminist Consciousness and Feminist Research*. London: Routledge.

STONE, E. and PRIESTLEY, M. (1996) 'Parasites, Pawns and Partners: disability research and the role of non-disabled researchers', *British Journal of Sociology*, 47(4):699-716.

TOURAINE, A. (1985) 'An Introduction to the study of social movements', *Social Research*, 52:749-87.

ZARB, G. (1992) 'On the Road to Damascus: first steps towards changing the relations of disability research production', *Disability, Handicap & Society*, 7(2):125-138.

CHAPTER 7

Researching Disability Employment Policies

Neil Lunt and Patricia Thornton

INTRODUCTION

Research is a multifaceted enterprise. Inquiry includes conducting surveys, using secondary data sets, as well as a range of more qualitative explorations. Positivist and interpretivist paradigms compete over the status of knowledge, the possibility of attaining objective knowledge, the role of the researcher in the research process, and the place of values and politics in research (Hughes, 1990; Blaikie, 1993; May, 1993).

What place does policy analysis occupy in these methodologies and methods? We draw on our experiences of one approach to policy analysis – a desk-based review of documentary material from 15 countries. The review was about national policies to promote employment of disabled people and, as such, was an example of 'disability research'. The commissioners of the research required us to report from the perspective of national governments, however, and not from the point of view of other actors in the policy process, such as disabled people's organisations. As effectiveness of policy was framed in terms of meeting 'national objectives' other, competing, objectives could not be addressed. We explore these and other constraints encountered in doing disability research in the policy arena. We address a series of interrelated questions: what was the background to the research; how was the study undertaken; what were the weaknesses in carrying it out; what were the outcomes of the project; and what impact did it have?

BACKGROUND

In 1992 the UK Department of Employment[1] commissioned the Social Policy Research Unit at the University of York to undertake a desk-top review in the field of disability and employment. The study aimed to 'provide an overview of legislation, schemes and services aimed at integrating disabled people into the workforce in all EC member states and also the United States, Canada, Australia and Sweden'. The UK was not included. The review sought to outline the types of provision in place within each country, look in greater detail at the implementation of different legislative and administrative approaches, and discuss their effectiveness in achieving the objectives within the national framework. The research specification anticipated that to attain an up-to-date picture of measures it would be necessary to study legal and research documents, often using non-English sources.

The study was commissioned in late 1992 and carried out over four months, with a further month devoted to writing and preparing the final document for publication. The report was published by the Employment Department in its Research Series in October 1993 (Lunt and Thornton, 1993).

This brief description of the commissioning, conceptualisation and conduct of the research can cover only some of the more significant nuances of the negotiation and research process: how the research contract was agreed; what decisions were taken in doing the research; and what constraints and difficulties arose.

The way in which the study was commissioned introduced an important 'stakeholder' into the picture and ensured the research was applied (aimed at addressing particular policy issues) rather than pure (aimed at furthering theory and knowledge for its own sake) (Rossi and Freeman, 1993). The relationship between research funder (in this case a government department)

[1] Now the Department of Education and Employment

and the researchers undertaking the study is central to understanding the conduct and outcomes of the research. Cantley (1992), in a discussion of relationships between contractors and researchers, identifies important factors that shape research negotiations between contractor and contracted: dominant paradigms and assumptions about the role of the researcher, academic context, assumptions about the use of the research, agency context, and funding arrangements. In this chapter we describe the ways in which our enquiry was shaped by factors such as these in the contractor-researcher relationship.

DOMINANT PARADIGMS AND ASSUMPTIONS ABOUT THE ROLE OF THE RESEARCHER

The impetus to undertake the review came wholly from the commissioning Department who negotiated with the contracted Unit. Here we enter the twilight world of contract research, where topics are rarely the choice of the researchers, and where work is commissioned to assist with policy development or service delivery (Richardson et al, 1990).

Why was the Social Policy Research Unit asked to undertake this particular study? The explanation probably lies with the Unit's 20 year track record in carrying out research studies for Government Departments, including Departments of Health, Employment and Social Security. It could be assumed that the Unit was sensitive to policy-makers' needs, and understood the conventions in researching, interpreting and presenting material. To draw on an analogy from the policy-making relationship between interest groups and government departments, the Unit was an 'insider group' in its dealings with central government (Jordan and Richardson, 1987). As Fletcher comments, 'bodies such as the Employment Service are often risk-averse when it comes to appointing researchers' (Fletcher, 1997, p. 179). For commissioners, standards and reliability may take priority over requirements that researchers have previously carried out disability research, are sensitive to disabled people, or are themselves disabled people. That said, the Unit was not unfamiliar with the political context and sensitivity of disability research (Baldwin and Parker, 1992).

It might have been reasonably assumed that the researchers were unlikely to raise troublesome issues and upset established power relations. As Lukes (1974) recognises, power is not only about the way decisions are taken, or issues kept off the agenda, but also about manipulation of interests and exercise of pervasive control. Some might argue that the Unit would perform to the required standards and forgo power and influence. On the contrary, we argue that the commissioner-contractor relationship does allow space for researchers to influence the shape, process and outcomes.

Why were the authors chosen to carry out the research? Perhaps choice is too strong a word – the research needed to be done immediately and we were available. The Unit had researched aspects of the employment situation of disabled people in the UK but the international dimension was quite new. As the researchers engaged to carry out the review, our awareness of the policy issues and debates was limited. We had no track record of comparative research. Labour market policy was a new field, as was employment law and the gamut of specialist legislation for disabled people; anti-discrimination legislation, employment quotas, and mainstreaming were relatively unfamiliar concepts. Our initial ignorance had some advantages. We were not encumbered with pre-conceptions or conventional analytical frameworks. We were open to new ideas and perspectives. One person's openness is another's idea of emptiness, however. How were we to know whether what we had to say was of interest, or had already been said?

The dominant assumption is that experienced researchers have technical skills and abilities that can be applied to new areas of enquiry and that a working knowledge of context is not a necessity. This paradigm sees research as a 'technical' process involving the systematic application of methods and techniques, rather than an exercise embedded in a social and political context (Gouldner, 1976). The underlying paradigm of the research study was that researchers can be dispassionate, removed and aloof. It highlights key differences between traditional (positivistic) scientific approaches to social research, and more interpretivist and critical understandings (Hughes, 1990).

ASSUMPTIONS ABOUT THE USE OF RESEARCH

The study was meant to meet current policy needs and provide a 'source book' for further Employment Department work on disability employment policies and services. At the time, employment of disabled people was rising on the policy agenda internationally. In the UK, campaigns were under way for anti-discrimination legislation to mirror the USA Americans with Disabilities Act. Disability activists suspected that the Government intended to abandon the quota system dating from 1944, which imposed obligations on larger employers to employ disabled people but remained unenforced and ineffectual in securing working opportunities for disabled people. UK policy trends indicated that the collective obligation to employ disabled people might be supplanted by promotion of individual responsibility.

Against this background, we pondered on how far the review would be used as evidence or ammunition in UK debates on new policy directions. Here important questions arise about the use to which research findings are put, and the control researchers have over dissemination and interpretation (Rule, 1978; Richardson *et al*, 1990).

AGENCY CONTEXT

It would be naïve to believe that policy-makers know in advance precisely what it is they wish to find out. The nature of the research task remains fluid, and precise issues and questions unfold as the investigation develops. Within broad parameters, researchers are able to exert a measure of influence on the shape and direction of the research project. Greater awareness and 'expertise' within an area increase bargaining strength. In the case of the disability and employment review, no one knew in advance what might emerge from such an exploratory study. Our preliminary investigation of the availability of information sources permitted us to formulate less ambitious aims.

Nor should it be assumed that commissioners are of a single mind. This project was jointly commissioned by the Department of Employment and its agency, Employment Services. The former was the lead partner in shaping the research specification, and more practically, meetings were held in London rather than Sheffield! Their requirements differed: the Employment Department wanted the study to report on policy and effectiveness; and Employment Services sought information to assist service delivery. Because of time constraints and the limitations of a desk-top study which could not adequately reflect what happens on the ground, we had more freedom to pursue policy dimensions rather than service delivery.

FUNDING ARRANGEMENTS: AROUND THE WORLD IN 80 DAYS

It could be argued that limited time devoted to the study prevented adequate investigation and analysis of the issues. We had to go around the world in 80 (working) days! We had to contend with one criticism that the researchers were pawns of an Employment Department paying lip-service to the idea of an international review through intentional under-resourcing. In fact, in terms of the Employment Department's research budgets, this was a relatively large piece of research and an essential condition was that it be completed before the start of the new financial year.

METHODS

The study drew on a range of sources including legislative texts, published documents, conference papers, working papers and assorted grey material. As May (1993) comments on the use of documentary methods, the sources utilised depend on the researcher's perspective, and the time and resources available. We drew on documents provided by international bodies such as the International Labour Organisation, European Commission, Council of Europe, and United Nations. Among them we found reviews of specific areas of our enquiry, such as legislation and sheltered employment, although not all were up to date or comprehensive. Other sources drawn upon included literature produced by pan-national disability organisations, such as the World Deaf Association and World Blind Association. At the national level we sought, often with difficulty, to include work of disability organisations and voluntary groups. We obtained general literature through database searches and abstracting services.

Documents produced by government authorities are the largest class of documents available to the social researcher (Scott, 1990). National sources included the various government departments with responsibility for some aspect of disability and employment, including departments of labour, welfare, health, and social security. Initially it was not always clear which departments to approach; some countries turned out to place responsibility for disability policy, including work and income, with health departments. Responsibility for policy and services typically was scattered across a number of departments and was not necessarily co-ordinated. Consequently, we did not know in advance who held useful information, and neither did departments know what was held elsewhere.

We also approached organisations responsible for monitoring and enforcing parts of legislation, as well as statutory and non-statutory service providers. Finally, we sought the assistance of individuals identified as being knowledgeable and well placed to describe developments in particular countries. In all cases, we asked for details of national legislation relating to the employment of disabled people, details of schemes and services which aim to implement the legislation and any official reports of the effectiveness of policy.

We pieced together fragments to gain a picture of the provision in each country. The view of disability employment policy was on the whole uni-dimensional. For example, there was a shortage of material on the disability-benefits interface, except in The Netherlands where responsibility lay with a single department. Little information was offered on housing, transport and education policies. Consequently, we were steered towards a narrow depiction of what constitutes disability employment policy. The logic of our information gathering meant that we tended to report on specialist and priority provision, and not on how disabled people were served by mainstream services. These deficits provoked us to consider how specialist and mainstream provision are inter-related. We were aware that work must be situated in a wider context than just employment policy.

PROBLEMS

Various problems and dilemmas arose during the study. In some study countries we obtained few published accounts of policy developments and their effects but personal communications provided potentially useful perspectives, frequently from disability organisations. We were constrained, however, by requiring referenceable sources, and faced difficulties in reporting the judgements and opinions of any national sources unless they were written down in a referenceable form. Consequently, as with most desk-top studies, we privileged the official accounts and focused upon policy intentions.

The problems of drawing on secondary sources were exacerbated by our limited understanding of the national context, the assumptions employed (including definitions and researchers' stance) and the language. These are discussed below.

The intention to review the effectiveness of various measures and their relationship to official objectives was difficult to achieve in practice. The first problem is the identification of policy objectives. Only when the legislation is recent and there is a distinct break with tradition are policy aims likely to be clearly stated. More often they develop incrementally. Official accounts of policy tend to be reproduced without much revision and we found ourselves describing official policy that locally based experts had difficulties in recognising!

Low importance was attached to evaluations. A major problem was how to access any evaluations of the impact of policy measures, and how to assess the relative significance of studies we did locate. It is one thing to put a policy in place, another for it to be effective. Reviewing the literature involves trying to match official and non-official accounts. Certain discussions of effectiveness and evaluation were more easily reported than others. There tended to be an emphasis on quantitative approaches, and on levels of spending on services. But a high number of people receiving services or placement does not mean there are high levels of consumer satisfaction or appropriate jobs. Further, the study emphasis was on access to employment, to the neglect of advancement of disabled people within employment.

A further constraint was that we looked at objectives of national policies and their effectiveness, and discounted initiatives that were not considered as national policy. Thus, we could not take account of what other social partners were doing. For example, employers' organisations sometimes undertook initiatives independently of national policy and legislative measures. Similarly, we could take no account of voluntary initiatives around supported employment and employment advice and counselling services. We were in danger, therefore, of getting only a partial picture of national provision. Fragmentation and privatisation of service provision were increasingly evident during the 1990s and thus crucial to the overall description. However, our assessments were entirely 'top-down' and could not take account of the influence of grass-roots movements, including how disability organisations contributed to policy formulation.

Language was a problem. As we knew only French and a little German we needed to rely mostly on English language sources. This reinforced our reliance on official accounts and limited access to material produced by disability organisations in the other languages. May (1993) has commented on the difficulty of understanding cultures different from our own. More particularly, he notes how difficulties of translation lead to a reliance on official publications, giving rise to the problem that:

'Any analysis based upon such documents may then produce partial and
incomplete theories. In other words, the stereotype of English visitors abroad
continuing to speak English, and simply raising their voices if not understood by
"those foreigners", has its research equivalent' (May, 1993: 162).

Comparative research has inevitable problems and this desk-top study was
no exception. As Hill (1996) notes, one of the main motives for comparative
studies is the desire to 'learn' from the experience of other countries. Thus,
comparative research tends to be research of a certain type; descriptive with
an emphasis on quantitative aspects, often removed from the national
context. It places emphasis on describing spending and institutional
arrangements and less on the comparison of outcomes and achievements.

Further dangers in comparative research include UK-centred
interpretation and lack of awareness of the ingrainedness of other national
approaches. Initially it is not easy to understand that Denmark does not
recognise disabled people as a distinct group, nor to comprehend the
pervasive system in France of assessing degrees of 'disability' and classifying
people accordingly. Such differences cannot be understood without looking at
the historical forces behind them. Comparative research needs to understand
traditional approaches to grasp the significance of, for example, associations
of disabled people in the policy process. Problems understanding terms and
definitions were compounded by the language problem: just what is meant by
'disabled people's organisations'?

REVISITING

From the 1993 review we became aware that disability and employment
was commonly an issue neglected by a range of stakeholders (and potential
stakeholders), including those with policy responsibilities within various
departments, organisations of disabled people, academics and others with
an interest in labour market issues. Moreover, this neglect was not peculiar
to any one country, but was a recurring theme across the majority of the
study countries.

Since the early 1990s, interest in issues of disability and work has been
growing. The disability movement and calls for choice and empowerment
began to place more emphasis on employment, particularly through the
campaigns around the introduction of anti-discrimination legislation.

Pressure on social security spending on long-term sickness and invalidity benefits began to lead to more active disability employment policies.

We decided to revisit the study in 1996. Feedback from various stakeholders suggested that the study had been useful. It brought together material previously dispersed across a number of countries, and prevented constant 'reinvention of the wheel'. We were told that the material was particularly relevant to countries developing disability employment policies and seeking guidance on competing ways forward, who were, for example, weighing up quota systems and discrimination legislation. The readership ranged from developing countries and economies in transition looking to develop new policies to countries with more established policies and traditions looking afresh at disability employment strategies. To obtain a national picture appeared a useful starting point. As May (1993) notes:

> 'One aim of comparative research, therefore, is to understand and explain the ways in which societies and cultures experience and act upon social, economic and political changes' (pp. 153-4).

Notions of anti-discrimination legislation and supported employment attracted particular attention. The interest in the international situation was not confined to government departments but also concerned organisations trying to influence discussions and debates.

For our own part, we were conscious that the policy picture was rapidly changing. Indeed our account of 1993 was quickly becoming outdated as new policy initiatives were being introduced. We wanted to report on these changes but also to take a closer look at the effectiveness of policy measures. There were inevitable gaps in the 1993 account that we sought to improve on.

Our approach and emphasis differed when revisiting the review in 1996. For a number of the countries we used national informants, who were grounded in the national context, to gather material and assemble the account. These individuals had critical perspectives on policy changes. We sought to place more emphasis on non-official accounts, and also understand the place of disabled people's, employees' and employers' organisations in influencing policy. There were particular issues and linkages that we sought to improve on, particularly the area of social security, which we recognised as intrinsic to any debate around work. We sought to extend coverage to an expanded European Union that now included Austria, Finland and Sweden.

We also included the UK in 1996. The funding in 1996 was provided by a grant from the European Commission, with additional support from the International Labour Organisation, rather than by any national government department.

OUTCOMES AND DISSEMINATION

Policy research of whatever type should be disseminated. As Richardson *et al* (1990) recommend, dissemination of research findings should be to the widest possible audiences, including attention to trade and voluntary publications, summaries and conference papers. The study was published as a full (208 page) report and a four page executive summary. Both were available free and distributed generously by the Employment Department. Over 100 copies were distributed to country sources, as an acknowledgement of their contribution. A descriptive article in a trade journal and two seminars to Employment Department staff followed publication. Outside the UK the report was widely distributed in paper form and accessible on the World Wide Web as part of the GLADNET international database of texts in the field of employment and training of disabled people.

We were keen to increase awareness of the study because we had come to realise that such a comprehensive compilation filled a gap, at least for English language readers. We were anxious that others should be freed from having to undertake a similar, now superfluous, task. But at the time we were uncertain about the use of such a piece of work. The material *might* help people to contribute to discussions around policy development, although such an effect clearly depends on the policy-making process and how we believe decisions are shaped in the policy arena. We were acutely aware of the lack of evidence on the effectiveness of some much vaunted policies and the problems of transferability of policy.

Subsequently, most of our dissemination effort was directed more at spreading the ideas which we had begun to develop in doing the work than at raising awareness of the 'facts' of national policies and services. We sought to stimulate debate around the disability and employment issues, encouraging policy makers and stakeholders to think about the whole and the parts of disability employment policy. We had identified important trends, issues and questions which we felt deserved further attention: were anti-discrimination and quota-type measures incompatible; how was service delivery likely to develop; how would newly recognised groups of disabled people alter the policy agenda? A further strand was to consider how employment fitted with the theoretical moves that have taken place around disability and to explore policy from competing sociological viewpoints (Lunt and Thornton, 1994). The study also prompted us to think more about the importance of the social security interface with employment, which we explored in a commission from the Joseph Rowntree Foundation (Lunt and Thornton, 1996).

At the most practical level the study's impact on UK national policy was at best indirect. The publication was used as a 'source-book' within the Employment Department when considering policy options. We did attempt, however, to build on the experience and knowledge we had acquired and offered a commentary on the changes under way in the UK (Thornton and Lunt, 1995).

NON-DISABLED RESEARCHERS DOING DISABILITY POLICY RESEARCH?

Given the sustained critique of non-disabled persons setting research agendas for, and doing research on, disabled people (*Disability, Handicap & Society*, 1992), how acceptable to the UK disability establishment is policy research undertaken by non-disabled researchers?

Two points are worth raising in relation to our work. First, we were not trying to interpret the experiences of disabled people. Nevertheless, one critique of interpretative methods may still be levelled against policy research; namely, that researchers render faithful accounts (albeit in our case 'policy accounts') and then move on to other issues, while disabled subjects (and issues) remain unchanged (Oliver, 1992). Such criticism would contend that as contract researchers undertaking short pieces of work, we raze the ground before moving on to more fertile grazing (or Foucauldian 'gazing') pastures. This is a strong critique, independent of the research methods used. Such practices are encouraged by the very nature of contract research and the paradigm of transferable skills. However, we have both identified disability and employment as a crucial policy issue and also maintained a professional interest. We believe it important that the issue gets the policy attention it deserves and continues to be debated. On the other hand, developing an ongoing policy interest in this area may itself be as controversial as the charge of 'transience'. Clearly, however, any study must compete in the market-place of ideas, where differing stakeholders will attach more or less value to the product that results.

The second, related, point concerns whether policy analysis of this nature has any value: does research facilitate change and make a difference? The relationship between research, policy development and social change is thorny, and encompasses ground which we cannot cover here. A distinction made by Bury (1996) is that research may not deserve the thrust of criticism reserved for it and that we should focus on political inactivity. He makes strong arguments for separating the two.

CONCLUSIONS

This chapter is a *post hoc* rationalisation of a research study. Looking back, we have identified the constraints encountered in doing disability research, including how the study was undertaken, the outcomes of the project, and the impact it had. Rarely is such detailed attention given to potential constraints in advance of a study; indeed, ongoing negotiation and problem-solving are the norm. Reflection, however, can be useful in helping identify what was difficult or problematic about the process. Reflection, although not changing the relations of research production, has the capacity to illuminate. Government Departments are slowly adjusting to a new understanding of what disability is and the implications for disability research and policy. Non-disabled researchers have a responsibility to engage in the wider debate, and, whenever possible, act as a catalyst in their dealings with central agencies.

Two questions remain: could the study have been done differently, and could it have been done better? As with any research project, the answers are inevitably 'yes'. For example, we have talked about disability as a homogeneous category, but clearly it is not. Variables of gender and race are missing from the review and subsequent update, and age is only partially addressed. 'National policy' was assumed to be synonymous with governments' interests and disabled people's role in its formulation is inadequately reflected. There is too little attention to job retention and career advancement, reflecting the policy interest in (re)entry to employment. Many essential aspects of the employment infrastructure are missing: education, transport, housing, health and social services. The focus is on special and priority policies and services for disabled people, ignoring the fact that disabled people are consumers of services which are open to all.

This does not mean that there was no value in undertaking the study. The issue of disability and employment is key and must be brought to the policy arena and gradually exposed to scrutiny and debate. A variety of interests and strategies can ensure this happens and that discussion remains high on the agenda. We would hope to contribute, if only in small part, to this process. In employment and disability policy there clearly remains work still to do.

REFERENCES

BALDWIN, S. and PARKER, G. (1992) 'Confessions of a jobbing researcher', *Disability, Handicap & Society*, 7(2): 197-203.

BLAIKIE, N. (1993) *Approaches to Social Inquiry*. Cambridge: Polity Press.

BURY, M. (1996) 'Defining and researching disability: challenges and responses', in C. Barnes and G. Mercer, eds. *Exploring the Divide: Illness and Disability*. Leeds: The Disability Press.

CANTLEY, C. (1992) 'Negotiating research' in J. Vincent and S. Brown, eds., *Critics and Customers: the Control of Social Policy Research*. Aldershot: CRSP/Avebury.

DISABILITY, HANDICAP & SOCIETY (1992) 'Special Edition: Researching disability', 7 (2).

FLETCHER, D.L. (1997) 'Evaluating special measures for the unemployed: some reflections on recent UK experience', *Policy and Politics*, 25 (2): 173-184.

GOULDNER, A. (1976) 'The dark side of the dialectic: Toward a new objectivity', *Sociological Inquiry*, 46: 3-16.

HILL, M. (1996) *Social Policy: A Comparative Analysis*. London: Harvester Wheatsheaf.

HUGHES, J. (1990) *The Philosophy of Social Science* (2nd edition). London: Longman.

JORDAN, A. and RICHARDSON, J. (1987) *Government and Pressure Groups in Britain*. Oxford: Clarendon Press.

LUKES, S. (1974) *Power: A Radical View*. London: Macmillan.

LUNT, N. and THORNTON, P. (1993) *Employment Policies for Disabled People: A review of legislation and services in fifteen countries*. Research Series 16, London: Employment Department.

LUNT, N. and THORNTON, P. (1994) 'Disability and employment: towards an understanding of discourse and policy', *Disability & Society*, 9 (2): 223-238.

LUNT, N. and THORNTON, P. (1996) 'Disabled people, work and benefits: a review of the research literature, Paper prepared for a Joseph Rowntree Foundation Seminar held on 12 November 1996', in House of Commons Social Security Committee *Incapacity Benefit: Minutes of Evidence and Appendices to the Minutes of Evidence*, London: The Stationery Office.

MAY, T. (1993) *Social Research: Issues, Methods and Processes*. Buckingham: Open University Press.

OLIVER, M. (1992) 'Changing the social relations of research production', *Disability, Handicap & Society*, 7 (2) : 101-114.

RICHARDSON, A., JACKSON, C. and SYKES, W. (1990) *Taking Research Seriously: Means of improving and assessing the use and dissemination of research*. Social Community Planning Research, London: HMSO.

ROSSI, P. H. and FREEMAN, H. E. (1993) *Evaluation: A Systematic Approach* (5th Edition). California: Sage.

RULE, J. (1978) *Insight and Social Betterment*. New York: Oxford University Press.

SCOTT, J. (1990) *A Matter of Record: Documentary sources in social research*. Cambridge: Polity Press.

THORNTON, P. and LUNT, N. (1995) *Employment for Disabled People: Social obligation or individual responsibility?*, Social Policy Reports 2, York: Social Policy Research Unit.

CHAPTER 8

Making Connections: A narrative study of adult children of parents with learning difficulties

Tim Booth and Wendy Booth

Parents with learning difficulties are widely presumed to present a high risk of parenting breakdown. Successive studies have reported high rates (40-60%) for the removal of children from the family home (Mickelson, 1949; Scally, 1973; Accardo and Whitman, 1990). Research also suggests that the children of parents with learning difficulties are at risk of developmental delay, maltreatment, neglect and abuse (Schilling, Schinke, Blythe and Barth, 1982). This evidence has contributed to the view that people with learning difficulties lack the competence to provide good-enough parenting, and is often used to support a general claim of parental inadequacy. Oliver (1977:19), for example, asserts that such parents 'continue to be incompetent rearers, whatever supportive treatment is offered' and Fotheringham (1980:35) too claims that few parents have the ability to provide 'conditions of care at the minimal acceptable level'. Accardo and Whitman (1990:70) argue that the only important question 'with regard to parenting failure of significantly mentally retarded adults would seem to be not whether but when'.

The study described in this chapter arose directly from earlier work, in which we documented the lives and struggles of parents with learning difficulties through personal accounts of their own experience of child-rearing and parenthood (Booth and Booth, 1994). This research showed that blanket judgements of parental incompetence are not grounded in the lives of parents themselves. The statistics on child removal owe as much to the decisions of professionals and the courts as to the behaviour of parents. The fact is that people with learning difficulties frequently fall victim to an expectation of parental inadequacy that is made real through the decisions and actions of those with the power to intervene in their lives. This 'presumption of incompetence' renders parents with learning difficulties vulnerable to discriminatory treatment and prejudicial judgements about their ability to cope with the demands of parenthood. From this point of view, parental competence is not just an attribute of the person but an attributed status that reflects the normative standards used for defining good-enough parenting by those charged with making the assessments (Booth and Booth, 1996b).

A common response to this research was that we had argued a case for parents that did not take account of the interests or welfare of their children (Schofield, 1996). What, people wanted to know, becomes of children who grow up in such families? This study began as an attempt to address this question.

THE TARGET GROUP

The study[1] was designed to explore what it means to be brought up by parents with learning difficulties through the experience of their adult children. The target group identified for inclusion in the study comprised

---

[1] The research was funded by a grant from the Joseph Rowntree Foundation.

men and women aged (preferably) between 18 - 30 years who had spent the greater part of their childhood living in a family where one or both parents had learning difficulties.

For research purposes, parents were held to satisfy the inclusion criterion if they were known to have received health, education or social services specifically designated for use by people with learning difficulties at some time in their lives or if a professional who knew them personally confirmed that they had been so-labelled. This was the only practical approach in the circumstances given that the parents themselves were not the subjects of the research, many were not seen or contacted and some were now dead. The expedient of using a person's current or former status as a service user as a surrogate for unobtainable test or clinical data in order to establish their learning difficulties has both a theoretical rationale (Mercer, 1973) and an administrative precedent, being the method used by many health authorities to identify those who are eligible for registration with their case registers (Farmer, Rohde and Sacks, 1993).

The decision to target adult children in the 18-30 age range was taken because we wanted respondents who were able to look back and reflect on their own childhood and upbringing from a position in the adult world, but whose memories were not too far distant from the events and experiences they described. Things did not quite turn out as planned. Difficulties in locating willing subjects and the way the introductions and interviews were set up (see below) meant that a number of younger and older people were admitted to the study. All in all, 18 of the 30 subjects fell within the prescribed band while 2 were below-age and 10 were over-age.

The research questions driving the study entailed that the adult children who took part had grown up mostly in the care of their parents at home, and had maintained contact with their family during any spell away from home. This requirement seriously limited the pool of eligible subjects. Twenty to thirty years ago, when our prospective subjects were born, it is arguably even less likely than today that the interests of the child would have been seen as best served by remaining in a family headed by parent(s) with learning difficulties.

Many adult children were located who had spent too long away from their parents to qualify for inclusion in the study. In the context of people's family lives it is not surprising that grown up children with relatively secure and stable home backgrounds were hard to find. Crises of family survival precipitated by poverty, broken relationships or official intervention were pandemic. Only half (15) of the study group had remained at home in the care of at least one parent with learning difficulties until they came of age or until they moved out to live independently. Five of our subjects had spent less than two years away from their parent(s), and a further three had been in care for two to four years. Of the remaining seven, all had spent more than four years in children's homes or residential schools but had remained in contact with their parents throughout this period. The majority of this group (5) had spent at least ten years of their childhood with their parent(s). The shortest time that anyone had lived at home was seven years, although in this case the lad went home from his residential school for weekends and holidays.

LOCATING THE SUBJECTS

Adult children of parents with learning difficulties constitute a hidden population for research purposes. There is no register of names through which they can be traced. Tracking them down presents the same problems as trying to trace the children of, say, parents who cannot read or write, or children whose mothers have epilepsy. There are too few to identify them through a general trawl of the population, and in any case such an approach would not be feasible given the sensitive nature of the subject and the difficulties of verifying people's responses. Consideration was given to placing a feature about the study in the local press inviting people to come forward but this idea was rejected because again there would be no way of validating the parents' status and also for reasons of interviewer safety.

The only practical means of overcoming these enumeration problems was to trace possible subjects through parents known to the services. Even this method was far from straightforward. Some professionals were noticeably reluctant or unwilling to label people as having learning difficulties. Data protection restrictions limit the possibilities for searching the records held by service agencies and in any case information about people's adult children was rarely available on file. No agency was in a position to supply a list of people with learning difficulties known to have children aged between 18-30 years. Legal hurdles aside, such information was usually known only to individual practitioners about individual clients. Accordingly, people working in the learning difficulties services were approached personally and asked if they knew directly or indirectly of any parents with adult children, or knew of anyone else who might know such a parent.

This method of using such 'key informants' (Whitman and Accardo, 1990) has a number of weaknesses. It excludes people who are not known to the service agencies; possibly over-represents the less competent parents or those with greater problems and fewer community supports; and is very time-consuming. Any bias resulting from the first two problems is likely to be small. Most parents with learning difficulties will probably come to the attention of the statutory services at some time when their children are growing up. The other limitation must be seen as part of the price for doing the research at all.

The key informant method took us into twelve local authority areas in search of our target quota of adult children. Enquiries were pursued and leads followed up through social workers and social services teams, adult training centres and social education centres, special schools, special needs tutors in further education colleges, community nurses and community learning disability teams, local case registers, clinical psychologists, educational psychologists, careers officers, Family Service Units, a range of voluntary organisations, and other personal contacts. The task of locating our subjects turned out to be a major logistical venture, and the difficulties we encountered were one of the main reasons why the fieldwork stage of the research took fifteen months to complete instead of the eight months we had initially planned. The process was more like private detective work than research sampling: more Raymond Chandler than Moser and Kalton. It involved tracking down sources, cold calling, getting a foot in the door, following up leads, checking out information, blundering down blind alleys, cultivating informants, using go-betweens and a great deal of legwork in pursuit of what in research terms were the equivalent of missing persons. Even so, obtaining the names of potential subjects was only the first step to establishing contact.

ESTABLISHING CONTACT

Finding the names of parents with learning difficulties known to have grown-up children was only a point of call on the way to our final destination. The next stage was to find out where the children lived and to arrange for an introduction. This was not so easy as it sounds. The sources who had come up with the parent(s) names were not always acquainted with the children, did not always know their home address and anyway could not usually divulge such information for reasons of confidentiality. In any case, given the nature of the study and the vulnerabilities of the families, we felt it was important that the initial approach should be made via people who were familiar and accountable, and in a way that left the initiative with the subject.

A number of leads fizzled out at this stage or had to be dropped. Some parents were found to have died and their children's whereabouts were unknown, or the children had left home and lost contact with their parents. Other grown-up children had emigrated or now lived in another part of the country. In a few cases the workers involved advised that family circumstances militated against the research (for example, because of a recent bereavement, illness, mental health problems, or a pending court case) or that the individual concerned was unable to communicate well enough to be interviewed. Some professionals refused to act as an intermediary or were instructed not to help us by their line managers. It is not possible to be sure how many potential subjects were lost in these ways, because the number of adult children in the family obviously could not be verified in every case, but at least fifteen families headed by a parent or parents with learning difficulties and known to have adult children slipped through the net before any attempt to contact them could be made.

Putting aside these setbacks, our principal line of approach was to establish contact through the good offices of an intermediary or third party already known to the person. In most cases this was a professional worker, although parents themselves or siblings were also used in this role. The only occasions when a third party was not used were where the subject was already linked into the researchers' network.

Where the third party was a professional or practitioner they were usually sent a brief outline of the study explaining what it was about and what it would involve, together with some notes aimed at anticipating any questions the subject might ask. They were left to decide when, where and how best to broach the matter. Initially people were simply asked if they would agree to see the researcher to talk about the project. They were told that participation was entirely voluntary and they could pull out at any time. Once consent was obtained the intermediary would either fix up a meeting at a time and place of the subject's choosing or seek permission to pass on the person's name and address to the researcher for arrangements to be made direct. In many cases (12), the third party came along to make the introductions at the first meeting.

The use of intermediaries in this way has its disadvantages. The researcher has no direct control over how the study is first presented and explained; people's feelings towards the third party might act as an uncontrollable source of response bias; and, where a practitioner is involved as the go-between, the researcher may be too closely identified with authority or officialdom. In practice, there was no way round these dangers if the study was going to get done.

Our previous research led us to anticipate that some parents might feel threatened by our enquiries. Most were likely to have experienced long-term surveillance from the statutory services, persistent intervention in their private lives, and various forms of system abuse (Booth and Booth, 1995). These experiences can foster an understandable insecurity and defensiveness. We offered to meet any parents who were made anxious or suspicious by our work, or who just wanted to know more about what we were doing. Third party intermediaries were made aware of our readiness to follow up such concerns. In effect, we allowed the parents a veto over the research: we would not proceed with the interviews if they were opposed even though their son or daughter had agreed to see us. In the event, 16 parents from 11 families were briefed personally about the study of whom 2 exercised their right of veto, in both cases after the first interview.

The process of establishing contact maintained a distance between researcher and subject until the latter's consent had been obtained. The third parties who acted as go-betweens had no cause to put any pressure on the people they approached and no obvious interest in trying hard to recruit them for the study. Equally the people themselves had no obvious incentive to take part in the study. On the contrary, there are many reasons why they might have preferred not to talk about childhoods that were likely to have been troubled. Both of these considerations pointed to the likelihood of a high refusal rate even when a possible subject had been tracked down. In fact, at least twelve people declined an invitation to participate in the study – around one in three of those approached.

Overall, our best estimate is that two people were located for every one who eventually agreed to be interviewed after allowing for the three main causes of attrition: people who turned out not to be eligible for inclusion in the study (primarily because they were too young or had spent too long away from their parents as a child); people who could not be contacted; and people who refused.

THE STUDY GROUP

Thirty people (16 men and 14 women) were finally recruited into the study. Their ages ranged from 18 to 42 years for the men and 16 to 37 years for the women with a median age for the group of 27 years: over half (57%) were between 20 and 30 years old.

The subjects divide evenly into people with and people without learning difficulties. The men and women are split equally between both groups. The number of people with learning difficulties exceeded what had been planned or expected. Indeed, one of the difficulties which prolonged the fieldwork was the necessity of ensuring adequate representation of unlabelled adults. Finding grown-up children with learning difficulties was relatively so much easier. This fact needs to be viewed in context. It is known that the genetic risk of parents with learning difficulties having a child with a clinically-diagnosable condition is no greater than for the general population (Tymchuk, 1990). Four specific factors, aside from heredity alone, seem to account for the problem. The first is an artefact of the study: adult children without learning difficulties were more likely to have moved away and less likely to be known by local service agencies or practitioners. Second, circumstantial evidence suggests that children are more likely to be removed from their parents if they do not have learning difficulties: partly because the risks to their welfare and development are seen as being that much greater and partly too because they more often present problems of control as they grow older. Consequently, fewer of them can be traced through their birth parents and more had to be excluded from the study for not having spent the greater part of their childhood with them. Third, the children of parents with learning difficulties face a high risk of developmental delay. Poverty is a major threat to their welfare. It undermines their health, their physical and intellectual development, their educational attainment, the quality of their family relationships and their emotional security. The high proportion who grow into adults with some form of learning difficulties shows what happens in the absence of effective supports designed to compensate for these deficits. Finally, the children in whom we were interested were much more likely to be excluded from mainstream school, channelled into special education and labelled as having learning difficulties because of the stigma attached to their parents.

Twenty-eight of the thirty informants had just one parent with learning difficulties, usually the mother (25 cases). Although most (24) people's parents had been living together when they were born, only 9 partnerships had survived death, divorce or separation and were still intact at the start of the study. Twenty-three informants had a mother or father with learning difficulties who was still alive at the time of interview, of whom all but one remained in regular contact.

The study group included six pairs of siblings. Eighteen people came from families of three or more children; and 8 people had no brothers or sisters. Eleven subjects were either married or divorced – including three women with learning difficulties – of whom all but one had children of their own. The two mothers with learning difficulties both had had their children taken into care. There was one couple in which both the husband and wife were involved in the study in their own right. Twenty-two people were unemployed at the time of interview (including all those with learning difficulties); six of the eight men without learning difficulties were in paid work. There were just three owner-occupiers in the group: 22 people lived in council accommodation and the remainder rented privately. Thirteen people were still living with their parents of whom nine had learning difficulties. Six people with learning difficulties were living independently in their own homes, all with some paid support.

THE INTERVIEWS

Eighty-two interviews were completed with the 30 people who took part in the study. The interviews were based on the narrative method of 'life review' in which people are invited to reflect on and appraise their past experience from their standpoint in the here-and-now (Birren and Deutchman, 1991; Magee, 1988). An *aide-mémoire* was used to provide a framework for the interviews and a checklist for marking off material that had been covered, and for pinpointing topics for discussion and information needing to be collected at a subsequent session. A few direct questions were included which it was felt should be asked in the same manner of all informants. Otherwise the interviews were conducted as free-ranging conversations in which the interviewer's prompting and questioning, though disciplined by the *aide-mémoire*, were driven by the storyline determined by the informant.

The interviews were not intended to produce factually accurate or verifiable accounts of lives; narratives whose details would stand up to cross-checking against independent evidence or other sources of information. A distinction must be made between the stories people tell and the lives they lead. The story does not simply 'display the life' (Plummer, 1990). People reconstruct their own past in the light of their present sense of who they are. Memories constitute one of the building blocks of identity and the meanings people give to their own past are intimately bound up with the image they choose to present to others. From this point of view, people's stories about their own childhood provide a way of conceptualising the link between their upbringing and who they have become in adult life. The methodological problems of trying to establish a causal connection between family processes and later outcomes for people brought up by parents with learning difficulties are probably insurmountable. The use of narrative methods opens up the possibility of establishing a bridge through people's subjective interpretation of their own lived experience.

The fieldwork was planned on the assumption that three interviews would be required with each informant in order to cover the ground mapped out by the *aide-mémoire*. The form and content of each of these interviews differed.

- *The first interview* was about making introductions, clarifying the purpose of the study, outlining what the interviews would be about and how the material would be used, answering any questions the person might have, assessing people's strengths and limitations as informants, finding out who's who in their family, and starting to build up a picture of their background and their life now. The aim was to leave as much as possible of the talking to the informant.

- *The second interview* placed more emphasis on the evaluative aspects of narrative (Kohli, 1981). As well as filling out the details of their life story, people were also encouraged to explore their feelings as a child (about, for example, their parents and grandparents, their schooldays, their family life, the problems they had gone through), to reflect on their experience of growing up, and to assess the significance of their upbringing in terms of their current situation. Information provided in the first interview often served as the cue for raising these topics.

- *The third interview* was used to go through the informant's story as recounted during the two previous sessions, make good any gaps (as pointed out by the interviewee or by reference to the *aide-mémoire* material), and address the issues of representation (ensuring the story is true to the person) and ownership (ensuring the person shares the version of their life as reported). More direct questioning was often called for at this stage. Also, people were by now usually a lot easier about the set-up and more trusting of the interviewer so making it possible to raise some sensitive issues that had been passed over in earlier interviews.

A full set of interviews was completed with 23 of the 30 informants (four interviews were necessary in the case of one woman with learning difficulties). A third interview was not obtained with five people: three called a halt after two meetings ostensibly because of new work commitments or starting college courses; one failed to turn up for their last appointment; and another man with mental health problems was evasive about fixing up a third meeting. A single interview only was had with two people: in both cases it was the informant's parents who decided to withdraw on their behalf.

The interviews were carried out in small batches of 7-8 informants at a time so that the interviewer could keep up with each person's story as it unfolded and grew more detailed. Although part of the initial fieldwork plan, such a staggered approach was in any case made inevitable by the difficulties encountered in locating and contacting subjects. No more than three weeks were allowed to elapse between successive interviews in order to maintain people's interest and commitment, and usually the gap was closer to two weeks. Almost all (79) of the 82 interviews were tape-recorded with the informant's consent and later transcribed. The one person who refused to be recorded readily agreed to notes being taken. Two sisters asked to see the text of their story, and another man agreed to having his interviews recorded after being offered a copy of the tapes. All informants were promised a summary of the findings once the study had been finished.

A number of ploys or devices in addition to direct questioning were used to unlock people's memories, gain access to their lives, elicit information and encourage them to talk.

Photographs

Asking to see people's family photos was an effective way of finding out about family members and family relationships, bringing back the past, triggering recollections, facilitating self-reflection, stimulating conversation, focusing discussion, and easing informants into their role. Photographs are useful to the interviewer in three ways. They help to take the spotlight off the informant (who is made to feel less self-conscious and more in control). They help to legitimise the asking of questions and the interviewer's curiosity. They also have a totemic significance by providing a visual representation of the nature of people's family ties: compare, for instance, the son whose sparse collection of family photos pictured no-one outside his immediate family unit, the woman who brought out five hefty albums full of snaps of family gatherings, group holidays, celebrations and set-piece wedding portraits, and the five people who had no photographs at all of their parents.

Writing Stories

Eleven people were asked to write a short story about an episode in their life of their own choosing, and seven of them delivered. The purpose was to see if people were prepared to reveal themselves through writing in ways they would not using the spoken word (Rowland, Rowland and Winter, 1990). The stories were not intended to present a complete picture or set of facts in themselves, but to open up the perspectives through which people made their own experience comprehensible and to identify topics which might become a focus for further enquiry. They also helped to verify or develop points raised in interview.

Shared Interviews

Ten interviews were conducted involving two sets of brothers and sisters, a pair of sisters and a married couple in which both informants were seen at the same time. These came about for reasons of design and necessity, including the wishes and convenience of the people themselves, the impracticality of meeting them alone, and the promise of better rapport. Shared interviews brought a number of benefits. They helped to give some people the confidence to talk more freely; allowed them to spark off each other; encouraged disclosure through mutual prompting and cross-questioning; made possible verification of factual data; and provided a measure of emotional support when talking about sometimes painful events. They also helped to illuminate the effects of such variables as birth order, gender and personality on people's experiences and their resilience in the face of adversity (Booth and Booth, 1997a). Bertaux (1981:39) says that 'a good life story is one in which the interviewee *takes over the control of the interview situation'* (italics in original). Such an occurrence implies a measure of self-assurance and fluency rarely encountered among most informants, least of all those with learning difficulties. However, shared interviews did tend to empower informants by making them feel less vulnerable to the interviewer's attention.

Switching Off the Tape-Recorder

Putting aside the tape-recorder for a spell during an interview was often a useful gambit, especially in the case of more reserved informants. Doing so served a variety of purposes: to relax the informant; to check whether the recorder was having an inhibiting effect; to mark the shift to a new and perhaps sensitive topic; and to give both parties a breather. Switching off made it possible to see if the person felt any easier about talking, and helped to 'break the ice' on a new topic before recording was started again. Issues that might require careful handling could be approached in an 'off-the-record' fashion. Also, though rarely acknowledged in the literature, the practice of recording puts a lot of strain on the interviewer, who is constantly aware of being 'on air' and playing to an audience (including the transcriber and any research colleagues). This knowledge exerts a subliminal pressure to say the right thing, keep the conversation flowing, stick to the point, phrase the questions appropriately, attend to leads and generally deliver a good performance. Switching off may be done several times during an interview for any number of these reasons.

ISSUES FOR NARRATIVE RESEARCH

People organise their experience and their memory mainly in the form of narrative (Bruner, 1991). This study set out to make use of this human capacity for 'storying' experience in order to capture something of what it means to be brought up by parents with learning difficulties. Stories invite the listener 'to imagine, and in imagining to experience, the worlds created in the words' (Scheppele, 1989:2074). Connelly and Clandinin (1990), for instance, suggest that a good story is one that can be lived vicariously by others. Our aim was to harness the power of narrative in order to depict the lives of our subjects at the level of feeling as well as understanding. The success of this venture obviously depended on the responsiveness of our informants. A number of inhibiting factors limited some people's ability to talk freely.

Inarticulateness

Inarticulateness refers to an inability to communicate fluently in words that goes beyond mere shyness, anxiety or reserve. It originates with restricted language skills, but is generally overlaid by other factors such as lack of self-esteem, learned habits of compliance, loneliness and the experience of social exclusion. Although more commonly encountered among our informants with learning difficulties, it was not confined to them. Inarticulateness does not present an insuperable barrier to people telling their story (Booth and Booth, 1996a). However, it does have implications for the role of the interviewer (who must expect to work harder) and for the way stories are turned into text (where the hand of the editor will be more apparent). Sometimes there was simply not enough direct speech to render a person's story in their own words. But third-person accounts of lives usually lose the immediacy and authenticity of the subject's own voice. In order to ensure the important emotional dimension of narrative is not lost with inarticulate subjects, researchers must be prepared to experiment with methods of reporting that allow more scope for the play of what George Eliot called 'the veracious imagination', including the fictional form (Booth, 1995; Clough, 1996).

Temporality

Talking about experience, as Clandinin and Connelly (1994:417) point out, 'is to talk temporally'. Time is what holds a life story together and gives it both structure and meaning. The self as narrator, however, exists only in the present. Language is necessary in order to abstract the self into the past (or an anticipated future). It is only through language that the self has a sense of itself in the past. For people with restricted language skills, like some of those with learning difficulties in our study, the inability to objectify the self found its expression in a strong present orientation and a concrete frame of reference that countermanded the tick-tock essentials of good storytelling.

The Reticence of Young People

Many of the younger adults in our study struggled to find a voice. Such reticence did not come about because they were unable to express themselves. They were just not sure they had anything worth saying. Lack of confidence in the validity of one's own experience is a characteristic of youth. People must first know what they know before they can begin to narrate their own stories. Informants who had less to say tended to be younger people (with or without learning difficulties) whose lives were still closely bound up with their parents or who, irrespective of age, had not yet fully negotiated the transition into adulthood. Dickerson and Zimmerman (1993) have conceived adolescence as a time when young people are living stories in which they are the protagonist rather than the narrator. Building on this insight, it may be that establishing an identity of one's own is a prerequisite for carrying off the role of narrator in the story of one's life.

Poor Recall

Some people seemed to have scant memories of their childhood. Why this should be is not immediately apparent although Bruner (1987) provides a possible clue. He suggests that story-telling provides recipes for structuring experience itself and for laying down routes into memory. The stories that constitute children and young people's lives are usually told for them by others. Autobiographical memories of childhood come from the sharing of such stories, primarily between parents and children. It is possible that parents with learning difficulties engage in less 'memory talk' of this kind with their children so limiting what their children know about their own past. The absence of family photographs may serve as one clue that such a store of remembering has not been laid down. People who lack fully storied lives may not be able to access their own experience through memory or know they have a story to tell.

Interview Cuckoos

The researcher was not always able to control who was present during an interview. Aside from the shared interviews, where two informants were seen together, twelve interviews involving ten people were conducted with someone else in the room for all or part of the time. Usually this was a parent, spouse or partner, although cuckoos also included a friend and various practitioners. Family members were present for two of the interviews with two people; in all other cases supernumeraries were only there for one of the three sessions. The other person was always present on the express wish of the informant. Although better avoided if possible, having an informed other occasionally sit in on an interview was not always a bad thing, especially given the problems of reticence and poor recall mentioned above. Parents in particular were sometimes useful for triggering early memories or raising issues that could be explored later when the subject was next seen alone. The essential flexibility of the narrative method provides a check against possible bias from this source: the same material can always be revisited at a later date or a further interview added to make good one spoiled.

'Writing about the past', Steedman (1990:245) says, 'must always be done out of a set of current preoccupations'. This study developed from our interest in the process of parenting by people with learning difficulties. We set out to investigate the link between family upbringing and family outcomes in families containing a parent or parents with learning difficulties through the experience of their adult children. The focus of the study was on their presently remembered past. A full account of the findings can be found in Booth and Booth (1997b; 1998).

The relevance of the study, however, extends beyond the immediate group of parents to which it refers. Looking at out-of-the-ordinary families throws new light on taken-for-granted assumptions about the process of parenting. Parents who break the rules help to define them more clearly. Observing children under pressure shows up the extent of their adaptability. Studying parenting on the margins of competence provides a new perspective on the limits of parental adequacy. From this point of view, the study highlights what is common to all parenting rather than what is different about parents with learning difficulties.

REFERENCES

ACCARDO, P. and WHITMAN, B. (1990) 'Children of mentally retarded parents', *American Journal of Diseases of Children,* 144, 69-70.

BERTAUX, D. (1981) 'Introduction', in D. Bertaux, ed. *Biography and Society: The Life History Approach in the Social Sciences,* London: Sage Publications pp.5-12.

BIRREN, J. and DEUTCHMAN, D. (1991). *Guiding Autobiography Groups for Older Adults.* London: The John Hopkins University Press.

BOOTH, T. (1995). 'Sounds of still voices: issues in the use of narrative methods with people who have learning difficulties', in L. Barton, ed., *Sociology and Disability.* London: Longman.

BOOTH, T. and BOOTH, W. (1994). *Parenting Under Pressure: Mothers and Fathers with Learning Difficulties.* Buckingham: Open University Press.

BOOTH, T. and BOOTH, W. (1995). Unto us a child is born: the trials and rewards of parenthood for people with learning difficulties. *Australia and New Zealand Journal of Developmental Disabilities.* 20 (1): 25-39.

BOOTH, T. and BOOTH, W. (1996a) 'Sounds of silence: narrative research with inarticulate subjects', *Disability and Society,* 11 (1): 55-69.

BOOTH, T. and BOOTH, W. (1996b) 'Parenting in context: policy, practice and the Pollocks', *Child and Family Social Work.* 1 (2): 93-96.

BOOTH, T. and BOOTH, W. (1997a) 'Risk, resilience and competence: growing up with Parents who have learning difficulties', in R. Jenkins, ed. *Culture, Classification and (In)competence.* Cambridge: Cambridge University Press.

BOOTH, T. and BOOTH, W. (1997b) *Exceptional Childhoods. Unexceptional Children,* London: Family Policy Studies Centre.

BOOTH, T. and BOOTH, W. (1998, forthcoming) *Growing Up with Parents who have Learning Difficulties,* London: Routledge.

BRUNER, J. (1987) 'Life as narrative', *Social Research,* 54 (1): 11-32.

BRUNER, J. (1991) 'The narrative construction of reality', *Critical Inquiry.* 18(1), 1-21.

CLANDININ, D. and CONNELLY, F. (1994) ' Personal experience methods', in N. Denzin, and Y. Lincoln, eds. *Handbook of Qualitative Research.* London: Sage Publications.

CLOUGH, P. (1996) ' "Again Fathers and Sons": the mutual construction of self, story and special educational needs', *Disability and Society*, 11 (1): 71-81.

CONNELLY, F., and CLANDININ, D. (1990) 'Stories of experience and narrative inquiry', *Educational Researcher*, 19 (5): 2-14.

DICKERSON, V. and ZIMMERMAN, J. (1993) 'A narrative approach to families with adolescents' in S. Friedman, ed. *The New Language of Change: Constructive Collaboration in Psychotherapy.* New York: Guilford Press, pp 226-50.

FARMER, R., ROHDE, J. and SACKS, B. (1993) *Changing Services for People with Learning Disabilities,* London: Chapman and Hall.

FOTHERINGHAM, J. (1980) 'Mentally Retarded Persons as Parents', Department of Psychiatry, Queen's University, Ontario, Canada (unpublished).

KOHLI, M. (1981) 'Biography: account, text and method', in D. Bertaux, ed., *Biography and Society: The Life History Approach in the Social Sciences,* pp.61-75. London: Sage Publications.

MAGEE, J. J. (1988) *A Professional's Guide to Older Adults' Life Review.* Lexington, USA: Lexington Books.

MERCER, J. (1973) *Labeling the Mentally Retarded: Clinical and Social System Perspectives on Mental Retardation.* London: University of California Press.

MICKELSON, P. (1949) 'Can mentally deficient parents be helped to give their children better care?', *American Journal of Mental Deficiency*, 53: 516-534.

OLIVER, J. (1977) 'Some studies of families in which children suffer maltreatment', in A. Franklin, ed. *Challenge of Child Abuse.* London: Academic Press.

PLUMMER, K. (1990) 'Herbert Blumer and the life history tradition', *Symbolic Interaction,* 13 (2):125-44.

ROWLAND, G., ROWLAND, S. and WINTER, R. (1990) 'Writing fiction as inquiry into professional practice', *Journal of Curriculum Studies.* 22 (3): 291-293.

SCALLY, B. (1973) 'Marriage and mental handicap: some observations in Northern Ireland', in F. de La Cruz and G. LaVeck, eds. *Human Sexuality and the Mentally Retarded*. New York: Brunner/Mazel.

SCHEPPELE, K. (1989) 'Foreword: telling stories', *Michigan Law Review*, 87: 2073-98.

SCHILLING, R. F., SCHINKE, S. P., BLYTHE, B. J. and BARTH, R. P. (1982) 'Child maltreatment and mentally retarded parents: is there a relationship?', *Mental Retardation*, 20 (5): 201-209.

SCHOFIELD, G. (1996) 'Parental competence and the welfare of the child: issues for those who work with parents with learning difficulties and their children. A response to Booth and Booth', *Child and Family Social Work*, 1: 87-92.

STEEDMAN, C. (1990). *Childhood. Culture and Class in Britain.* London: Virago.

TYMCHUK, A. (1990) 'Parents with mental retardation: a national strategy', *Journal of Disability Policy Studies*, 1(4): 44-56.

WHITMAN, B. and ACCARDO, P., eds. (1990) *When a Parent is Mentally Retarded*. Baltimore: Paul H. Brookes.

CHAPTER 9

Involving Disabled People in Research: A study of inclusion in environmental activities

Sarah Beazley, Michele Moore
and David Benzie

INTRODUCTION

The need for research which gives disabled people as much control as possible over the questions it asks, the way these are investigated and over what happens to the eventual project outcomes, has been firmly established in recent years (Barnes 1996; Moore *et al.*, 1998; Oliver, 1992; 1993). However, a range of difficulties face researchers who wish to hold on to these principles, and in this chapter we illustrate some of the practical dilemmas we have met in our own work. The notion of 'taking the lead from disabled people' has become extremely important in the context of political and theoretical debates surrounding disability research, but there are many problems in making this happen. This chapter addresses these issues by examining one of our own studies which ran into difficulties measuring up to the expectation that disabled people must have a central involvement in all aspects of research relating to their lives.

We would like to point out that our comments are not intended to judge individuals involved in the research being examined, but to make explicit the tensions which can permeate a research situation. There is invariably a problem with re-examination of research situations because other people implicated have no opportunity to have their say and we cannot be certain to protect personal or institutional anonymity. There are, however, many lessons to be learned from looking back and reviewing specific attempts to actively involve disabled people in research.

The aims of the chapter are:

• to illustrate the obstacles researchers may face in trying to maximise disabled people's involvement in research
• to examine interpersonal dynamics within research, with special reference to situations where communication is neither easy nor effective;
• to consider questions of researcher accountability for involvement of disabled people; and
• to prompt further consideration of how researchers can resist sidelining disabled people in the process of enquiry.

Discussion relates to the earliest stages of setting up a small project, funded by an agency concerned with environmental issues, to evaluate innovations for widening inclusion of disabled people in its schemes (Benzie et al, 1997). We have chosen to focus on preparatory research activity such as defining the potential agenda (or agendas) and getting the process of enquiry going. We illustrate how each part of the research act involves processes within a process and how recognition of structural, ideological and institutional barriers and differences of view is essential before the slow course of dismantling barriers to the involvement of disabled people in the research process can begin.

CONTEXT

The environmental agency wished to put research in place at short notice, and this obliged us to draw up proposals which would outline sensible plans for mounting a useful investigation while also leaving open the possibility of following alternative directions. Although the initial agency request was vague we wanted to respond positively for several reasons, and as others have said, it is incumbent upon researchers to acknowledge their personal purposes for becoming involved in a particular project (Shakespeare *et al.*, 1993). First, we had been nominated as a disability research team by a service provider who had previously sub-contracted research to our team, and with whom we wished to keep good links. This person had already set up a number of joint ventures at branch level between his organisation and the environmental agency which had provided people with learning difficulties opportunities to join a walking club or go on courses in horticulture or conservation. It was felt that these projects needed to be evaluated. Secondly, we are under the same constant pressure as all academic researchers to bring funds into our University (Barnes, 1996). Thirdly, at a personal level we had various interests. One of our research team is disabled and would like greater opportunities and choice in environmental activities. One of us has a disabled sister, keen to be outdoors and involved in the countryside, along with a background in Environmental Sciences which provided further affinity with this project.

These motivations are not intended to excuse our willingness to launch straight into disability research without subjecting the reasons behind a project to more rigorous scrutiny. They may however shed light on the reasons why we found ourselves, as no doubt other researchers do too, more than willing to assume a level of mutual agreement about disability issues in order that research might go ahead. Clearly, at the start of the collaboration we knew little about the nature of the work being done by the agency, nor about how they were including disabled people, and this was a risky point of departure. As Stone and Priestley (1996) have noted, researchers can find themselves in awkward situations if the work they carry out turns out to be at odds with the preferred approach of disabled people and their representative organisations. The research circumstances we were moving into were ambiguous, and so we committed ourselves to a fairly loose plan of research, specified only as :

a short-term intensive research project to monitor and evaluate access for disabled people to environmental activities with a view to (i) maximising the participation of disabled people in environmental activities and (ii) developing policy and practice in this area.

The project was to run over a five month period on a three days a week basis.

GETTING STARTED

Once funding had been approved, a meeting was held with the service provider who had recommended us and the director of the local branch of the environmental agency commissioning the project. Whilst all such preliminary meetings are bound to be tentative, there was understandably some trepidation on all sides due to the unusual situation of having the funding in place before the different stakeholders could get to know each other or reach points of agreement about their priorities. Despite the common ground of the proposal, the director of the environmental agency knew little about our research reputation and further distanced himself by claiming little personal knowledge of disability issues. For our part, we had to seek clarification about the particular context to be investigated before we could begin to work out a way forward.

It emerged that the environmental agency branch director wanted several things from the project. As the agency was regularly seeking research funding there was an interest in defining a long-term research programme. Further aims included developing initiatives for disabled people, and opening up possibilities for working more closely alongside other service providers. Additional priorities for our team centred on ensuring that the views of disabled people were central and encouraging disabled service users to put forward their own ideas. At this early stage we agreed to focus on access to environmental activities created by a conservation course attended by disabled and non-disabled students and run at an urban parkland area used for practical involvement of people in the rejuvenation of city spaces. In addition, we agreed to draw together some strategies for seeking funding which would build on the findings from the course evaluation.

We had a plan of action now and arranged to meet the lead tutor on the course, who was employed by the environmental agency. The incidents which unfolded next go some way towards explaining the importance we attach to evolving crystal-clear strategies for facilitating disabled people's access to the research process. What we have found is that acceptance by service providers that service users *should* have opportunities to participate in research does not necessarily mean that participation will not be obstructed. Disabled people's rights to research involvement are often smothered by others who exercise strong and complex positions of power over their lives. Luck and good judgement alone will not ensure that researchers can effectively resist obstruction by various individuals who set themselves up as the gatekeepers of disabled people's well-being.

SELF-DETERMINATION OF ACCESS TO THE RESEARCH PROCESS

It was arranged that the research assistant should join the course for a period of time and thus get to know the context and also the students. The students would also become acquainted with the research assistant and his personal approach before deciding whether to participate in the project. After this 'getting to know you' phase, the students would be invited to group discussions. They would also have the opportunity of individual interviews at which they could contribute their views of the environmental course and what it meant for them generally and in relation to their future life and career plans. The information gathering settings were to be informal, the specific topics and mode of discussion to be defined by the students, and any involvement optional.

A phone call the following week brought the newly started project to an abrupt halt. It turned out that there were other agencies involved with the disabled students. These included a training agency associated with students with learning impairments and a voluntary project associated with some of the Deaf students, both of which asked for the research to be delayed. The agencies had only just found out about the project and whilst their representatives indicated they were willing to become involved, and did not seek to undermine our professionalism or the professional and ethical codes which we were operating under, it was argued that the research proposal would have to go through their own vetting procedures. In addition, the training agency independently set in motion a procedure for using support workers to secure agreement to the participation of the disabled students.

There are many frustrating issues for disability researchers here. The need to mediate consent through third parties was not mooted in relation to non-disabled students whose views we would be seeking; no agency was brought forward to determine (or ostensibly 'protect') their decision as to whether they were to participate. The disabled students were being singled out and denied their right to learn about the research first-hand. It seems to us that much of this problem stemmed from the newness of our link with collaborating service providers who appeared to have decided that issues regarding consent and the gaining of permission could not safely be left to the research team. Unfortunately, the service providers did not know that one of the researchers had concurrent experience as a communication support worker. This information might have added greatly to our credibility and skills. Equally, we had made certain assumptions about the link service providers, for example, that they would be aware of the sensitive politics of research situations, and were best placed to let key people know about the project. Progress was suddenly out of our control, and time, on such an intensive project, was very much against us.

Members of the research team endeavoured to make conciliatory phone calls. However, it emerged that those blocking progress were genuinely interested in pursuing the work but wanted to ensure that appropriate institutional protocol was followed. Nevertheless, this meant that the research was being determined more by the needs of non-disabled service providers than the needs of disabled service users. The importance of personal integrity became uppermost. For example, the person working with the Deaf students was conscious of the political nature of disablement and rightly concerned only to proceed once matters of anonymity had been clarified. The key person at the training centre had concerns which we found less acceptable, commenting for example, that it was 'pretentious' to seek the views of people with learning difficulties and expressing the view that 'lots of care' rather than skill is needed to work with 'these people'. Our beliefs about which of the barriers to the research were reasonable could easily have started to displace our professional investment in retaining business-like relations with all participants. We kept quiet about our objections because we wanted to generate co-operation, but were thus engaged in reproducing disablement.

This highlights the diversity of personal understandings of disability which disabled people meet throughout their lives. For researchers, the broad range of philosophies held by different people drawn together in setting up a disability research project must be acknowledged and contextualised. Just how difficult these issues become in practice, how compromise in the name of co-operation can render the researcher part of the problem in the sense of perpetuating disablement through polite acquiescence, and how our responses to the diverse positions assumed by others, all deeply infuse the way in which we are dealt with by those who have power over a project. At this point, the issues of if, when and how researchers challenge disabling assumptions presented by others came to the fore. Homan (1991) has described how the role of gatekeepers is particularly questionable in relation to involvement of disabled people in research and we were now confronted with the enormity of ethical issues bound up with the freedom and rights of the students whose experiences we were hoping to uncover.

The time-scale for meeting our contractual obligations for project completion was being severely disrupted by individuals who were seeking to control disabled people's access to the research. This meant our original goals were looking distinctly unattainable and we had to consider urgently alternative ways forward. We wondered whether to conduct some interviews with professionals or with non-disabled students in the meantime, as there were fewer barriers to arranging this, but such a move would conflict with our commitment to having the directions of the research established by disabled students. The strong accountability we felt to disabled people may seem rather self-important and pretentious, but personal commitments to disabled family members and colleagues made it impossible to draw back from securing the adequate and primary inclusion of disabled people's own voices. We acknowledge that we also feared losing the confidence of the service provider who had introduced us to this project and was funding other of our research activities. We decided against involving non-disabled before disabled participants but had to raise the time delay with the commissioning agency, while finding other ways of making up for lost time.

MOVING THE RESEARCH GOAL POSTS

It seemed a period of deferment was necessary, rather than a headlong dash to cram 'active research' of any available sort into the time vacuum that was looming. We needed to find alternative ways to fulfil our research obligations. Mid-way through the funded research period then, we decided to change tack and switch our focus more towards the interest of the environmental agency branch director in developing future bids for funding. We hoped this change of plan might open up new avenues for investigation in which we could hang on to our personal objective of evolving routes through which disabled people can influence research agendas and, at the same time, still respond to the needs of service providers. We wrote a progress report in order to clarify the change of direction and reframe our role. From here-on our aim was 'to act as facilitators and to elicit ideas from key stakeholders about what they feel should be explored in future projects looking at disabled people's access to the environment'.

Mid-project goal shifting is rarely countenanced within conventional academic research. Our own wide research experience suggests that disability researchers must be prepared to be very flexible in responding to the obstacles which are thrown in the way of disabled people's participation. We make no secret of the difficulty we encountered in trying to achieve this flexibility both when writing research proposals and in the fieldwork stage. In the case of the focal study, it was necessary and appropriate to revise the plan of activity in order to try and safeguard the central position of disabled people. Not until these changes had been settled did things start to feel comfortable again. But the problem of having to gain consent for disabled people to participate through third parties continued to cast a cloud over the issue of access.

RIGHTS TO KNOWING ABOUT THE RESEARCH PROCESS

We now hoped that, since the research could no longer be construed as evaluative, those preventing the participation of disabled students might relent, but this did not happen. In discussions about who should receive the progress report, and/or be notified of the changes of direction, the disabled student's 'right to know' was denied. This placed us once more in the role of reinforcing the oppression of the disabled students. Relevant service providers seemed unconcerned about this and remained satisfied that we were doing our job in an acceptable manner. However, the function of the progress report, as we saw it, was to create a veneer which would make them and us feel comfortable about research progress, but which offered nothing at all for advancing the rights of disabled people to meaningful involvement in research.

Researchers also have to consider many issues of accountability. There is obviously no blue-print for knowing exactly to whom disability researchers are accountable *in situ*. There are many hazy areas, such as the one we were now in the middle of, over who should be consulted about shifts in research focus and direction, especially if these consultations further exclude disabled people. Critics might regard us as naïve for not knowing whose permission would be needed for reports (including progress reports) to be produced and disseminated. It was only in retrospect that we began to recognise how far these issues are critically entwined with the ethical considerations of 'informed' consent and gaining of permission. There is clearly an argument that researchers should know the precise answers to these questions before research plans are agreed. In the focal study, one of the service providers working with Deaf students was especially anxious about anonymity because many of those to whom the report would be circulated – not least those who commissioned the project – might recognise the identities of agencies and individuals. This illustrates how spending time to lay down ground-rules in advance would have made for greater effectiveness in the long run. We ended up having to provide assurances that circulation of the report would be limited, but this of course, contravened the rights of many significant others to know what was (or was not) going on. In any event, confidentiality never could be total. What is at issue is the denial of disabled people's right to know about the existence of research activity concerning them.

EVOLVING RESEARCH RELATIONS

Eventually, after a long period of negotiation, the research assistant was permitted to join the students on the course, doing some digging and hedge planting. He attended the conservation course over a period of a month, taking part in day-to-day activities, with a view to building relationships with prospective participants. Immediately, another difficult set of issues arose about the involvement of disabled people in research. Some of those who were prospective participants were disabled in social contexts because of communication barriers and through long experience of exclusion. Our problem was in knowing when and how the researcher/researched relationship could be deemed 'good enough' for meaningful conversations to take place. Although the researcher became friendly with all of the students met on the course, the short time period involved meant that the researcher could not establish relationships of sufficient familiarity and skill to allow easy and effective communication. This was made more difficult because the research assistant did not have qualifications in British Sign Language (BSL), or training for communicating with people experiencing mental illness. Such barriers placed a heavy constraint on the opportunity for self-expression among disabled participants (Booth *et al*, 1990). Moreover, one of the service providers felt that, given these obstacles, it would be inappropriate for the research assistant to hold project-related discussions with the disabled students. Once again, students were not given the chance to give their views on what should happen. In the end, a manager of one of the voluntary agencies involved undertook to talk to some of the disabled students along with their communication support worker, herself a Deaf person. The voluntary group manager spent some time gathering relevant information about the aims of the research. Unfortunately, things went from bad to worse, however, when this person then became ill and was off work for the duration of the study.

We had no alternative but to contact the communication support worker to ask if she could find out the views of the disabled students. We recognised that accessing disabled people through third parties was hazardous, but had little option. Given that the communication support worker was Deaf and no textphone was available, contact was made by fax rather than telephone, but this limited the exchange of information. However, it was suggested that the communication support worker was well acquainted with the goals of the project and could be further assisted in addressing the students by having access to a preliminary set of questions which we were in the process of putting together to guide eventual discussions with service providers. We wanted to reduce barriers between ourselves and the communication support worker and provided this provisional list of questions. However, what was intended as a starting point for discussion was used instead as a questionnaire. The responses thus obtained by the communication support worker, being structured, were constrained, and respondents had not been invited to exercise their prerogative of establishing the agenda in any way.

The effect of conducting the research by proxy was that our methodological aspirations could not be realised and this is a source of difficulty for the research team. The complexity of technical difficulties is evident in relation to factors such as phrasing, or the amount of time dedicated to posing a question, which in turn influence the response obtained. For example, the communication support worker reported in response to the question 'what hobbies/activities do/would you like?' (taken literally from the written draft of possible prompts) that 3 students answered 'private'. This might, of course, legitimately comprise the view of the respondents, but their replies could also be a product of BSL/English mismatch. For example, a signer might, if attempting to simplify the vocabulary, ask 'what do you like to do in your own time?', or 'what do you like to do yourself at home?' No researchers were present to observe or monitor the discussion sessions. Perhaps in hindsight, video-recording would have been useful, though we suspect that gaining permission for this might well have proved difficult. The point is that disabled people's involvement in research may not necessarily be maximised by placing the methodological and conceptual tools of research in the hands of disabled people. Even where disability researchers meet with very little active political resistance, the process of handing over the tools of research can, in reality, be tainted by a lack of commitment or ambivalence. Certainly our attempts to ensure that any third party presentations of the research maximised the interests of disabled people were hampered because we were obliged to hand over part of the process which, through illness of a key player, was then handed on again.

Further concerns arose in relation to the role of communication support workers in our study. It was standard practice on the conservation course for some of the disabled students to use communication support workers to facilitate dialogue with unfamiliar people. Several points are worth making. First, communication support workers can facilitate better access for disabled people to the research process by enabling them to choose their preferred interactive medium and language. Second, both disabled research participants and researchers have to trust the judgement and skill of the communication support worker and vice-versa. Subtle changes of meaning frequently occur in the process of moving from one language to another. There is conspicuous powerlessness on all sides in such mediated interactions (Moorehead, 1997). The third point is really an extension of the first two in terms of self-determination in research. When using communication support workers, researchers have restricted access to disabled people's own articulations. Those acting as communication support workers may, subconsciously or consciously, introduce shifts linked to their own value systems and beliefs or to a desire to represent one or other of the parties in a certain light. There is inevitably a level of dependency which will influence proceedings and it is important for researchers to be prepared for such pitfalls when communication is indirect. Finally, there are hazards if either party wishes to discuss things which may unsettle relations either with the communication support worker, or within relevant social groups.

We were left wondering just how effective any communications in the course of a shared research process can be, and unclear about how critical it is that they are. Is the process of handing over research design and implementation essential to ensure power is properly devolved, and does the handing over guarantee that disabled people's rights will be adequately respected? When sharing control over research what are the risks of a project becoming so 'designed by committee' that it loses direction? Who needs control of disability research to ensure it will generate outcomes in sympathy with the human rights agenda as defined by contemporary disability rights movement? And to what extent are researchers bound to impose this agenda upon disabled people who are as yet untouched by it – or perhaps even disagree with it? Whilst the demands are for disability research to be enabling and empowering and take its lead from disabled people, this is plainly not a soft option.

RELATIONS WITHIN THE RESEARCH TEAM

Another category of relations within the research community concerns those between members of the research team, and in particular, the relative positions of those who are disabled and those who are not. The researchers in our own team can be placed on a continuum ranging from personal acquaintance with impairment to indirect experience through disability in the family. The disabled/non-disabled divide is one we experience as blurred and indeterminate and is a source of vulnerability and unease. We have had to look carefully at what this means in practice and how the distinction impacts upon the way we do things. The project under discussion involved some difficulties in this respect.

It will be obvious by now that the environmental activity project was fraught with problems and that our team was fearful that failure to resolve these might mean that people who valued us as researchers might begin to think twice about continuing their support. There were internal, as well as external pressures, which culminated in an uncomfortable decision that the person with most research experience in the team, who happened to be non-disabled, would have to take the reins and steer the project efficiently towards a specific set of pre-determined tangible outcomes. This conclusion is clearly not in accord with recommendations that disabled people should have ultimate control over the research process. We knew full well that the reason why non-disabled people so often occupy the most powerful positions within research teams is because of the long years of disablement experienced by colleagues who have impairments, but were compelled to take realistic account of where the buck should stop in our own setting. We have had to discuss at length whether we could have dealt with things differently or better. It should not be thought that the research team was ducking proper recognition of the call for disabled people to be at the helm of disability research projects and others too have heeded the difficulties of making each and every disability research endeavour wholly collective (Campbell and Oliver, 1996; Oliver, 1996; 1997). The reallocation of tasks came about as the result of an ordinary everyday management problem which meant that the input of the disabled researcher from the environmental access project was even more crucially required on another of our disability studies (Skelton et al., 1997).

Part of the problem for us, related to the fact that the key disabled member of our team felt they had little professional experience with learning disabled and/or Deaf people who were the focus of the study, whereas the non-disabled researchers have more. We were agreed that the distance between researchers and those disabled people who were to be the researched was most appropriately reduced by recognition of the nearness of experience to those in the specific community being examined and this need not be impairment-led. We feel that the role of disabled people in research teams is a broad one bringing both personal and political dimensions to the team's understanding, but it is misleading to assume that individual disabled researchers can be, or wish to be, representative of and answerable to disabled people in every circumstance.

Our concern is that in making the decision for a non-disabled person to take charge, even for straightforward time-management reasons, commitment to placing disabled people firmly in the driving seat of research is jeopardised. This highlights the wide gulf between the rhetoric of commitment and practical issues facing the disability researcher.

Critics of non-disabled disability researchers may suggest that our account reveals yet another example of disabling and oppressive research. We hope, however, to have shed some light on the practical difficulties which can sometimes explain the origins of such shortcomings in everyday disability projects. Disability researchers often have to take account of their own needs and roles. There is considerable variability with regard to what we are doing, and whether what we are doing is what we ought to be doing. This points to the urgency for coalitions between both disabled people and researchers, and between research teams as well. Even as we seek to close our reflections on disabling barriers in this one example of our work, we are left with many questions which must similarly trouble other researchers.

A particular concern of this chapter has been to explore the role of disability researchers. If we are to act simply as facilitators, taking up ideas from key stakeholders and providing a vehicle for the collection and dissemination of information they prioritise, we must explore the implications for keeping the interests of disabled people clearly in view. What position are researchers in if initiatives for disability research do not stem from disabled people in the first place, or if oppressive dimensions slowly unfold once a project is under way? Do we refuse to participate in such enquiries or become involved on a best-endeavours basis, hoping to be part of a drip-drip process which will stimulate less oppressive activity? How much personal political commitment can be usefully exposed? In what circumstances does it become imperative to disclose the disability research principles which we hold dear, and to whom must we communicate these principles? What about funding bodies, service providers, disabled people or their representative family members? How should our research commitments be articulated? What is practical and what is necessary? It may be tempting to gloss over the finer considerations raised in answer to these questions when setting up a research contract, but they all invest disability researchers with critical obligations, which, as the preceding discussion aims to show, usually need facing up to sooner rather than later.

CONCLUDING REMARKS

We have acknowledged elsewhere that disability research involves debate, listening and earning the respect of others, particularly in relation to the voices of disabled people (Moore et al., 1998). Nevertheless, in this chapter we have had to describe how even well-intentioned research acts can leave disabled people outside of, and alienated from the research process. Our account shows that there is no room for complacency on the part of disability researchers and that we are ever and always embroiled in, and required to openly resist, the politics of oppression.

Within our own research teams we are agreed that there is no turning back on the issue of maximising the role of disabled people in research. Yet the conditions in which disability research originates and later takes place can, as we hope to have illustrated, quickly swamp prospects for securing a central role for disabled people. We agree with Oliver (1997) that researchers must be mindful of the damage their work can do to disabled people's lives and recognise and support the role of research in resistance. But carving out a pivotal role for disabled people at all levels in a disability research project is a task which should not be oversimplified. Barriers to maximising the involvement of disabled people are many and far-reaching as we have tried to show.

It is also important to admit that agitation for changes in the way disability research is done can imbue researchers with an intense sense of powerlessness. Our activities are caught up in seemingly immovable institutional and structural factors. Recognition of the barriers to greater involvement of disabled people, both as researchers and those whose lives are being researched, does not necessarily lead to resistance to those barriers. Disability research must challenge oppression, but it is not easy to engage with such lofty obligations in the political world of everyday research. What we hope to have reinforced is the need for critical attention to, and personal resistance of, those attitudes, situations, events and behaviours which continually threaten to undermine the rights of disabled people. Important as resistance by individual researchers and research teams will be, it is only through collective resistance that platforms for change will eventually emerge.

REFERENCES

BARNES, C. (1996) Disability and the myth of the independent researcher, *Disability and Society*, 11 (1) : 107-10.

BENZIE, D., BEAZLEY, S., MAELZER, J., MOORE, M. and PATIENT, M. (1997) *Disabled People's Access to the Environment : setting up relevant research*. Manchester : Manchester Metropolitan University Disability Studies Team Project Report.

BOOTH, T., SIMONS, K. and BOOTH W. (1990) *Outward Bound : Relocation and Community Care for People with Learning Difficulties*. Milton Keynes : Open University Press.

CAMPBELL, J. and OLIVER, M. (1996) *Disability Politics : Understanding Our Past, Changing Our Future*. London : Routledge.

HOMAN, R. (1991) *The Ethics of Social Research*. London : Longman.

MOORE, M., BEAZLEY, S. and MAELZER, J. (forthcoming, 1998) *Researching Disability Issues*. Milton Keynes : Open University Press.

MOOREHEAD D. (1997) 'Meanings of Deafness', *Deaf Worlds: Deaf People, Community and Society*, 13 (1) 2-8.

OLIVER, M. (1992) Changing the social relations of research production?, *Disability, Handicap and Society*, 7 (2) : 101-14.

OLIVER, M. (1993) Re-defining disability : a challenge to research, in J. Swain, V. Finkelstein, S. French, and M. Oliver, eds. *Disabling Barriers : Enabling Environments*. Milton Keynes : Sage.

OLIVER, M. (1996) *Understanding Disability: from Theory to Practice*. Macmillan : Basingstoke, Hampshire.

OLIVER, M. (1997) 'Emancipatory research : realistic goal or impossible dream?' in C. Barnes and G. Mercer, eds. *Doing Disability Research*. Leeds: The Disability Press.

SHAKESPEARE, P., ATKINSON, D. and FRENCH, S., eds. (1993) *Reflecting on Research Practice : Issues in Health and Social Welfare*. Buckingham: Open University Press.

SHAKESPEARE, T. (1996) Rules of engagement : doing disability research, *Disability and Society*, 11 (1) : 115-9.

SKELTON, J., BEAZLEY, S., MAELZER, J., MOORE, M. and PATIENT, M. (1997) *Learning Disabled People and Older Care-Givers*. Manchester: Manchester Metropolitan University, Disability Studies Team Project Report.

STONE, E. and PRIESTLEY, M. (1996) Parasites, pawns and partners: disability research and the role of non-disabled researchers, *British Journal of Sociology*, 47, (4): 699-716.

CHAPTER 10

Reflexivity: The dilemmas of researching from the inside

Ayesha Vernon

INTRODUCTION

My starting point for doing research was Oliver's recommendation that:

> 'Disability research should not be seen as a set of technical objective procedures carried out by 'experts' but part of the struggle by disabled people to challenge the oppression they currently experience in their lives' (1992: 102).

The focus of my research was to understand the nature and extent of oppression experienced by disabled Black women given that we are simultaneously subject to disability, 'race' and gender oppressions. Hence, as a disabled Black woman myself doing research on other disabled Black women, I am, both 'inside' the culture and participating in that which I am observing. In other words, my research is as much about my own experiences as it is about others. A similar point has been made by other feminist researchers researching women's experiences (e.g. Oakley, 1981; Ribbens, 1990).

This is an important point to bear in mind since no research is ever completely free from bias as Wheatley points out:

> 'Ethnographic relations, practices and representations as well as the metaphors we use to make sense of them are contextually contingent - their character is shaped by who we look at, from where we look, and why we are looking in the first place' (1994: 422).

In fact, the closer our subject matter to our own life and experience the more we can expect our own beliefs about the world to enter into and shape our work, to influence the very questions we pose and the interpretations we generate from our findings.

Moreover, it is argued that there is a thin dividing line between identification with one's research subjects and their exploitation (Reay, 1996). Thus, reflexivity, the examination of the ways in which the researcher's own social identity and values affect the data gathered and the picture of the social world produced, is a critical exercise for those researching the experience of oppression, particularly to insure the avoidance of colluding with the established hegemony. Gramsci (1971) used the concept of hegemony to describe a situation where the values of an elite group stand dominant within a society who, through the construction of an all pervasive ethos, maintain their own interests while subordinating those of others. Thus, reflexivity is as important for those researching from the 'inside' as anyone else for as Barton has rightly observed 'intent is no guarantee of outcome' (1996: 6).

My research was based on two assumptions. First, that there is a political nature to all we do: our work, its process and products are never neutral. Hence, our research efforts always have implications for the redistribution or consolidation of power (Maguire, 1987). Secondly, I agree with Freire (1970) that the fundamental theme of our epoch is domination which must mean that its opposite, the theme of liberation, must be the aim of all research on the oppressed.

This chapter will outline what prompted me to carry out the research on disabled Black women, why I believe research on the experience of oppression is critical, what strategies I employed to carry out my research in the light of the debate on emancipatory disability research and the dilemmas I encountered. I do not intend to discuss my personal experiences here since these have already been adequately discussed elsewhere (Vernon, 1996a). Suffice it to say that my personal experiences of living as a disabled Black woman in a society which defines 'normal' as being 'able-bodied', white and male and those who deviate from this highly valued norm as 'abnormal', coupled with the realisation that I was a 'stranger in many camps' as those who deviate in several ways are also often rejected by those who are themselves rejected by the privileged (Hill-Collins, 1990; Renteria, 1993; Vernon, 1996c, 1997), have formed the core of my experience and the primary reasons for my research in this area. My need to make sense and consolidate my experience with other disabled Black women was intensified by the fact that there was so little existing literature documenting and analysing our experience.

WHY RESEARCH?

Research is very powerful in that it can either be a significant aid in the maintenance and perpetuation of oppression or it can be a critical tool for eradicating oppression depending on how research is carried out, for whose aims, who it is carried out by and on whom. Miller (1976) explained how the state of subordination in society can be reinforced through the research process: a dominant group, inevitably, has the greatest influence in determining a culture's overall outlook – its philosophy, morality, social theory and even its science. The dominant group, thus, legitimises the unequal relationship and incorporates it into society's guiding concepts (Miller, 1976 cited in Oakley, 1981: 39).

Hitherto, feminists felt the inadequacy of much of earlier research to capture their experience which was instead 'added on' to masculine viewpoints (Oakley, 1981). This pointed to a necessity for women to engage in research to explain from the 'inside' of what it is like to be a woman in a male-dominated world. Subsequently, Black women felt the inadequacy of much of feminist research which primarily focused on women's experience of sexism and, therefore, excluded or added on the simultaneity of gender, 'race' and class in their lives (Bhavnani and Coulson, 1986; Carby, 1982; King, 1988). Whilst there is now more awareness among feminist researchers and theorists of the need to include Black women's issues (Ramazanoglu, 1989), to date, disabled women continue to be excluded in feminist literature (Morris, 1992).

Moreover, disabled women's concerns are marginal in research on disabled people which, it is argued, is 'mainly about white disabled men' (Morris, 1992). This is because for disabled women the desire for social integration goes far beyond the economic sphere emphasised by disabled men (Lonsdale, 1990). The existence of gender stereotypes which define the role of women as wives and mothers interact with prevailing disability stereotypes of dependency and helplessness (Barnes, 1992b) to exacerbate their experience of oppression (Lloyd, 1992). At the same time, disabled men are also subject to the prevailing masculine image of 'strong' and 'virile' men which is again undermined by disability stereotypes. A recent development in this debate has been the assertion that given the number of feminist writers discussing issues of sexuality, imagery, gender identity and relationships in relation to disabled women (for example, Campling, 1979, 1981; Deegan and Brooks, 1985; Fine and Asch, 1988; Keith, 1994; Lonsdale, 1990; Morris, 1989; Saxton and Howe, 1988), compared with only one article on disabled masculinity (Gerschick and Miller, 1995) that it is disabled men's experience which is underrepresented rather than disabled women's (Shakespeare *et al.*, 1996). This, it is argued, is a consequence of the fact that disability studies has 'downplayed the personal and focused on the structural' reproducing 'the wider split between the public and the private' (p.7).

However, such an assertion overlooks the fact that we live in a patriarchal society in which men rarely, if ever, experience institutional or individual discrimination on the grounds of their sex. Women, on the other hand, are frequently the targets of sexual discrimination both institutionally (for example, in education and in the labour market) and individually (for example, through sexual harassment at work, violence in the home and rape on the streets). Consequently, although disabled women are considered to be less 'feminine' and 'desirable', just as disabled men may also be considered to be less 'masculine' and 'virile' (Lloyd, 1992), like non-disabled women, disabled women are also often targets of male sexual curiosity and sexual harassment in a way that disabled men are rarely likely to be (Vernon, 1996b). As in other areas of academia and key positions of power, the academic highground of disability analysis is dominated by men who have focused on the structural aspects of disability such as employment, income, housing, etc. While these issues affect all disabled people equally in determining the quality of their lives, the difference between men and women is centred on the question of priorities. For disabled men the economic consideration of employment and income is the number one priority for being a 'breadwinner' is the expected role of men in society. A man who has a job has proved to society that he has the means to be a successful husband and father. In contrast, women's priorities are said to lie in the domestic arena as wives and mothers. Disabled women are not considered to be adequate to fulfil this role even if they wish to do so. Moreover, disabled women who aspire to be economically independent are likely to face a bigger hurdle than disabled men in consequence of their additional penalty of gender stereotypes. For example, Lonsdale (1990) demonstrated that the number of disabled women in unskilled jobs was proportionately higher than disabled men or non-disabled women. Furthermore, whilst disabled men were found to earn on average almost a quarter less per week than their non-disabled male counterparts (Prescott Clarke, 1990), disabled women were found to earn on average a third less than disabled men (Martin, White and Meltzer, 1988). Mainstream disability academics have so far omitted to analyse how gender and disability oppressions combine and interact in the experience of disabled women and their potential impact on disabled women's lives.

The impact of racism on disabled people's lives is also overlooked in disability studies (Hill, 1994; Vernon, 1997). Moreover, disabled Black women's experiences have been, and continue to be, neglected by academic researchers and theorists on disability, 'race' and gender. It is as though the assumption has been made by all concerned that what we experience is the same as all other women, Black people and/or disabled people, or worse, that we do not exist. Therefore, my need to research disabled Black women's experience in order to make sense of the complexity of our situation and to challenge our total exclusion is similar to the need felt by earlier feminists to engage in research to challenge the distortion and exclusion of their experience. Research is involved in the production of knowledge and, thus, it is a critical field of struggle through which oppression can be perpetuated or resisted. Emancipatory research (that is research which seeks to alleviate oppression) is critical in exposing the mechanisms for producing, maintaining and legitimising social inequities and domination. Having thus far described how I came to choose the particular research topic in question and why it is important to carry out research, in the remainder of this chapter I will turn my attention to discussing the particular strategies I employed in my research on disabled Black women.

RESEARCH STRATEGIES

The planning phase of the study and the literature review on research methods indicated the need to incorporate the principles of the emancipatory research paradigm. These include: involving participants from the outset in a research project which focuses on their experiences. This I did in the initial phase by carrying out in-depth semi-structured interviews with four of the women involved in the study to decide what aspects of their experience the research should focus on. From this it emerged that education and paid employment were the areas in which they had major concern which warranted further investigation. This is not surprising since education and employment are the main arenas through which power, wealth and influence are distributed and, hence, they are also the main arenas through which inequality and oppression are perpetuated.

Other principles of emancipatory research include socialising rather than individualising. For example, locating the causes of their 'problems' in the structures of an oppressive society rather than blaming the individual (Oliver, 1992). This was done in a variety of ways: by a careful phrasing of the questions asked in the interview, by sharing my own experiences (where relevant) so that they felt they were not alone in what they had experienced. And, finally, in collectivising their experiences through an in-depth analysis of the data and disseminating this information both to the women in the study and to the wider community through written publications (e.g. Vernon, 1996a).

Initially, 25 women were asked if they would like to take part in the study. Two women declined (one due to lack of time and one disagreed with the social model of disability) and one dropped out after an interview for fear of being identified. Identification was a particular concern in my research because relating examples of discriminatory practice in the workplace can, if identified, have adverse consequences on their employment prospects. With this in mind, all the women were informed at the outset about the use of pseudonyms which they had the opportunity to choose for themselves as well as the fact that they will have a chance to read through the interview transcript and change or take out anything they are unsure about.

SELECTING THE SAMPLE

In the absence of a suitable sampling frame for the random selection of disabled Black women in Britain, a combination of organisational contacts, publicity in the disability press and word of mouth through networking were used to obtain access to and select women for interviewing. The criteria for inclusion was fairly straightforward. Namely, all disabled Black women who have worked, are working, or seeking work, within the age range of 16-60. Initially, several notices were placed in the disability press with requests for disabled Black women to get in touch for an informal chat on some possible research on their experiences. Only two women responded as a result of the press coverage. It is difficult to say precisely why the press adverts attracted so little response. It may be that after years of being targeted for disability research with little positive effect on their lives, disabled people are no longer prepared to be pawns in a project which is of little or no benefit to them. It may also be an indication of the lack of political awareness around disability, in particular the lack of willingness among some people with impairments to identify themselves as disabled because of the negative connotations attached to disability. Certainly the two women who responded to the publicity were very politicised on all three issues. It is also possible that there are only a small number of disabled Black women who read the disability press on a regular basis or even know of its existence which is particularly likely if they are not politicised around disability. Attempts to place adverts in the ethnic minority press were unsuccessful as they did not even get printed which may be another indication of their lack of awareness around disability issues.

Secondly, organisations of disabled people were contacted with requests for a circulation of a flyer to members who are disabled Black women. The most fruitful of which proved to be a London based organisation which provided six contacts. Four other women agreed to take part after my meeting with them at various disability events. My major source of contacts came from some of the women in the study who provided me names and addresses (after they had first checked with them) of the women they knew who may be interested in taking part (these were not necessarily friends of the women but rather those they knew either through working in the same field or being involved with disability organisations).

DATA COLLECTION

A three-stage model of research and validation of data was followed. First, informal conversations were held with all the women, usually by phone, although, some were also face-to-face – unfortunately, time, distance and the cost of travel (the research was part-time while working full-time and self - financed) prevented me from doing this with all the women in the study. Issues discussed in the initial contact included establishing rapport by telling them about me, finding out about them, what the research was about, indicating what would be required of them and asking if they were willing to participate in the research.

Some gap was usually left between this and my second contact with them when I did the interview. The time and place of the interview was selected to suit their convenience. For example, they were asked if they would prefer to come to my house in which case I would pay their travel costs, or would they like me to meet them somewhere that is convenient for them. Three interviews took place in the participants' workplace, three in my home and the rest were at the participant's own home. Of the three women that came to my house, only one accepted my offer of travel expenses and one stayed the weekend with me. She wanted to stay for a weekend because she was going through a difficult patch with her family at the time and she welcomed the opportunity to be able to talk it through with another person of a similar background to herself.

Although, the primary focus of the research was on the experience of education and employment, participants were asked to talk about their personal biographies during the interview in order for them to have some control in what was discussed and to gain a deeper and more comprehensive understanding of the women's lived experiences. My sample comprised of a range of impairments including three deaf women and one with a learning difficulty. However, all interviews, except one, were in one-to-one direct communication. One deaf woman was interviewed through a sign language interpreter.

The interviews were taped. During our first contact I asked if they would mind my taping our conversation. None of the women did. The advantages of taping were that I was left free to listen and respond to what they were saying without worrying about taking notes and being accurate. Interview times ranged from half an hour to three and a half hours, the average being two hours. The taped interview was transcribed into print and given back to the participant with the request to add, delete or change anything as they saw fit. This was important in order to avoid manipulation and exploitation of the interview situation for it is often easy for research participants to get carried away in talking about their lives, particularly if a good level of rapport has been established. It is also necessary to check descriptive and interpretative validity as well as a means of giving them the opportunity to reflect on what they said.

A few days after the transcripts were sent, I contacted them by phone to see if they had received it and how they felt about it. Overall, a majority of the women said that it was fine as it was. Although, one was a little anxious about what she had said because 'in case people get the wrong idea about what I am saying' and as a result of this she decided to opt for a pseudonym which she originally did not want. One transcript was returned to me with 52 amendments, the majority of which were grammatical corrections but there was one additional piece of information (an actual example of where she had experienced further discrimination). Another woman sent me back her transcript after reflecting on it at some length and making several changes, mainly clarifying existing points.

When I sent them the interview transcript I had made it clear that they could either phone me their comments through and I will make the specified adjustments to save them time and inconvenience or, if they wished, they could write to me. Consequently, four women dictated me changes over the telephone which I was able to do with the aid of a mobile phone perched between my shoulder and neck while I typed the changes at the computer. Although, not requested by them, I sent these four women a revised copy of their transcript to reassure them that the changes had been made and for them to keep a copy of it for future reference if they wished.

INVOLVEMENT/EXPLOITATION

Hitherto, researchers have assumed the role of 'experts' over the research subjects and, thus, reinforced the dominant power structure of society (Oliver, 1992). In order to shift the balance of power from the researcher to the researched, there have been calls for greater involvement of research participants at every level of the research process. For example, Barton (1988a: 91) asserts that the research participants should be involved in the choice of topic for investigation as well as the uses to which the findings should be put. Some feminist writers have even argued for involvement at the point of conceptualising and writing up (Lather, 1987). This is an attractive and commendable aspiration. However, there are practical difficulties. I found that the main limitation in realising this aspiration has been one of time constraint, particularly from the viewpoint of the research participants. For example, if they are to have a say on the final content and shape of the study, they would need to receive a full draft of the report for them to read and reflect on before commenting. This would require a great deal of their time and attention which the majority of them were unlikely to be able to give to it. I was concerned that making such a demand of them may give rise to feelings of resentment or exploitation. Therefore, I tried an alternative method of dissemination by attempting to bring all the women together in order to share and discuss the findings. Again, this proved difficult for several reasons. The participants were geographically spread out into different parts of the country and travelling on inaccessible public transport is a major constraint for many disabled people, and for those who could overcome this with difficulty, it was impossible to find a time that was convenient to all concerned. Thus, even this modified aspiration had to be abandoned in favour of disseminating a summary of the findings in order to give them a picture of the collective experience and obtain their comments.

Ultimately the researcher is responsible to the sponsoring institution for framing the analysis, contextualising the findings and writing up the final report and, thus, forcing her/him to do it in the way she/he deems most appropriate (Ribbens, 1990). Moreover, for me, the need to involve the women in the study raised the issue of exploitation particularly as it is the researcher who benefits the most out of completing a research project. For example, Sue Wise (1987) points out the inescapable power that we as researchers have over our research data when she states:

> 'The research products are produced by the researcher and it is her version of reality that is seen to have cognitive authority ... no matter how we deny it we are still operating within an environment where the ethic prevails that those who publish research are experts and those who are written about are not' (p.76).

A further dilemma I reflected on was over the question of conflicting interests, which has not yet been addressed in any discussion of emancipatory research. For example, what if there was no consensus among the women in my sample about what aspect of their experience should be researched? This is a particularly important question since not all disabled people perceive their experience as defined by the social model of disability. We may think that rejection of the social model is a form of internal oppression (Rieser and Mason, 1990).

However, if they are not aware of the model, and many disabled people are not, do we take on the role of an educator? And, if we do, are we, then, not imposing our own value judgements and interpretation of the world on their realities? In my own research, there were those who did not recognise what disability, racism or sexism were, even though they gave me examples of where they claimed to have experienced such discrimination. In such situations, it was left to me to interpret the specific meaning of what they had related to me. This left me wondering, at times, if I was not imposing my own political and theoretical way of viewing the world on their reality.

HOW EMANCIPATORY WAS IT?

In summary, emancipatory research is about the 'changing of the social relations of research production' (Oliver, 1992). In other words, shifting the control from the researcher to the researched which requires researchers to learn to put their knowledge and skills at the disposal of the researched for them to use in whatever way they choose (Barnes, 1992a). Although, as stated earlier, my research is as much about making sense of my own experience as those of the women who took part in my study, the research was for a PhD and the decision to proceed was solely mine as well as how to undertake the interviews and the analysis.

However, because there has been very little research on disabled Black women, once I started to approach other disabled Black women with the idea of doing research on our experience, their enthusiasm was clearly encouraging. Thus, I was in control, although, a small number of participants (four) were initially consulted on what aspect of our experience should be researched.

Following earlier feminist writers Oliver (1992) identified three essential principles of emancipatory research as being reciprocity, gain and empowerment. Below I discuss how I tried to achieve these and the limitations I encountered.

RECIPROCITY

Feminist researchers have defined reciprocity in different ways. First, it is argued that the researcher must be prepared to answer direct questions regarding the mutual exchange of personal information and, thus, secondly, introduce some vulnerability through self-exposure in the same way as we are asking the research participants (Ribbens, 1990). However, as Ribbens (1990) points out, not all research participants want to hear about the researcher and that if we volunteer the information without being asked, it may be seen as 'making demands of them'.

The issues of reciprocity and researcher vulnerability are also complex as each individual differs in how they view the world and its social interactions. In my research, I found that I soon learnt from the messages I was receiving from the women themselves so that I knew when it was okay for me to share my experiences and when it was not. If my experiences were similar to theirs, then I shared them and in return I usually received the response that 'it's nice to know that I am not alone'. In general, however, I waited until they asked me about myself. Although, I let them know at the beginning that I was prepared to answer any questions they may have. Some women wanted to know something about my experience before talking about themselves. Others asked me questions about myself after they had finished telling me about themselves and, yet others, asked me during their accounts to compare and contrast their experiences with mine. I agree with Ribbens (1990: 584) that:

> '...we should ...take our cue from the person being interviewed for they may not always wish to know and it may detract them from talking about themselves'.

Oakley (1981) identified a third level of reciprocity in that she developed long-term friendships with some of the women in her research project. Indeed, this happened in my own study in that I too have made several lasting friendships. However, this is not something that is in the general control of the researcher as we must take our cue from the research participants as to how much they wish to enter into our lives and for us to enter into theirs.

I believe that reciprocity is an inevitable result of an 'insider' researching the lived experiences of the group to which she belongs: through the mutual exploration of the research topic which is of common concern to them both. For example, when we were discussing difficulties encountered at job interviews, it became mutually convenient to share strategies for deflecting overt cases of discrimination from potential employers. Moreover, several women in my study were, to my immense embarrassment and discomfort, grateful to me for my having listened to them and for 'caring' about their issues. For example, Jackey phoned me after reading her transcript to comment:

> 'I wanted to put my real name down because I am proud of who I am, a black woman with a learning disability and I hope that we as disabled black women can help each other. I would like to thank my mother, and the Lord for helping me and thank you for interviewing me because if it wasn't for women like you no-one would care what happens to us at all'.

And, Jo said that she had never been able to talk to anyone about her entire experience and feel understood as now because her non-disabled Black friends only understood issues around racism. Often, they were so pleased to have been listened to about 'the whole' of their experience that they were hugging me when I left with pleas to keep in touch as though I was some long lost friend. Furthermore, for research to be fully reciprocal, the researcher must be prepared to listen and help in matters that may not be directly relevant to the research project in question. As researchers we often seek to hear about specific experiences in isolation of others. It is, of course, necessary to have a rough outline of the areas that research is going to focus on to avoid confusion and lack of clarity. However, experiences are not compartmentalised in the way that researchers seek them out and interpret them. Some of the women in my study felt free to say during the interview that 'this is highly confidential, I don't mind telling you but I don't want it included in the research'. When they said this I usually switched the tape recorder off even though they did not ask me to do so and I switched it on later after asking the women's permission.

WHO GAINED?

Throughout my research, I frequently asked myself: I know what I am getting out of this but what are they getting out of it? Undeniably, I was the main beneficiary in that I obtained the data to complete a PhD and the resulting publications. Although, on the latter, it is worth noting that all participants were asked if they would mind my using their material for written publications. None of them did. In fact, some commented that, at long last, disabled Black women's issues will start being discussed.

I also gained a better understanding of my own personal biography through exploring others' experiences and seeing similarities in my own. This latter point was also shared by several of the women who made it clear to me that they valued having been given a copy of the interview transcript because it led them to reflect on their experience and make sense of it. For example, Lisa commented that:

> 'It is emotionally good to receive this. I didn't realise until now exactly how much I had been through because you usually push it to the back of your mind and get on with your life and try not to think about it'.

This is precisely the kind of passive acceptance that emancipatory research can help to avoid through opportunities to talk about and reflect on one's experiences as well as sharing them with others to identify common threads. Furthermore, knowing all along that I was going to be the main beneficiary of this research, I was particularly concerned by the need to avoid exploitation. Thus, I let all the women know that I would be pleased to hear from them either socially or to help in any way I could. To this end, several of the women have kept in touch with me by phone, and sometimes by letter, either to discuss specific things such as job search and interview skills or simply to ask me how the research was going. For example, one woman asked me to give her some feedback on a job application and another asked to help in arranging a work placement which I was able to do. Two other women asked me to speak about disabled Black people's issues at two separate national events and a third has offered to translate the study into Sign Language for the British library for deaf people.

HOW EMPOWERING WAS IT?

This was more difficult to assess since empowerment is something that people do for themselves collectively (Oliver, 1992) or, indeed, individually – for example, by joining or even forming a local coalition of disabled people and by learning to become more assertive. It could be argued that because my research was initiated from the 'inside', that the decision to carry out the research and make our experiences known was, in itself, a form of self-empowerment and the fact that several of the women who took part in the study were keen to provide me with other contacts to interview is also evident of the same self-empowerment.

Karl (1995) observes that a sense of empowerment comes from 'being recognised and respected as equal citizens and human beings with a contribution to make' (p. 14). Of course, if the prior experience of the research participants is that they have not been treated as equals – which is the case with many disabled people living in a disabling society, and particularly for disabled Black women who are 'a multiple Other' (Vernon, 1996c)– then a research relationship which treats them as equals, is likely to increase their self-confidence and self-esteem which is the first step towards empowerment. Thus, the first seeds of empowerment may be sown by allowing the research participants to speak for themselves about their experiences and concerns and, thereby, engendering a feeling of being valued.

Disabled Black women are a minority within a minority. Hence, frequently, one disabled Black woman does not know another. Thus, the opportunity to share experiences can quite literally be 'empowering'. In isolated situations experiences are individualised as 'problems' of the individual frequently by people around them and sometimes by the individuals themselves. This can result in a particularly damaging form of disempowerment as dissatisfaction with the self can result in colluding with one's oppressors.

CONCLUSION

I wish to highlight three main points arising from the discussion in this chapter. First, like many other feminists I chose to do research which was central to my own experience, made all the more necessary by the continued exclusion of disabled Black women's experiences from all three academic agendas of disability, 'race' and gender. My proximity to my research subjects resulted in a constant sense of insecurity about the need to avoid exploitation and bias in the interpretation of the data. Not surprisingly, I found that there were many similarities as well as differences between my experience and those of the women who took part in my study. Hence, I lay no claim to objectivity. Although, it has been argued that objectivity is the word our oppressors use to impose their way of seeing the world on us while they suppress our way of seeing the world (Oakley, 1981) and that empowerment involves rejecting the dimensions of knowledge that perpetuate objectification and dehumanisation (Hill-Collins, 1990). The affirmation of finding myself at the core of some women's accounts was enormously empowering. Although, my fear of distorting the often similar experiences of the women whom I interviewed generated a constant sense of insecurity which in turn served to underline my power as interpreter. I often found myself feeling immense anger and hurt at the horrendous tales the women told about rejection and discrimination at school, at work and at home. At times, I wondered if I was conflating their many varied experiences with my own. In the end, I came to the conclusion that there is no neutral ground in researching the experience of oppression. One is either on the side of the oppressed or the oppressors and for me as an 'insider', there was no question as to which side I would rather be on. Therefore, my need to avoid reinforcing oppression in the research process was magnified with an acute sense of treading on egg shells in order to avoid overstepping the thin line between identification and exploitation.

Secondly, although I was committed to working within the emancipatory research paradigm, ultimately, it is true to say that 'the social relations of research production' remained unchanged in that I initiated the research and I was in control and not the participants in my study. However, it could be argued that because I was participating in that which I was observing (in that my research was as much about own experiences as those of other disabled Black women), that the control of the project was not as far removed from the participating group as it would otherwise have been. My hope is that the research will act as a much needed starting point both for bringing disabled Black women's issues out into the open and, more importantly, to begin the consideration of how disability interacts with other oppressions in disabled people's lives on the mainstream agenda of disability research and analysis.

Thirdly, the objectives of emancipatory research can be achieved through uncovering how oppression manifests itself in the day-to-day realities of those oppressed. However, it is important to bear in mind that exposing the workings of the mechanisms of oppression is no guarantee of bringing about change for the better. Changing the attitudes which are deeply ingrained in an individual's subconscious (as well as institutional policies) is a slow and laborious task. As Maguire (1987) has observed 'transformation is a process, not a one time event' (p. 242) and it is important not to lose heart. Taking part in research will seldom result in immediate collective action. However, it is only through understanding our experience as an oppressive situation and through the realisation that one is not alone that we can identify ourselves with others in the same situation and in so doing begin the journey towards our empowerment.

REFERENCES

BARNES, C. (1991) *Disabled People in Britain: A Case For Anti-Discrimination Legislation for Disabled People*. London: Hurst/BCODP.

BARNES, C. (1992a) 'Qualitative Research: Valuable or Irrelevant?', *Disability, Handicap and Society*, 7 (2): 115-24.

BARNES, C. (1992b) *Disabling Imagery: An exploration of Media Portrayals of Disabled People*. Halifax: Ryburn/ BCODP.

BARTON, L. (1988) 'Research and Practice: The Need for Alternative Perspectives', in L. Barton, ed. *Disability and Dependency*. Lewes: Falmer.

BARTON. L. ed. (1996) *Disability and Society: Emerging Issues and Insights*, London: Longman.

BHAVNANI, K-K. and COULSON, M. (1986) 'Transforming Socialist-Feminism: The Challenge of Racism', reprinted in M. Evans, ed. (1994) *The Woman Question*. London: Sage.

BRITTAN, A. and MAYNARD, M. (1984) *Sexism, Racism and Oppression*. Oxford: Basil Blackwell.

CAMPLING, J. (1979) *Better Lives for Disabled Women*. London: Virago.

CAMPLING, J., ed. (1981) *Images of Ourselves: Women with Disabilities Talking*. London: Routledge & Kegan Paul.

CARBY, H. (1982) 'White Woman Listen! Black feminism and the boundaries of sisterhood', in Centre for Contemporary Cultural Studies (1982), *Empire strikes Back: Race and Racism in 70's Britain*. London: Hutchinson/ CCCS, University of Birmingham.

DEEGAN, M. and BROOKS, M., eds. (1985) *Women and Disability: The Double Handicap*. New Brunswick, Transaction Books.

FINE, M. and ASCH, A. (1985) 'Disabled Women: Sexism Without the Pedestal', in M. Deegan and M. Brooks, eds. *Women and Disability: The Double Handicap*. New Brunswick, Transaction.

FINE, M. and ASCH, A. (1988) *Women With Disabilities: Essays in Psychology, Culture, and Politics*. Philadelphia: Temple University Press.

FREIRE, P. (1972) *Pedagogy of the Oppressed*. Harmondsworth: Penguin Books.

GERSCHICK, T. J. and MILLER, A. S. (1995) 'Coming to Terms', in D. Sabo and D. Gordon, eds. *Men's Health and Illness*. London: Sage.

GRAMSCI, A. (1971) *Selections From the Prison Notebooks*. London: Lawrence and Wishart.

HILL-COLLINS, P. (1990) *Black Feminist Thought: Knowledge, Consciousness and the Politics of Empowerment*. London: Unwin-Hyman.

HILL, M. (1994) ' "They are not our Brothers": The Disability Movement & the Black Disability Movement', in N. Begum, M. Hill and A. Stevens, *Reflections: The Views of Black Disabled People on their Lives and Community Care*. London: CCETSW.

KARL, M. (1995) *Women and Empowerment: Participation and Decision Making*. New Jersey: Zed Books.

KEITH, L. ed. (1994) *Musn't Grumble*. London: Women's Press.

KING, D. K. (1988) 'Multiple Jeopardy, Multiple Consciousness: The Context of a Black Feminist Ideology', *Signs*, Autumn, pp 42-72.

LATHER, P. (1987) 'Research as Praxis', *Harvard Educational Review*, 56 (3): 257-73.

LLOYD, M. (1992) 'Does She Boil Eggs? Towards a feminist model of Disability', *Disability, Handicap and Society*, 7 (3): 207-21.

LONSDALE, S. (1990) *Women and Disability: The experience of disability among women*. Basingstoke:Macmillan,.

MAGUIRE, P. (1987) *Doing Participatory Research: A Feminist Approach. The Centre for International Education*. Boston: University of Massachusetts.

MARTIN, J., WHITE, A. and MELTZER, H. (1989) *Disabled adults: services, transport and employment*. London: OPCS.

MORRIS, J. (1989) *Able Lives: Women's Experience of Paralysis*. London:Women's Press.

MORRIS, J. (1992) 'Personal is Political: A feminist perspective on researching women with physical disabilities', *Disability, Handicap and Society*, 7 (2): 157-66.

OAKLEY, A. (1981) 'Interviewing Women: A Contradiction in terms', in H. Roberts, ed. *Doing Feminist Research*. London: Routledge and Kegan Paul.

OLIVER, M. (1992) 'Changing the Social Relations of Research Production', *Disability, Handicap and Society*, 7 (2): 101-14.

PRESCOTT CLARKE, P. (1990) *Employment and Handicap*. London: Social and Community Planning Research.

RAMAZANOGLU, C. (1989) *Feminism and the Contradictions of Oppression*. London: Routledge.

REAY, D. (1996) 'Insider Perspectives or Stealing The Words Out of Women's Mouths: Interpretation in the Research Process', *Feminist Review*, no 53, Summer, pp.57-73.

RENTERIA, D. (1993) 'Rejection' in R.Luczak, ed. *Eyes of Desire: A Deaf Gay & Lesbian Reader*. Boston: Alyson Publications.

RIBBENS, J. (1990) 'Interviewing - an "Unnatural Situation"?', *Women's Studies International Forum*, 12 (6): 579-92.

RIESER, R. & MASON, M. (1990) *Disability Equality in the Classroom: A Human Rights Issue*. London: ILEA.

SAXTON, M. & HOWE, F. (1988) *With Wings: An Anthology of Literature by and about Women with Disabilities*, London: Virago.

SHAKESPEARE, T., GILLESPIE-SELLS, K. and DAVIES, D. (1996) *Sexual Politics of Disability: Untold Desires*. London: Cassell.

VERNON, A. (1996a) 'A Stranger in Many Camps: The experience of Disabled Black and Ethnic Minority Women', in J. Morris, ed. *Encounters With strangers: Feminism and Disability*. London: Women's Press.

VERNON, A. (1996b) 'Disabled Women in the Labour Market', Conference paper: Self Determined Living for Disabled Women, 15-18 August 1996, Munich.

VERNON, A. (1996c) 'Deafness, Disability and Multiple Oppression'. Conference paper to the PSI and ADSUP conference Deaf and Disabled people: Towards a New Understanding, 7-8 December.

VERNON, A. (1997) 'Multiple Oppression: A Minority Interest or a Majority Experience?' Seminar Paper to the series on Dialogues in Disability, City University, London, January.

WHEATLEY, E. (1994) 'Dances with Feminists: Truths, Dares and Ethnographic Stares', *Women's Studies International Forum*, 17 (4) : 421-3.

WISE, S. (1987) 'A Framework for discussing ethical issues in feminist research: A review of the literature', Writing Feminist Biography 2: Using life histories. *Studies in Sexual Politics*, no. 19, Department of Sociology, University of Manchester.

CHAPTER 11

Researching Disabled Sexuality

Tom Shakespeare

In 1996, two years after we commenced the research, Cassell published *The Sexual Politics of Disability: Untold Desires*. For Dominic Davies, Kath Gillespie-Sells and myself it was the end of a hard slog, a real moment of pride, but also an occasion for trepidation: what would other people think? How would the disability movement react? What difference would our book make? Had we done the right thing?

Researching and writing is largely under the authors' control. Of course, it is true that unexpected developments or problems may shape the development of the process, there is room for disagreement among collaborators, and books rarely end up exactly as they were intended. However, we exercised choice and control over the project, in negotiation with Cassell, which was relinquished once the book emerged on the market. At that stage, we could only wait and worry.

Post-structuralist writers have identified what they call 'the death of the author'. By this is meant the openness of a text to multiple interpretations. While the writers may have specific ambitions and intentions, once the book is in the public domain, others are free to read into it their own values and feelings, and to use the arguments and evidence it provides to promote ends which may be contrary to the authors' intentions. There is no way around this danger. For example, free market libertarians on the Right have adopted the anti-institutional emphasis of the disability movement to argue that day centres and other provision should be closed down. A progressive demand for autonomy and integration is converted into cuts in public services and rolling back of the state.

Nothing this extreme may result from our book on disabled sexuality. However, unscrupulous readers might find the description of disabled sex titillating: we felt it was very important to capture the creativity and energy of disabled people's sexual expression, but doing so runs the risk of supplying non-disabled voyeurs with material for erotic fantasies (not a usual danger of academic writing). More importantly, perhaps, we might have mis-represented disabled people's experiences or desires, or distorted the evidence to provide an account which is unduly negative or positive.

It is unusual to be given the opportunity to reflect on the research process, to justify our work, and to correct any misapprehensions which have arisen. The reflexive discussion which follows is representative only of my views: my colleagues have not participated in writing this chapter. It has been difficult to avoid sounding either too defensive and apologetic, or too self-congratulatory. The important judgements about the work are those of other disabled people.

WHY DID WE WRITE IT?

There are cynical answers to this question, which would be inaccurate, but cannot entirely be discounted. These include: personal ambition; desire for financial gain; voyeurism; academic credibility; opportunism. The altruistic answers might include: political commitment; perceived need; intellectual curiosity; professional development. The truth lies somewhere between these positions, and includes a considerable degree of pragmatism.

The original idea was Dominic's: we were to collaborate on a collection of accounts by lesbian and gay disabled people. Kath Gillespie-Sells was invited to join the team to bring a feminist and lesbian perspective. We shared a common commitment to sexual liberation and empowerment in general and to lesbian and gay rights in particular. When I made contact with Cassell, who publish widely in this field, the commissioning editor steered us towards a more general book about the sexual politics of disability as a whole. This was a daunting prospect. Rapidly we moved away from a collection of essays on aspects of the issue, towards a book based on personal accounts, which we would gather from friends and strangers in the disabled community.

For me, there were various subsidiary intellectual reasons, with personal and political dimensions. My own concerns and politics focus as much on sexuality as on disability, and I have always worked in areas which are of direct interest to me and relevance to my life. A book which looked at identity, sexuality, relationships and parenting was of great interest to me, and also offered a chance to put my previous intellectual work on disability theory into practice. Moreover, having been trained as a sociologist at the University of Cambridge, my work had largely been within social theory, which I increasingly felt was unhelpful and largely irrelevant to ordinary life. Inspired by the Chicago School, by Erving Goffman, and by feminist research, I wanted to do some 'proper sociology', by which I meant interviewing real people about their lives, and creating new knowledge, rather than criticising or recycling other people's work.

As we argue in the book, disabled people have usually been degendered and regarded as asexual, and we felt that the literature on disability had an absence around sexuality. There are various dimensions to this. Traditional literature on disability has been discredited by the emergence of the disability movement and the disability studies perspective, which is based on the social model and a disability equality approach rather than a medical tragedy assumption. While there are books which discuss disability and sexuality, they fall within the limitations of the traditional literature (Shakespeare *et al*, 1996: 1).

However, there was no existing book which effectively dealt with sexuality within the disability studies literature either. Key texts (e.g. Oliver, 1990) hardly mentioned the issue at all, and even feminist work (e.g. Morris, 1991) skirted round the issues. Although other accounts (e.g. Morris, 1989; Oliver, 1983; Hunt, 1966) do mention sexuality, there was still no book specifically and exclusively discussing the issues, drawing on qualitative research with disabled people. In general, with the exception of the feminist literature on disabled women, there has been little emphasis within disability studies on the realm of identity, personal experience, and private life. For us, the personal is political, and while we understood that the priority had been to explore structural relations and social barriers in the public spheres of life, we felt it was high time to redress the balance.

I have a suspicion that the disability community has had a reluctance to explore sexuality. Milton Diamond discusses the way that families and agencies avoid the issue, in terms which may be relevant to the disability movement itself:

> 'While they recognise that these are valid issues, they generally wish the sexual concerns to be ignored; they want them to sort of "go away", since they are ill at ease dealing with them, and don't really know how to handle the issues' (Diamond, 1984: 210).

The American writer Ann Finger, argues that the disability rights movement has not put sexual rights at the forefront of its agenda:

> 'Sexuality is often the source of our deepest oppression; it is also often the source of our deepest pain. It's easier for us to talk about - and formulate strategies for changing - discrimination in employment, education, and housing than to talk about our exclusion from sexuality and reproduction' (Finger, 1992: 9).

It was our experience that disabled people – like everyone else – often summed up their life ambitions in terms of 'a job, a partner, and a family'. We felt that the disability movement had made an effective challenge on the first issue, but not on the rest. British disabled feminist Liz Crow's comments echo our own opinions:

> 'I've always assumed that the most urgent Disability civil rights campaigns are the ones we're currently fighting for - employment, education, housing, transport etc., etc., and that next to them a subject such as sexuality is almost dispensable. For the first time now I'm beginning to believe that sexuality, the one area above all others to have been ignored, is at the absolute core of what we're working for.(...) It's not that one area can ever be achieved alone - they're all interwoven, but you can't get closer to the essence of self or more "people-living-alongside-people" than sexuality, can you?' (Crow, 1991: 13).

A final set of issues arose for me during the research. These related to my growing academic interest in narrative and biographical sociology. A particular example of this is Ken Plummer's book, *Telling Sexual Stories*, which is discussed in the book's conclusion. His work echoed my views and reinforced what we were trying to do with our research. He suggests:

> 'Rights and responsibilities are not "natural" or "inalienable" but have to be invented through human activities and built into the notions of communities, citizenship and identities. Rights and responsibilities depend upon a community of stories which make those same rights plausible and possible. They accrue to people whose identities flow out of the self-same communities. Thus it is only as lesbian and gay communities started to develop and women's movements gathered

strength that stories around a new kind of citizenship became more and more plausible. The nature of our communities - the languages they use, the stories they harbour, the identities they construct, the moral/political codes they champion - move to the centre stage of political thinking' (Plummer, 1995: 150).

Connecting with my previous work on identity, my interest in agency, and my philosophical allegiances with post-structuralist thought, Plummer's work was the benchmark for my writing.

HOW DID WE GO ABOUT IT?

Working together, we decided to research a book which covered the range of issues in a coherent and fairly comprehensive way. This involved drawing up a loose schedule of areas to be explored in interviews with as many disabled people as possible. We looked at what little was already available, and we brainstormed from our own experience: we felt that our own lives and feelings were very relevant to the process. Rather than trying to achieve some spurious objectivity or distance, we acted as key informants and research participants.

Our sample was drawn from people of our own acquaintance, and from people who answered adverts or followed up requests published in a range of journals, including *Disability Now* and *The Pink Paper*. Eventually, it comprised 44 people: almost exactly equal numbers of men and women, but as many gay, lesbian and bisexual respondents as heterosexual. Clearly the British population does not comprise equivalent numbers of gay and straight individuals: the sample was skewed by our own contacts and biographies, and by the fact that gay people seemed more likely to come forward, and more willing to talk, than many straight people. We were not unduly alarmed at this situation: a greater concern was the small number of Black or Asian respondents, and the fact that the majority of participants were active in the disability movement. We made efforts to redress these imbalances, and were explicit about these limitations in the final publication: our lack of time and resources prevented us doing more to equalise the sample. We have never claimed to be representative, in a statistical sense: we are not saying 'this is the experience of all disabled people', we are saying 'this is what some disabled people have experienced, and these are our conclusions'.

As time went on, we used a greater variety of methods: we included letters which people wrote to us; some people made tapes of their own; we used progressively less structured formats. It was our intention to document the lives and experiences of disabled people, and we felt a commitment to the individuals involved, rather than the social scientific community or a particular sense of methodological rigour. In this we felt supported by developments such as the work of Ken Plummer (1995) and Tim Booth (1996), both of whom have espoused narrative techniques and the gathering of personal stories within sociology. Perhaps the most obvious sign of this focus on life-story are the personal accounts between each chapter in the book: we decided to include these in order to convey the richness of the material we had gathered, and to give participants a chance to speak for themselves, and also, it has to be admitted, to achieve the target length which the publishers had set for us.

This last point indicates the pragmatism which underlay our methodology. As long as we were faithful to the participants, by which we meant basic ethical commitments not to misrepresent, betray confidentiality, or distort, we were content to follow their interests and allow the project to develop organically. The scope of the research was very broad: in an area which had not been investigated before, and with the paucity of records of disabled people's lives, we felt that we could afford to cast our net wide, and to sacrifice some rigour and some exactness. Many topics are not adequately explored: pregnancy and parenting, for example, or sexual abuse. Other people are generating more comprehensive accounts of these areas.

Certain problematic issues surfaced during the research process. For example, we had to deal with disclosure of sexual abuse from a number of participants, which was a topic we felt that we did not have the time or expertise to cope with effectively. We agreed that we would not ask questions, probe or analyse responses about sexual abuse, although we would include material in the book. This aspect of the work was one of the most distressing features of the research, and we would support the new initiatives which have developed to combat abuse.

A second issue concerns the willingness of participants to discuss matters of personal relationships and sexual activity. The disability community as a whole does not readily discuss these private dimensions of life as a disabled person in our experience. We have argued that this area is as political as many of the issues which we do discuss and campaign about. Disabled people, in general, may lack the language or confidence to discuss matters of sex and love: this is a product of disempowerment, and a lack of effective sex education, and the minimal expectations of family, friends, carers and professionals. If interventions are made – for instance, SPOD (Sexual Problems of the Disabled), they are often unhelpful because they are mechanistic, depoliticised, and outdated. In Britain, as a whole, discussion of sex is largely taboo: we are a nation of prudes, subject to immediate embarrassment over personal matters. Initiatives such as the Outsiders Club, on the other hand, aim to sexualise disability but run the risk of exploitation, voyeurism and abuse by failing to work within a disability equality perspective.

We found that many respondents were able to talk in general about their lives, and in abstract about issues of identity and imagery and barriers, for example, but found it difficult to talk specifically about relationships or sexuality. Some respondents would only respond to issues in political terms: they would talk about what they believed to be an appropriate and correct response to sexual matters, rather than about their own feelings and desires. However, enough respondents felt comfortable and willing to discuss the details of their sexual lives to enable us to include discussion of such personal experiences, although these were more likely to be women than men, and lesbian or gay people than straight people.

A third problem was represented by the small minority of respondents, all men, who reported behaviours with which we could not empathise: behaviours which were restrictive of other people's sexual and civil rights, and sometimes verged on abuse. Examples might include use of pornography or prostitution, or exploitative relations with other people. Given that our first commitment was to representing the views and experiences of disabled people faithfully, we felt anxious about censoring or judging the accounts provided by disabled people. However, we also felt that integrating disabled people in society, enabling access, and achieving civil rights should not be at the cost of oppressing other people in society, particularly women. We attempted to balance such testimonies, then, with other accounts by disabled people which were explicitly anti-sexist or opposed to abusive relationships, rather than excluding any material. Moroever, in the chapter on "Bad Sex", we explored our own ethical standpoint on inappropriate sexual relations. This was not without its complications, however, as we ourselves held a range of views about what constituted a healthy or positive sexual relationship:

none of us necessarily advocated monogamous pair-bonding as the only option, but we had different opinions as to the value of non-committed or casual encounters.

Other differences between authors inevitably occurred during the writing period, as our various biographies influenced our response to the material, and our feelings about the style and direction of the text. One of us is predominantly a trainer, organiser and activist; another is a psychotherapist and counselling lecturer; a third is an academic. These differences meant that we approached the material in different ways, and had different aims for the final book. We would probably argue that this range of experience, wedded to a common concern for disability equality and sexual liberation, ensured that the book was balanced and broad in its appeal. However, at various times it led to differences over our authorial voice: how political could we be? How informal? How academic? Given that Cassell had commissioned a book with a predominantly academic readership, it was the sociological criteria that generally won through, although we would hope that the text is also both accessible and political.

WHAT DID WE HOPE TO ACHIEVE?

This account of the research underlying *The Sexual Politics of Disability* may sound complacent, and lacking in academic professionalism. However, it was our intention to pave the way for others, and to produce a readable text which gave a voice to disabled people, not to provide the final word on this topic. It was our hope that a variety of people would read the book, and would think of disabled people differently as a consequence. We set out to demonstrate that disabled people can be just like other people; that physical restrictions are not the main issue in disabled sexuality; and that the sexual rights of disabled people need to be met, just as much as the civil and political rights.

We thought of our audience as a broad one: lay readers, academics, professionals, but most of all disabled people. We hoped that disabled people would recognise their own experiences, and would feel validated by the accounts we published. We placed the research within our broader understanding of empowerment, which for us is as much about personal and emotional developments as it is about political and structural change: in the book, and in our professional work, we balance a need for barrier-removal and civil rights, with a need to support individuals to develop a more positive self-image and a sense of pride and self-worth. To orient ourselves towards the early origins of the disability movement, we work within the tradition established by the Liberation Network of People with Disabilities, as much or more than that represented by the Union of Physically Impaired Against Segregation.

It is difficult to say whether these ambitions have been fulfilled; voices and reactions filter back to us which are largely positive, from women and men who understand and respect what we have tried to do. Reviews have thus far been positive, sometimes deliriously so. It is particularly heartening that people included in the book have found it accurate and helpful. There has certainly been considerable interest in the book, as well as some scepticism from the more ideologically rigorous members of the disability movement who pick up on semantic details (describing the social model as "an analysis of the experiences of disabled people" did not go down well). But the true mark of the book's success in achieving its ambitions will be a more long-term appraisal and response from disabled people in general, and in the extent to which it challenges the prevailing view of disabled people as asexual, which is an intangible consequence which we will never be able to measure.

Of course, the research and writing has been a learning experience. There are many ways in which I would do things differently in future. Most of these are minor points: the major ones are about being systematic, not being too ambitious, allowing enough time. I'm not sure I would do this type of research and writing collaboratively again: we succeeded, but I feel a need to exercise more control over projects than I was able to on this occasion. I'm now more likely to work with just one other person. I stick with my view that it is important to gather primary data and to give disabled people a voice, and that analysis and theory is secondary to that. However, in my current work on disabled childhood, because it is a more sociological project, there will be more analysis and discussion.

CONCLUSION

The million dollar question remains: is *The Sexual Politics of Disability* emancipatory research? To be honest, I don't know and I don't really care. I am a pluralist, and would rather follow my own intellectual and ethical standards, rather than trying to conform to an orthodoxy. I don't follow recipes when I cook, and I'm not keen on following imposed rules when I research. However, I think I share the basic commitment which underlies the notion of emancipatory research, although it is for others to judge by the results.

My editor has asked me to answer three questions:

1. Is the research initiated by disabled people rather than by academics?

Well, yes and no. Two of the authors were not academics and one was. We are all disabled people. We had political objectives, namely disability equality and civil rights. However, no representative self-organised group of disabled people initiated the project.

2. Does the research adhere to the social model of disability?

Everything I do adheres to the social model of disability, according to my own interpretation of it. I'm not prepared to ignore issues such as impairment, but in general I think I can answer yes. The book opens with a chapter on social barriers, after all.

3. Does it involve unprecedented levels of participation, accountability and reciprocity?

Not really. We were broadly accountable to our research participants. We let them shape the research interviews, in many cases to write their own accounts, and their own priorities influenced the format and scope of the final text. We talked to other disabled people, organisations and academics. I was not, and am not, prepared to let other people control what I write, or dictate the appropriate political stance. In this project there was not enough time or resources to enable people to check over the text or comment on it. While I would always welcome advice and feedback, I'm not sure I'd ever want to be accountable to anyone other than my publisher and my conscience.

I have a certain scepticism about the notions of emancipatory research developed by Mike Oliver (1992) and Gerry Zarb (1992), among others. Different forms of social research may be more or less applied or pure, and more or less allied to the needs of particular groups within the disability movement. While disability studies emerged from the disability movement, it is not contiguous to it: there are obviously major areas of overlap, and a general ideological commitment to the ideals of the disability movement on the part of disability studies academics, but it would be wrong to see disability studies as only providing policy interventions or social analysis for political goals. We need to have a range of models for the connection between theory and practice.

The Politics of Disablement, for instance, is a sociological work, without direct recommendations or policy points (Oliver, 1990). However, it has had a major impact on the lives of disabled people, because it gave intellectual credibility to the social model, and validated the analysis and direction of the disability movement. It may be fairly inaccessible, but thousands of disabled people have read it, and their consciousness has been altered as a result. This has enabled them to become activists in the movement, to argue more forcefully for disability rights, and to campaign for a better deal for disabled people. Other works, for instance Colin Barnes' Disabled People in Britain and Discrimination (1991), offered social policy evidence for the extent of disabling barriers in society: it was a critical tool in demonstrating the reality of social exclusion and the need for anti-discrimination legislation, as Rachel Hurst has argued (Hurst, 1995). Therefore research differs in the way it affects policy and practice – some operates directly, some indirectly.

It is my belief that the criteria which Mike Oliver presents for emancipatory research are too strict, and that he is naïve or disingenuous in believing that his work has benefited nobody other than himself. He may have profited financially, by a few thousand pounds, and he may have developed a reputation as a widely published and cited academic. However, as an academic, he could have made a living out of lecturing and researching on any number of topics: he did not have to choose disability. He has used his status and his position to support and develop the disability movement, and his books have contributed both directly and indirectly to disabled people's increased political consciousness, and to their success in grasping specific goals.

There is a certain tendency within the disability movement, which I have nicknamed "Maoism" (although the term in not used in a strict ideological sense), which is suspicious of academic work, and venerates the activist and the grassroots at the cost of the researcher and the writer. From this perspective, academics are parasites on the movement, who would be better off on the streets or staffing their local organisations of disabled people. The movement is the key, and the academics are an optional extra. All research with disabled people is suspect, and organisations should not cooperate with those who are 'seeking to make a career out of exploiting disabled people'. It may be guessed that I do not find this a helpful or constructive approach.

I do not believe that academics should be spokespeople for the disability movement: the voice of disabled people are the representative organisations of the disability movement, not individuals regardless of expertise or experience. However, academics have a valuable part to play in the development of our understanding of the world as experienced by disabled people. It is a very privileged position: it depends on being able to stand back, and to observe, and to think and reflect. It depends on time, and space, and money. And it would be a pretty poor disability studies researcher who did not repay that privilege by devoting time and energy (and money) to supporting and building the organisations of the disability movement.

The precedent which I offer for the relationship between researchers and the movement is the way in which other scholars – feminists and lesbian and gay writers are those with whom I am most familiar – have worked within identity politics. While there have been tensions, I do not observe in these parallel contexts the same demands being made of intellectuals, or the suspicion and resentment that sometimes seems evident in the disability movement. Perhaps that is because disabled people have a tradition of being exploited by researchers; or perhaps that it is because the relative poverty of most disabled people, and the relative wealth of most academics, is more stark a difference than the comparable gap between feminist women and feminist researchers or lesbian/gay people and writers. However, I do hope that disability studies does not repeat that precedent too closely: rather than following feminism and lesbian/gay studies into the academy and into increasingly complex and arid discussions of theory, I would hope that disability studies research retains its accessibility for ordinary readers, and its commitment to documenting the lives and priorities of disabled people. This form of openness is my main priority. I want my work to make a difference, but I have no illusions about its impact. Books don't change the world. People do.

REFERENCES

BARNES, C. (1991) *Disabled People in Britain and Discrimination*. London: Hurst and Co.

BOOTH, T. (1996) 'Sounds of still voices: issues in the use of narrative methods with people who have learning difficulties', in L. Barton, ed., *Disability and Society*. London: Longman.

CROW, L. (1991) 'Rippling Raspberries: Disabled Women and Sexuality', unpublished MSc dissertation, South Bank Polytechnic.

DIAMOND, M. (1984) 'Sexuality and the Handicapped', in R.P. Marinelli and A. Dell Orto, eds, *The Psychological and Social Impact of Physical Disability*. New York: Springer Publishing.

FINGER, A. (1992) Forbidden Fruit, *New Internationalist*, 233: 8-10.

HUNT, P. (1966) *Stigma*. London: Geoffrey Chapman.

HURST, R. (1995) 'International Perspectives and Solutions', in G. Zarb, ed., *Removing Disabling Barriers*. London: Policy Studies Institute.

MORRIS, J. (1989) *Able Lives*. London: Women's Press.

MORRIS, J. (1991) *Pride Against Prejudice*. London: Women's Press.

OLIVER, M. (1983) *Social Work with Disabled People*, Basingstoke: Macmillan.

OLIVER, M. (1990) *The Politics of Disablement*, Basingstoke: Macmillan.

OLIVER, M. (1992b) Changing the social relations of research production, *Disability, Handicap & Society*, 7 (2): 101-114.

PLUMMER, K. (1995) *Telling Sexual Stories*. London: Routledge.

SHAKESPEARE, T. GILLESPIE-SELLS, K. and DAVIES, D. (1996) *The Sexual Politics of Disability: Untold Desires*. London: Cassell.

ZARB, G. (1992) 'On the road to Damascus; first steps towards changing the relations of disability research production', *Disability, Handicap & Society*, 7 (2): 125-38.

CHAPTER 12

Uncovering the Shape of Violence: A Research Methodology Rooted in the Experience of People with Disabilities

Marcia H. Rioux, Cameron Crawford, Miriam Ticoll, Michael Bach

BEGINNING: A HUNCH

Our research agenda at the Roeher Institute is aimed at understanding the social and economic construction of inequality and the conditions for full citizenship and the exercise of human rights. Within this research agenda the study of violence and abuse experienced by people with disabilities provided us with an opportunity to reflect on the way in which research questions are constructed, often unconscious of the importance of a disability perspective. It also provided us with an opportunity to examine the relationships of specific forms of inequality faced by people with disabilities and the forms of violence and abuse this subjects them to.

One consequence of disadvantage is that issues affecting a group of people – issues that should be self-evident – are overlooked or ignored. This is not necessarily a deliberate omission but more likely the result of a failure to be sensitive to those who have traditionally been excluded. When we began this study violence and abuse in general had burgeoned into areas of concern in social policy and government spending and programs in Canada. However, only a very few studies had investigated the incidence of violence and abuse among people with disabilities. And although these studies provided some striking findings about the vulnerability of people with disabilities to abuse and violence, they also raised questions.

The stories we were hearing did not seem to be reflected in the studies we were reading on violence and abuse. And the safeguards and protocols and precautions that we would have expected in situations of high vulnerability were not only non-existent but were not even identified as needed. It was reminiscent of the silence that surrounded violence against women in the home long after it ought to have been a public issue.

The reasons behind the silence and the indifference to the circumstances of people with disabilities prompted us to undertake a study in this area – a study that was subsequently published as *Harm's Way: The Many Faces of Violence and Abuse against Persons with Disabilities* (Roeher Institute, 1995).

As we reviewed the literature and conducted preliminary interviews with people with disabilities as part of the development of our research design, it was evident that not only were traditional assaults and abuse not being investigated and resolved but that another whole area of investigation needed to be addressed. We could not find information on how people with disabilities themselves characterized abuse. In other words, as with so many aspects of their lives, in this area the experiences of people with disabilities were being appropriated and interpreted from the perspective of others.

A starting point for this study[1] was that we live in a society in which people with disabilities experience forms of marginalization solely due to their disability. Our interest was in the relationship between marginalization and their experience of abuse and violence. Moreover, this study was an effort to give people with disabilities a voice in naming violence and abuse. It provided an opportunity for speaking of their own experiences and of those events and actions that are abusive from the insider's perspective.

Within the parameters of the study people with a variety of disabilities from across Canada were interviewed in depth. The research instruments and interviews were designed to enable people to tell their stories. They were given an opportunity to say how various violent or abusive actions affected them, how the acts made them feel, how such acts had an impact on their lives and their self-esteem, and how these acts created a susceptibility to further acts of violence. The culture of being disabled in an ableist society resulting in a lack of confidence and control, isolation and desire for human contact and affection and lack of a sense of self-worth emerged in the chorus of voices and words.

From that perspective, violence and abuse look somewhat different. In the experience of those with disabilities, it is not only the traditional acts of hitting, sexually assaulting or verbally abusing a person that are being defined as violent. It is, in fact, a wide gamut of actions or lack of actions that create suffering or trauma. It is being pulled into an uncomfortable position. It is being isolated at home and not being allowed to go to school. It is being forced to eat or being denied food. It is being given medication that takes away one's sense of control. It is being left sitting on a toilet for long periods of time.

FROM A HUNCH TO A RESEARCH DESIGN

A literature review was carried out as a basis for determining the feasibility, need and design of the research. The literature review revealed a number of things. First that there was very little research with regard to people with disabilities and violence. Second, that the research that had been carried

[1] This study was carried out with the generous funding support of the Family Violence Prevention Division of Health Canada, the Women's Programme of Human Resources Development Canada and the Status of Disabled Persons Secretariat of Human Resources Development Canada.

out tended to look at the problem from the standpoint of conventional categories, such as sexual abuse and sexual and physical assaults. From that perspective the results showed that disabled people experienced those forms of violence faced by others, but that they were at a disproportionately greater risk than many other people within society to even these conventional forms of violence. Third, the literature survey revealed that while existing research indicated that people with disabilities are particularly vulnerable to violence, very little comprehensive cross-disability research had not been carried out. Therefore it was difficult to estimate how widely such acts occurred.

The literature review was followed up by a series of interviews with people with disabilities to get a preliminary sense of their perception of what constituted abuse and violence and the circumstances in which they found themselves most vulnerable. The sample was purposive but provided us with a way to determine whether in fact the preliminary hypothesis we were working with was worth pursuing.

Adding to the challenge of understanding violence and abuse against persons with disabilities was the fact that research studies carried out in the fields of sociology, criminology and psychology had been based on small samples. That made it difficult to generalize with confidence about the extent of the problem even when measured by conventional standards[2]. Moreover, much of the research was from the United States. The profile of violence in that country is somewhat different than in Canada, for example, homicide rates are much higher, firearms are far more prevalent, etc. In addition, legal provisions, social policy and social programs differ on the two sides of the border, which may have resulted in different conditions of risk and abuse for persons with disabilities in Canada.

Several large sources of Canadian research data available at that time were unable to shed light on violence and abuse against persons with disabilities. The data were not organized in a way that allowed for the systematic gathering, retrieval and analysis of this kind of information. For example, national crime statistics provided by police departments to Statistics Canada concerning complaints, arrests and convictions had not

---

[2] Some researchers had estimated that persons with disabilities are about one-and-one-half times more likely to encounter violence against themselves than the population at large. (Sobsey, 1994; Crosse et al., 1993; see also The McCreary Centre Society, 1993: 5-6.)

been classified according to whether the survivors had disabilities. These data did not, therefore, reveal the extent to which various actions proscribed by the federal Criminal Code were occurring in the lives of persons with disabilities. This limitation stemmed in part from the structure of Statistics Canada's Unified Crime Report format, which drives police data gathering and reporting for statistical purposes. As a result, few police departments had the means to systematically input and extract data from crime incident reports that related to persons with disabilities; few departments had set about to collect this data by other means[3].

Research into patterns of criminal victimization based on large interview samples, such as Statistics Canada's General Social Survey on personal risk, did not, at that time, include questions about whether crime victims had disabilities. The electronic data for the Statistics Canada survey entered the public domain too late for analysis and inclusion in the report. The measurement of violence was limited to actions that were prohibited under the federal Criminal Code[4].

Large databases with a specific focus on persons with disabilities, such as Statistics Canada's Health and Activity Limitation Survey (HALS), provided data on whether respondents' particular disabilities were caused by violence but not whether respondents with disabilities had been victimized since the onset of disability.

Another difficulty in assessing the nature and scope of violence and abuse against persons with disabilities were the contradictory research findings. For example, Westcott (1991) and the Roeher Institute (1988) had found that children with disabilities were at a high risk of abuse compared with other children. However, Benedict et al. (1990) found no such correlation between disability and victimization.

There were positive signs, however, that attention in the research community was beginning to shift towards violence and abuse against persons with disabilities. Statistics Canada, for example, in its recent survey

---

[3] Most of these data limitations continue to exist in Canada.

[4] The structure of the survey instrument also made it difficult to differentiate between violence that occurred in prisons and violence that occurred in other institutional settings, such as rehabilitation facilities or hospitals. Patterns of violence at these various sites were considered likely to be different and persons with disabilities more likely than others to be involved with hospitals and rehabilitation facilities. It would make more sense for the survey questionnaire not to lump together all institutions as if they are equivalent in terms of risks and harms that they present to their residents.

on assault and sexual assault against women, collected raw data on female abuse survivors who had ongoing health problems that affected their daily activities. The data indicated that adult women aged 16 years and over with a disability or disabling health problem[5] were considerably more likely than females without such limitations to be physically or sexually assaulted by their partners over the course of their married lives (39 as compared with 29 per cent)[6]. Examining the extent to which women in Canada had ever in their adult lives (i.e., since the age of 16) experienced one or more forms of assault or sexual assault as proscribed by the current Criminal Code[7], the survey indicated that women with disabilities were more likely than women without disabilities to be subjected to violence of some kind: 60 per cent compared to 50 per cent[8]. However, no other research and analysis concerning the victimization of women with disabilities had yet been conducted on the basis of that survey data[9].

Although the current state of research provided only limited insight into the extent and dimensions of violence and abuse against persons with disabilities, it was nonetheless illuminating. The sheer accumulation of independent findings strongly suggested that, even when looked at from the perspective of conventional measures of violence and abuse, there was a problem of considerable magnitude (Stimpson and Best, 1991; Sullivan, Vernon and Scanlon, 1987; Jacobson, 1989; Jacobson and Richardson, 1989; Ammerman, Lubetsky et al., 1989; Statistics Canada, Centre for Justice Statistics, 1994; Pillemar and Moore, 1990; Ulicny et al.,1990).

THE RESEARCH OBJECTIVES

The literature review, the initial set of interviews as well as the focus groups indicated that people with disabilities are often at increased risk of similar forms of violence as other groups of people, as well as additional forms of

---

5 At the time this report was prepared, Statistics Canada had not completed classifying respondents' particular disabilities. All that was known was that the respondents had some kind of condition or health problem that limited their daily activities.
6 Statistics Canada, Canadian Centre for Justice Statistics, 1994c: 6. The survey, however, did not clarify whether respondents sustained their disabilities as a result of the abuse or before or after the abuse as a result of other factors such as auto accidents or work injuries.
7 That is, the respondents experienced violence regardless of whether it was perpetrated by their husbands or male partners.
8 The Canadian Centre for Justice Statistics provided a special cross-tabulation to the Roeher Institute on this issue.
9 Because of the difficulties encountered in classifying respondents' disabilities, the data set was not available at that time when the research was undertaken.

violence. The lack of previous comprehensive research suggested a need for the development of knowledge about violence from the perspective of people with disabilities to understand all the forms of violence and abuse they experienced as well as their particular vulnerability. Four specific objectives for the research were identified:

1) To gain an understanding of the forms of violence and abuse experienced by people with disabilities;

2) To examine those factors associated with the forms of violence and abuse experienced by persons with disabilities;

3) To examine the mechanisms that exist to respond to violence and abuse; and

4) To examine how gender differences of victims of violence affects differences in the experience of violence, the factors associated with violence, and the responses to incidents and victims of violence.

METHODOLOGY

Because a central aim of this research was to gain an understanding of the subjective experience of violence, a methodology was needed that brought a focus to the experience of violence, without pre-determining or pre-structuring the categories of violence about which the research would inquire. Having recognized that people with disabilities had been left out of much of the research on violence and abuse, and acknowledging the particularities of their marginalized status, we needed an approach that would enable a view of the world from their standpoint. An open-ended interviewing process, driven by the categories of violence and abuse in the current Criminal Code, or drawn from existing research, feminist and otherwise, was not adequate to the research task on hand.

For this reason, a 'narrative' research approach was intentionally chosen. As Mishler (1986) has pointed out, a narrative approach to research interviewing departs in important ways from traditional quantitative and qualitative data collection. Research interviewing is usually cast in terms of a 'stimulus-response' model, where the interviewer provides a 'stimulus' in the form of a question ('Have you ever been physically hit by a caregiver?') and waits for the response ('yes', 'no', 'I don't know'). As Mishler points out, this model of research establishes the researcher's frame as the dominant one, leaving the respondent to either find a place in that framework or remain silent. As Booth and Booth suggest in relation to people with learning disabilities, the predominance of such an approach has meant that 'informants with learning difficulties have been regarded mainly as sources of data for researchers' narratives rather than people with their own stories to tell' (Booth and Booth, 1996:56).

A narrative approach to research places the onus on the researcher to create an environment in which the respondent can begin to tell his or her story. The approach recognizes that people live their lives and construct their identities in narrative terms (Taylor, 1989), and that they make sense of their experiences as events that contribute to their own script(s), the plots that constitute their lives. Unless one is able to 'emplot' events within a broader life history and life story they have little meaning. Cognizant of the risks of re-traumatizing individuals in the process of interviews about their experiences of violence, we also felt it important that the interview respondent control the dialogue so that they could bring as much meaning as possible to their experiences. Providing them an opportunity to recount in narrative terms their experiences was one way of doing this.

Interviews were conducted across Canada with self-selected individuals with disabilities. Respondents were interviewed in each province. The interview sample was constructed in consultation with a large number of disability and advocacy organizations. The organizations were asked to make the initial contact with individuals whom they knew had been victimized and who would feel comfortable being interviewed about the situations in which they had been abused. Only individuals who volunteered to participate were invited to take part in the interviews. We considered the self-selection of respondents to be an essential ethical safeguard to avoid the possibility of re-victimization.

An effort was made to ensure an even balance between male and female interview respondents with disabilities. This proved more challenging than anticipated. It was more difficult to identify males who had been victimized and were prepared to discuss it. This may reflect the possibility that females are more likely than males to be victimized, or that males feel more inhibited than females discussing situations in which they have been abused. It may reflect a difference in how men and women think about abuse and how they characterize violence. Until statistical analysis based on a large sample of persons with disabilities is conducted, it is not possible to determine precisely why more females than males seem prepared to talk about violence and abuse in their lives.

An effort was also made to include interview respondents who represent Canada's racial diversity. Several Aboriginal persons were interviewed. However, people of colour and Aboriginal persons have a limited presence in the disability and advocacy organizations that provided assistance to the project. Therefore, the interview sample does not fully reflect the country's diversity. The statistical sources that were consulted, however, do include all individuals with disabilities in Canada. The statistical data and analysis provide insight into the social and economic situation of persons with disabilities as a group.

The open-ended narrative nature of the interviews required that interviewers be experienced and be trained to be as sensitive as possible to the responses of interviewees and to respect any limits required by interviewees who had been victimized, including wanting to end the interview. Although these precautions were taken, it was not possible to entirely shield interview respondents from the pain of reliving violent situations. Seventy-one persons with disabilities took part in the interviews and several of the interviews were terminated because the incidents were too painful for the respondents to recount. At least one of the interviewers used American sign language and all the interviewers were trained to interview people with intellectual and psychiatric disabilities.

Interviewers were told to probe any circumstances that the person being interviewed identified as abusive and to include any of the following:

• common forms of physical, verbal and psychological violence to which many persons in society are susceptible (date rape, crime in the street, family discipline, for example);

• those forms of violence to which people with a disability are more susceptible (for example, where they can't protect themselves, where they are isolated or where they depend on numerous caregivers in situations where there is a high turnover, etc.);

• those forms of violence which are considered socially acceptable or socially justifiable because the individual has a disability (for example, aversive therapies, withholding of medical treatment for newborns, sterilization, social isolation and segregation).

In particular we were looking for information that answered such questions as:

- What forms did violence against persons with disabilities take?
- What practices were associated with these forms of violence, and who was involved in violent victimization of persons with disabilities?
- In what environments did persons with disabilities experience forms of violence?
- How did forms of violence get understood by the victim, the family, the service system, the criminal justice system?
- What were the impacts of violence on the victim?
- What were the factors or set of factors associated with the occurrence of violence and abuse and what was the relative significance of various factors in explaining the nature of the abuse and its impacts?

Interviewers were specifically instructed to include emphasis on seeking, through the interview process, gender differences in experiences of violence and abuse, and responses to violent victimization.

It was anticipated that some individuals would experience emotional stress while telling their stories, particularly in face-to-face interviews. Arrangements were made for the necessary counselling and other emotional supports and in several cases these supports were used. It was also expected that interviewers might experience stress and anguish while listening to people tell their stories. In some instances, interviewers were appalled at the level, scope and impact of the violence and abuse that had invaded the lives of interview respondents. Interviewers often felt remorse at having to leave participants in situations that were far from ideal. Emotional supports were made available for interviewers.

Given that a qualitative research methodology was used in the interviews, the project proved to be a learning experience. A detailed interview guide was designed to capture both brief and discursive interviewee responses concerning the abuse they had encountered and others' responses to their victimization. The development of the guide involved considerable deliberation and care with respect to ensuring that questions were appropriately and respectfully worded, given the sensitivity of the subject. The interview questionnaires were also reviewed by a number of people with disabilities who were advisers on the project. Due to the sensitive nature of the subject and the depth of feeling and scope of memory that opened up, many of the interviews, as expected, took on a life of their own.

Interviewers sometimes used the guide in one of two ways. In some instances, it served as an interview questionnaire. In others it served as a reminder to pursue issues that did not surface during the natural flow of the conversation. After the interviews were concluded, many of the respondents' comments were classified according to the data categories used to design the guide. However, several kinds of interviewee response were not anticipated during interview design and pretesting and so could not be made to fit into the established structure. Coding procedures were revised to include these responses.

Another development during the interviews was the readiness of not all, but many, participants to tell their story. It was initially assumed that respondents would perhaps need some time to feel comfortable and safe enough to respond to questions concerning abusive and violent actions they had personally experienced. Participants were asked several questions as ice breakers, which had them speak about their life in general and about abusive situations that had occurred to one or more people whom they knew. Several participants were impatient with this approach and wanted instead to get to the details of their own stories. Interviewers moved with the natural dynamic of the interviews. In most cases, the interviews went beyond the ninety minutes initially planned.

Interviews and focus groups were also conducted with counsellors and social workers involved in fielding complaints of abuse and violence against persons with disabilities. Several of these individuals also had disabilities. Interviews and focus groups were held with a sample of police officers and police administrators from across the country, as well as with community advocates, administrators and service providers attached to community agencies that serve persons with disabilities. Family members of persons with disabilities who have been subjected to violence were also part of focus groups and interviews. In all, the interviews and focus groups involved 120 respondents.

In addition to a two-day orientation and regular debriefing sessions with interviewers, a day-long session was conducted with the interviewers towards the end of the interview process. This allowed them to share with the research team and one another some of the insights that emerged during interviews. The transcript of the discussion served as another source of data that enriched the primary interview data. The discussion also helped in the development of a critical perspective from which to analyse these data.

SECONDARY RESEARCH SOURCES

The literature review distinguished identification, intervention and prevention as the three categories of responses made within the judicial system, the support service system, the treatment service system and the legislative system. Secondary analysis was carried out to look at the capacity of these systems to respond to violence and abuse as well as the nature of the responses. Included in these were self-regulatory professional standards, ethics review procedures, personnel policies, complaint review procedures, and laws and regulation.

A review of federal, provincial and territorial legislation was conducted to examine statutory protections and sanctions against abuse and violence. The review included provisions that dealt with physical abuse, sexual abuse, verbal and emotional abuse, harassment, neglect and other criminal and civil offences proscribed under the *Canadian Charter of Rights and Freedoms*, the federal Criminal Code, federal, provincial and territorial human rights legislation and numerous pieces of social service and mental health legislation. Statutes covering the provision of evidence in courts of law were also included in the review, as were laws relating to guardianship and adult protection. All pertinent federal, provincial and territorial laws were examined.

A select, yet reasonably comprehensive and detailed, review of case law was conducted. Again, federal case law and case law from each province and territory was examined. The purpose of the review was to identify and analyse principles the courts used in judgments and sentencing in cases involving violence, abuse and other violations against persons with disabilities.

A select review was made of policy and program arrangements at the provincial, territorial and community level that had a bearing on the conditions that place individuals at risk, that affected the reporting and detection of abuse and violence, and that could shape responses to violence once it had been identified. The purpose of this review was to gain insight into the diversity of current policy and program arrangements, not to provide an exhaustive policy and community program analysis.

Statistics Canada's 1986 Health and Activity Limitation Survey (HALS) data were analysed as a basis for identifying the prevalence of social and economic conditions associated with risk in the case of people with disabilities.

FINDINGS

'Violence is a result of our so-called "idea" of where people fit in the hierarchy. These people [people with disabilities] are at the bottom. Consequently, doing violence to them isn't a big issue because they're not worth anything anyway ....We live in a violent society. And people who for one reason or another are unable to assert their own needs or their rights, or protect themselves - many of whom have a disabling condition - are susceptible to violence. Except they can't run away. They don't have any place else to go. Police don't necessarily listen to them, so the institutions that are supposedly there to protect us simply don't pay attention....So protection must come from their own efforts. And if they can't mobilize their own resources, or if there are no resources to mobilize, there's nothing anyone can do' [taken from an interview].

On the basis of the interviews, a working definition of violence and abuse of disabled persons was constructed:

'Acts of violence and abuse are defined as conscious and deliberate acts that cause, or that threaten to cause, harm. They are public or private acts that seriously violate the principle that disabled persons, like other persons are to be equally valued and protected as citizens. They are acts that ignore or hold in contempt the voice of a person and that exploit a power imbalance, or that on other grounds are contrary to the free and informed consent of the person abused. Typically, these actions result in the suffering of the abused person, whether emotional or physical. Extreme violent or abusive actions result in the injury and even death of the person affected.'

Violent and abusive acts against persons with disabilities were found to involve any of the following:

- physical force (e.g. beating; aggressive caregiving);
- physical actions that take the form of care (e.g. administration of medications, restraint or other treatments);
- sexual assault or other forms of sexual abuse (e.g. non-consensual touching or fondling);
- the denial of rights, necessities, privileges or opportunities by persons in a position to promote or safeguard the well-being of the person affected;
- patterns of communication that may not involve physical contact but which are perceived as threatening (e.g. explicit threats or stalking), as tormenting (e.g. harassment), or as insulting (e.g. 'speaking down to' or using derogatory terms in conversation); and
- lack of proper action (e.g. the neglect or failure to respond effectively to harmful incidents).

The research found that people with disabilities are more likely than others to be subjected to acts of violence and abuse that are proscribed by criminal and civil acts. They are also subjected to acts of violence and abuse that do not meet legal definitions of violence but that the survivors perceive as harmful. These may include acts that are perpetrated in places where the abuse is shielded from the arm of the law. Contributing to the vulnerability is society's inability or unwillingness to clearly name and prohibit the problem. But equally important are the often radically unequal social and economic position of persons with disabilities that place them at a disproportionate risk, as well as the lack of individual control and choice that makes it difficult for the individual to avoid and escape situations of risk.

Many circumstances obstruct survivors from disclosing acts of violence and abuse against themselves. The lack of proactive community and system measures to anticipate and look for signs of potential abuse and violence prevents the problem from coming to light. The responses from family members, social workers, educators, counsellors, law enforcement officers and the courts to respond to the problem, in a particular case and generally is random. Some individuals encounter empathic and effective assistance while the perpetrators are convicted, others face outright denial of the abuse and little if any assistance while the perpetrators go free.

The study concluded that the existing legal, policy and program framework is not working effectively, measured by the scale of violence and abuse and the reported response. It recommended that a holistic approach be initiated to address the issues, starting with a public commitment and recognition of the principle that assuring people with disabilities freedom from violence and abuse and proper redress is not a matter of charity but a matter of individual and citizenship rights. The legal and political structure entitles citizens, including those with disabilities, to live in safety and security and to be respected and treated equally[10]. From that perspective, directions for change (see Roeher Institute, 1995: 183-203) were identified in social policy, administrative and programs coupled with community development initiatives that would strengthen the capacity of communities to identify and address abusive situations and circumstances. Statutory reforms were also recommended as well as effective public education and public awareness and systematic data collection and research.

[10] Canadian Charter of Rights and Freedoms

FOLLOWING UP

We recognized that the release of the research report was an opportunity to spark public concern and awareness so we mounted a national press campaign which involved a press conference and wide distribution of the study. The press conference not only provided the research results but a number of people from the disability community told their own stories – people with a diverse perspective on the issue. In advance we sent out the press release and copies of the publication to all the major national disability organizations and alerted them to our press strategy. This enabled the study results to provide a forum for disability organizations to get some local press as well, and in the process raise the profile of disability rights advocacy generally.

Approximately 1000 copies of the report have been distributed. Of those about 100 were sent to journals – disability journals, social policy journals, feminist journals, and journals which have some interest in abuse. The rest have been distributed through our distribution service.

Since the publication of the study, which provides a blueprint for further action, we have used the information in it to create plain language information sheets, to run seminars about abuse and violence for disability organizations and for generic sexual assault centres as well as to facilitate police training and information seminars. In the past month, a plain language safety guide, *Out of Harm's Way,* has been published which provides a method of assessing risks in the physical, policy, and personal environment in which people with disabilities find themselves. An issue of the magazine, *entourage,* which we produce was devoted to the issue and we continue to work with advocacy organization to bring about change in federal criminal law, administrative procedures and protocols to be put in place to provide the protections to which all persons should be entitled in Canada. Several legal cases which were initiated by people after they were interviewed for this study are proceeding through the courts and one abuse shelter for people with disabilities and others has been established as a result of the study.

The piece of research would not have been possible without the co-operation of those interviewed and those who were willing to carry out the interviews. Canadians owe a great debt to these people and to those who continue the fight to ensure that all Canadians can live in security and dignity in our country.

REFERENCES

AMMERMAN, R., LUBETSKY, M., *et al.* (1988) 'Maltreatment of Children and Adolescents with Multiple Handicaps: Five Case Examples', *Journal of the Multihandicapped Person,* 1(2): 129-39.

BENEDICT, M., WHITE, R. *et al.* (1990) 'Reported Maltreatment in Children With Multiple Disabilities', *Child Abuse and Neglect,* 14(2): 207-17.

BOOTH, T. and BOOTH, W. (1966) 'Sounds of Silence: narrative research with inarticulate subjects', *Disability and Society,* 11(1): 55-69.

CROSSE, S. B., KAYE, E. *et al.* (1993) *A Report on the Maltreatment of Children with Disabilities.* Rockville, Baltimore, Md: Westat, Inc.

JACOBSON, A. (1989) 'Physical and Sexual Assault Histories among Psychiatric Outpatients', *American Journal of Psychiatry,* 146 (6): 755-58.

JACOBSON, A. and RICHARDSON, B. (1987) 'Assault Experiences of 100 Psychiatric Inpatients: Evidence for the Need for Routine Inquiry', *American Journal of Psychiatry,* 144 (7): 908-13.

MISHLER, E. G. (1986) *Research Interviewing: Context and Narrative.* Cambridge, Mass: Harvard University Press.

PILLEMAR, K. and MOORE, D.W. (1990) 'Highlights from a Study of Abuse of Patients in Nursing Homes', *Journal of Elder Abuse and Neglect* 2 (1-2): 5-29.

RIOUX, M. and BACH, M., eds. (1994) *Disability is not measles: New research paradigms in disability.* North York, Ontario: The Roeher Institute.

ROEHER INSTITUTE (1988) *Vulnerable: Sexual Abuse and People with an Intellectual Handicap.* North York, Ontario: The Roeher Institute.

ROEHER INSTITUTE (1995) *Harm's way: The many faces of violence and abuse against persons with disabilities.* North York, Ontario: The Roeher Institute

ROEHER INSTITUTE (1997) *Out of Harm's Way: A Safety Kit for People with Disabilities Who Feel Unsafe and Want to Do Something About It.* North York, Ontario: The Roeher Institute.

SOBSEY, D. (1994) *Violence and Abuse in the Lives of People with Disabilities: The End of Silent Acceptance?* Baltimore, Maryland: Paul H. Brookes Publishing Co.

STATISTICS CANADA (1994) *Violence against Women Survey.* Ottawa: Canadian Centre for Justice.

STIMPSON, L. and BEST, M. (1991) *Courage above All: Sexual Assault against Women with Disabilities.* Toronto: DAWN.

SULLIVAN, P. M., VERNON, M. *et al.* (1987) 'Sexual Abuse of Deaf Youth', *American Annals of the Deaf,* 32 (4): 256-62.

TAYLOR, C. (1989) *Sources of the Self: The Making of the Modern Identity.* Cambridge, Mass: Harvard University Press.

THE MCCREARY CENTRE SOCIETY (1993) *Sexual Abuse and Young People with Disabilities Project: Results and Recommendations*. Vancouver, B.C. The McCreary Centre Society.

ULICNY, G., WHITE, G. *et al.* (1990) 'Consumer Exploitation by Attendants: How Often Does it Happen and Can Anything Be Done About It?', *Rehabilitation Counselling Bulletin,* 33 (3): 240-46.

WESTCOTT, H. (1991) 'The Abuse of Disabled Children: A Review of the Literature', *Child Care Health and Development,* 17 (4): 243-58.

CHAPTER 13

From the Research Notes of a Foreign Devil: Disability research in China

Emma Stone

INTRODUCTION

In July 1995, the *British Journal of Sociology* accepted an article for publication. The authors: Emma Stone and Mark Priestley. The title: 'Parasites, pawns and partners: disability research and the role of non-disabled researchers'. The text: the emancipatory paradigm, its why, its what, its implications for us, our fieldwork and our PhDs. The sub-text (for myself at least): doubts regarding the practicability, the necessity, even the desirability of an all-or-nothing emancipatory research paradigm.

As I re-read the article, I am transported back to that time 'Before Fieldwork' when the motivated postgraduate is initiated into the inner circles of social science through ritual exposure to research methodology. Having come from Oriental Studies through Development Studies, I was unprepared for the delights which awaited me in a Sociology and Social Policy department. I drank in as much as I could of epistemology, ontology, triangulation, validation, evaluation ... until the fear of months away from my husband and home seemed nothing compared to the terror of being labelled parasite, of being put along with my research design and data in the methodological dock upon my return. Emancipatory research was hardest to imbibe ... not because I didn't like the look of it I like radical, I like uncompromising, I like principles which point at privilege and salute visions of a new world – why else do Chinese and Development Studies? – but because I could not see how I could square my research on disability in China within an emancipatory research framework.

Long before I came across the emancipatory paradigm, I determined to do participatory action research in line with current thinking on fieldwork in developing countries. But, to echo Zarb (1992) and Oliver (1992), emancipatory research is more, much more than those. Central to the emancipatory paradigm are a reversal of the social and (ultimately) the material relations of research production and a grounding of agenda, analysis and action in the social model of disability. I took those ideals on board and in so doing I became increasingly anxious: the chances of realising the paradigm's ideals seemed so slim as to make me question the decision to proceed. Encouragement from Mark and from my supervisors Colin Barnes and Delia Davin ensured that my unease did not stop me researching. But nor did my unease stop. Thankfully, I found relief in a good friend and fellow postgraduate, also in China, for whom home-grown methodologies seemed similarly unreal. We were each other's partner in research crime, each other's reminder that all you can do is your best and what do people back home know anyway.

Eighteen months on and having spent half of that time in China, it is time to reconsider my research methodology with balanced hindsight rather than fearful anticipation. Give me another eighteen months and I might be less scathing of research methodologies – but at the moment my mind is in the reality of doing research in China. And it is something of that reality that I want to communicate here. The paper explores the three issues of researcher identity, the social relations of research production and the applicability of the social model in a cross-cultural context. My discussion of these topics is very much the product of my own fieldwork experiences, so I illustrate my points with reference to fieldwork I undertook in two rural counties in China: Heping County and Shanlin County (renamed to protect confidentiality).

HALF-DEVIL: RESEARCHER IDENTITY

'People in the field will also seek to place or locate the ethnographer within their experience' (Hammersley & Atkinson 1983: 77).

Chinese people have a name for foreigners: yang guizi, the foreign devils, predominantly white and western, most definitely Other. Such an apparently indiscriminate grouping does not render nationality obsolete, hence the almost inevitable opening line of a first encounter: what nationality are you? I am British. British Smog. British Empire. Hong Kong. Thatcher. Mad Cows. Documentaries.

My arrival in China followed hard upon the second and extended showing of a documentary on China's orphanages. This was British television filmed by young British journalists, undercover as charity workers. And there I was. Young, British and interested in disability – a matter for social welfare and therefore for the same Ministry that is responsible for China's orphans. At national, municipal and county level, doors closed. There was a revived awareness of the dangers in associating with foreign devils. Association means responsibility and responsibility incurs risk: risk for the cadres that permit access; risk, too, for international organisations which have invested years in building relationships with those cadres. I had arrived in Beijing airport with a Government Warning invisibly tattooed on my forehead: Foreign Devils Can Seriously Damage. And it dawned on me that my preoccupations with doing disability research as a non-disabled researcher were of minor importance in China. Here it was nationality that mattered. Somehow I had to disentangle myself from the very negative images evoked by my British identity, lest my research should fail before it had begun.

Constructing an appropriate self, or selves, in order to facilitate data collection has been coined 'impression management' by Hammersley and Atkinson (1983) and it is largely unavoidable for any researcher engaging in cross-cultural research where colonial and neo-colonial ties operate. Those who wish to avoid being tarred with the colonialist brush naturally employ strategies to confound such perceptions (Hammersley and Atkinson 1983; Devereux and Hoddinott 1992; Francis 1992). Success in this endeavour depends on skill and luck – or a fortuitous combination of attitude and ancestry in my own case.

Attitude

> 'Researchers who are concerned about appearing judgmental or ethnocentric tend to present themselves as bland, pleasant individuals who never disagree with anyone' (Devereux & Hoddinott 1992: 19).

For a time, I dressed down, I looked down, and I toned down all my research questions. I was so concerned not to play the arrogant expatriate that I over-compensated.

As regards data collection, I was desperately anxious not to cause embarrassment through inappropriate questioning. When I first arrived in China, I hardly dared mention the words 'disability research' for fear that it would create tension or that I might find myself on the next plane back to Heathrow. It was some time before I realised that I was treading on eggshells where the ground was often hard as iron.[1] My images of China, doubtless distorted by the western media, were such that I imagined – as maybe you do now – that it would be impossible to inquire about disability discrimination let alone eugenics. How wrong I was! This is not to argue a case for the insensitive researcher. There are times and places for asking questions and it is right that a researcher should respect those. But it is imperative that a researcher learn them first.

Excessive caution, based on my own prejudices rather than informed experience, placed similar inhibitions on my personality and behaviour. Initially, I took on a meek and mild persona. I wasn't comfortable in that role, but I thought it would be less threatening to Chinese research subjects and friends. That is as may be, but it was also far less interesting for them as my karaoke (or ka-la-OK! in Chinese) career illustrates: my début was on the Beijing karaoke scene. Self-effacing apologies ('I am an awful singer and far too shy') which would work in Britain failed to impress in China. When I did take the microphone, I failed even more – my voice was so quiet that no-one could hear me and my hosts were most definitely disappointed. So once in Heping County, when I found myself in a factory's ballroom, I knew what I had to do. I took my place beneath the mirrored disco globe and forty sets of intrigued eyes fixed on me. Microphone in one hand and plastic flowers in the other, I gave it all I had in an ear-blasting, lung-bursting rendition of

[1] See Lockwood (1992), Hoddinott (1992) and Francis (1992) for similar accounts of real and imagined sensitivities when researching in developing countries.

ABBA's 'Dancing Queen'. It was a triumph and my research relationships soared! And so I discovered that when Robert Chambers (1983) writes of the need for humility in research and overseas development work, this should not be equated with bowing and scraping and staying in the background. True humility can entail performances of the most unlikely and flamboyant kind.

It seems that I became adept at the art of impression management. I learnt what went down well, what conversational gambits would amuse or relax or impress; I asked for advice and I was honest and direct in interactions. But what is particularly interesting about this process is that as I became more true to what I felt to be my everyday British self (karaoke excepted), my hosts believed that I was taking on more Chinese attributes. Therein lay the interface between my attitude and my ancestry.

Ancestry

Ancestors occupy an important place in Chinese lives. Through accident of birth (this is where luck rather than skill takes over) I have distant Chinese ancestry. My maternal grandmother was born in Hong Kong in 1904. She lived in Hong Kong until her husband's death in the late 1960s, whereupon she journeyed to England to live with my parents, my sister and myself. My grandmother belonged to the Eurasian strata of Hong Kong society: a mix of Orient and Occident, a weaving together of the Middle East, Europe and China, wealthier than local Chinese but kept at arms' length by the colonial élite. Her death, in October 1995, brought me back home. I have always loved to talk about my grandmother and never more so than when I returned to China to resume fieldwork in 1996.

I believe now that my ancestral claims go a long way towards explaining the ease with which I gained trust and support, the readiness with which I was introduced to others and brought into confidences. As someone with Chinese blood ties, my passport nationality proved less problematic. Indeed, my ancestry took on a wholly new significance. My ability to speak Mandarin, my interest in all things Chinese, the gusto with which I consumed Chinese food, even my sense of humour, opinions and values were frequently attributed to my ancestry. And, out of emotional need rather than cunning, I played along. Asserting the Chinese side of my identity enabled me to maintain a bond with my grandmother. I was a willing accomplice in a beautiful act. At the same time, my hosts were glad to find additional grounds for trusting me and to explain why it was that I didn't conform to their perceptions of white, western Other. Less flattering images of foreign devils remained intact.

In summary, I derived legitimacy from my Chinese ancestry in much the same way that I imagine disabled researchers doing disability research derive legitimacy from disability status or gay researchers doing research on gay issues derive legitimacy from their sexuality and so on. Yes, identity does make a difference but it is far from the last word on what makes a good and trustworthy researcher. Ancestry would have counted for little had I been that arrogant expatriate. It was ancestry and attitude *together* that enabled me to disentangle myself from some of the more negative aspects of my initial ascribed identity. Finally, it is important to stress that in drawing on, some might say exploiting, my heritage, I was not looking to go native. Impression management is not about living an Other's life. It is about giving face, showing respect, earning confidences, creating bonds. It is in this context that what might otherwise seem like small and silly things take on an inestimable importance.

DANGEROUS LIAISONS: THE SOCIAL RELATIONS OF MY RESEARCH PRODUCTION

'There is no independent haven or middle ground when researching oppression: academics and researchers can only be with the oppressors or with the oppressed' (Barnes 1996:110).

Two assumptions underpin this statement. First, that it is possible to draw a clear dividing line between the oppressors and the oppressed. Secondly, that the nature of research on oppression is analogous to a zero-sum game, whereby the oppressors win and the oppressed lose or vice versa, depending on whose side the researcher plays. The extent to which a researcher has a choice in the matter is limited, as Barnes (1996), Bury (1996) and Shakespeare (1996) concur in their exchanges on disability research and independence. Most obviously, choice is restricted by fundholders and academic peers. Nonetheless, Bury and Shakespeare view independence, carefully defined, as a necessity, whereas for Barnes independence is at best mythical and at worst counter-emancipatory where the researcher holds onto control which might otherwise be devolved to disabled research subjects.

What would any of them make of my research? Although I could have taken advantage of the relative freedom afforded a PhD candidate, I chose instead to do research which would make it impossible to devolve full control to research subjects and equally impossible to exercise full control myself. In addition to the standard triangle of fundholders, academic peers and researcher, I added disabled people, parents of disabled children, grassroots project workers, local government cadres and two international organisations. If that wasn't enough, I elected to formalise local-level partnerships with government officials in using a team approach to conduct research. Thus, in deciding to do research in Heping and Shanlin counties, I entered a situation in which I did not know whether the inevitable compromises would be validated. I took the risk and placed others at risk in so doing.

The following is an outline of the main partnerships formed, compromises made in accordance with those partnerships and my justifications for straying from the paths of maintaining independence or devolving control to disabled research subjects.

International Organisations

In Heping and Shanlin, my first partnerships chronologically speaking were with an international non-governmental organisation and a multilateral aid agency. Prior to research taking place, the potential for channelling both the research process and outcomes into programme development was discussed and both organisations felt that process should be as, if not more, important than outcome. As regards process, we agreed on the primacy of participation and of using the research as a relationship- and capacity-building exercise with local government counterparts. As regards outcome, I agreed to write reports to include recommendations for programme development in the respective counties and to lead a workshop on participatory action research for national-level Chinese counterparts of the multilateral agency in Beijing. There was little need for compromise in the research process but it is understood that publications arising from my finished thesis should be cleared with the respective organisations first. Some of my biggest compromises might still be to come.

Government Cadres

The work of both organisations is at the invitation of and in partnership with local Civil Affairs bureaux. Inevitably, therefore, my research followed suit. In Heping, negotiations with local officials were straightforward since everything was arranged through an intermediary (the relevant Program Officer) and before my arrival in Heping. The specified time-frame was one week: any longer and local authorities would question our motives since standard evaluations lasted little more than a day. I submitted a research design. Heping officials faxed us their's. We proposed further revisions, some of which were taken up and others weren't. At the time, I was overjoyed at the extent to which some aspects of my initial design had been taken on board: a team of three local co-researchers under my direction; home-visits to meet with disabled adults and families with disabled children; visits to welfare factories incorporating focus groups with disabled workers. However, certain departures from my original schedule proved very problematic.

I had proposed to spend one day in each of two selected factories researching the situation of disabled factory workers in one-to-one interviews and a focus group discussion. Heping officials, by way of spreading the foreign guest and evaluation burden more thinly, made arrangements for visits to eight welfare factories. They were unwilling to renege on these arrangements. As a result, time was limited in each factory and divided between a management briefing and a focus group discussion; one-to-one interviews could not be accommodated. This limited the extent to which focus group discussions could realize their potential. More difficult still was the highly skewed sampling which meant that the majority of disabled adults I encountered were welfare factory workers and male.

In Shanlin, negotiations and compromises seemed tougher still. At the end of my previous visit in July, local cadres agreed that I could return in the autumn to do collaborative research. Accordingly, I returned in November hoping that the three weeks allocated would be used in training and leading a local team in participatory research. On arrival, I presented my ideas. I would lead a team drawn from local disabled people, parents of disabled children and government cadres in conducting interviews in three sites in the county, each site exhibiting a different socio-economic level. We would spend five or six days in each site, with two focus groups per site in addition to one-to-one interviews. Interviews and discussions would be taped with participant consent. Content would relate to the needs and aspirations of local disabled children, adults, their families and their communities as well as general socio-economic data on the region and information on existing services.

Within hours of laying out my ideas, relevant phonecalls had been made, three sites and a team had been selected (which included a young disabled woman and might have included a young disabled doctor but for a case of mistaken identity) and I was invited to start training and teamwork the next morning. However, frequent interruptions from officials during the training sessions made it clear that higher permission would be required unless I drastically reduced the scope of my proposed research. I had neither the time nor faith to await provincial consent and I was unwilling to throw my hands in the air and cry 'forget this, I'm going back to Beijing' since such a gesture could have jeopardised relations between local counterparts and the involved international organisation. So I compromised, guided by more and less subtle hints from local officials. The outcome: two days in each of two sites (neither of which was a poor area although we did interview people from relatively poor households), interviews with disabled adults, parents of disabled children, local teachers and doctors but no interviews with local cadres and only one focus group per site, no tape recording and only supervised photography, and no questions pertaining to general socio-economic data.

Research Teams

In Heping County, the team was small and was eager to follow my lead in the formulation of questions and data collection methods. I had been brought in to lead the team and to train them in evaluation techniques so there were limits to the degree to which they were willing to suggest alternatives. In Shanlin County, on the other hand, the research team was made up of nine permanent members and three representatives from each of the original sites. The formulation of research questions and methods was a more participatory exercise which meant that reaching agreement sometimes proved very difficult. One of the most articulate members of the team (not, incidentally, a cadre) felt that nothing short of a closed questionnaire was good enough. 'Questionnaires are scientific and objective', he told me. His views were held by others in the team. In the end, we produced a guide-sheet and two activity sheets (uncomplicated tasks which required participants to circle sources of support and information and to draw comparisons between their own life-chances and those of other disabled people or families in the area). The method worked relatively well but would have been more successful had time been no object: a total of four days meant that a pilot was out of the question. Working with such a large team magnifies the problems involved with using research assistants, particularly where the nature of research is such that more than enumeration is required (Devereux & Hoddinott 1992b). Validity, reliability and comparability of data are all liable to suffer in the process.

Disabled Children, Disabled Adults, Their Families

Inevitably, perhaps, forming links with the more powerful members of a community inhibits relationships with less powerful members. Whilst I maintained what Truman and Humphries (1994: 1) describe as 'a conscious partiality with those who are margnialised or invisible', the extent to which that partiality was visible and therefore meaningful to disabled research subjects and their families is open to debate. In the context of interviews and focus groups, I used every opportunity to demonstrate that partiality through words and attitude, but it is impossible to know whether or how far I succeeded. What is beyond doubt is that occasionally my desire to involve disabled people and families with disabled children in a meaningful way was frustrated by the unanticipated working-out of that desire.

My biggest regret is that I was not party to the selection of research subjects. In China, as Manion (1994) notes from her own research, sampling for large-scale surveys let alone for one-to-one interviews is invariably biased. My concern, however, lies less in statistical bias than in the process of participant selection. The request for participants would have been made by local cadres or, in Heping, by employers and was not therefore a request that would be easy for anyone to refuse. While some participants (to judge from body language and vocal participation) relished the opportunity to voice aspirations and share life stories in the presence of a foreigner and entourage of cadres, others were clearly alienated by the whole process.[2] In my eagerness to practice participation-friendly methods and in my hosts' desire to fulfil my expectations, the wishes of research participants were relegated.

[2] See Thomas Gold (1989) on the pitfalls of officially arranged research in China.

In Heping, I had assumed – wrongly and naïvely – that participants would participate only if they wanted to. It is good fortune alone that most seemed happy to be involved. I wonder if it is possible to balance the alienation of the few with the eager involvement of the many and come out with a half-way clear conscience? In Shanlin, I endeavoured to reduce risks of alienation by advising cadres that only people who were willing should participate, and by dividing the interviews between three teams thereby reducing the official entourage and the intrusive presence of a foreigner. Even so, there was still one occasion when a research participant was evidently tense and unsure as to what answers were acceptable, in spite of a village cadre's personal assurances that there would be no 'contradiction' and he could speak freely. (How far he believed that is impossible to say, although it is entirely possible that the cadre meant what he said.) I also tried to create more space for scrutiny by disabled participants or family members by structuring the two focus group discussions around analysis and planning rather than around individual lives (this was possible in Shanlin because focus groups built on one-to-one interviews). But these are small gestures compared to the ideals of emancipatory research.

Multiple partnerships: rights and wrongs

Quite a list of liaisons and compromises, then. With hindsight, there is much that I would have done differently but I would not change my decision to make multiple partnerships. I have good reasons.

First, working with government cadres enabled as well as inhibited the *participation* of disabled individuals and their families. It would have been impossible for me to knock on the doors of ordinary people in Heping or Shanlin and expect to be invited in without some form of official introduction. Local officials were the principal gatekeepers and I could not have involved disabled people and families without them.[3]

Secondly, there would have been no possibility of research leading to *action* without linking with officials and international organisations. In certain contexts (and China is currently one of them) the replicability and sustainability, let alone implementation, of development projects depend on

---

[3]Commonly, overt fieldwork in most developing countries requires working within an official framework (Devereux & Hoddinott 1992) although some researchers avoid this (Gold 1989, Harriss 1992).

local government involvement. Co-operating with officials significantly increased the likelihood that research would make a difference in the lives of local disabled children, adults and their families. That was something all of us wanted to achieve.

Thirdly, given the role of civil affairs cadres in the lives of Chinese disabled people, conducting collaborative research was an excellent way to learn about local government responses to disability. There is a dearth of *information on local responses* to disability in China thereby encouraging the dangerous view that nothing goes on.

Fourthly, although social relations reflected real world hierarchies, there was still scope to *challenge power relations* and to highlight the importance of service provision with rather than for disabled people and families. Involving disabled individuals and their families at all was a significant departure from standard approaches to planning and evaluation in China.

Fifthly, in working with international organisations it has been possible to channel information to them on local conceptualisations of disability, family responses to disability and existing government services. International organisations need and want to know this information in order to *make international intervention relevant.*

Finally, for all the compromises involved in using a team approach to data collection, the rewards are unbeatable. It made infinitely more sense in terms of *capacity-building and community-development* to pass on evaluation and analysis skills rather than enter the field to gather data in haste and depart taking all the data and skills with me.

To sum up, having multiple partnerships is a messy business. Moreover, it cannot easily be squared within an emancipatory paradigm since the more powerful one partner, the less room there is for meaningful participation by less powerful partners. This can lead to a situation whereby ideologically significant partnerships are invisible outside of the interview bubble, research report or researcher's head. In this way, the view that research on oppression is a zero-sum game has some truth to it: research is not like the miracle of feeding five thousand with three loaves and two fishes. There is only a fixed amount of control to go round and the more partners you have at the picnic, the greater must be the host's skills in careful and ceaseless redistribution. This makes research more demanding and less emancipatory, but not less valid. As the reasons laid out above illustrate, the undeniable difficulties which arise from multiple partnerships do not confirm the universal necessity and desirability of seeking a single research relationship with disabled research subjects to whom all control is devolved. Nor is it necessarily helpful to categorise research relationships with more and less powerful partners as synonymous with siding with the oppressor or the oppressed.[4] I do not doubt that I made dangerous liaisons but in the final analysis I believe that the risks proved worth taking.

COLONIAL MANTLES: THE SOCIAL MODEL AND CROSS-CULTURAL RESEARCH

> 'Disability research, therefore, has reinforced the individual model of disability ... seeing the problems that disabled people face as being caused by their individual impairments ... Hence they fail to accord with disabled people's own explanations of the problems of disability which argue that these are caused by society' (Oliver 1992: 108).

The emancipatory research paradigm is inseparable from the social (oppression) model of disablement. But what if 'disabled people's own explanations of the problems of disability' do not conform to the social model? In such circumstances, how should the researcher reconcile differences between disabled people who espouse the social model of disability and those who do not without compounding oppressive approaches to impairment on the one hand or compounding oppressive approaches to research subjects (by overriding their conceptualisations) on the other?

We identified the potential for conflict between participants' analysis and the social model in 'Parasites, pawns and partners...' and questioned how far the researcher could or should act as an advocate for the social model without risking charges of proselytisation (Stone & Priestley 1996). At that time, we concluded that the researcher should defer to her or his theoretical and political standpoint:

> 'This need not run counter to the goals of emancipatory research, since taking the initial decision to adopt a social model of disablement as the theory which drives our research is in itself taking an important step in establishing our political

[4]With regard to Mozambique, Hanlon criticises those outsiders who castigate fellow outsiders as 'supporters of the "wrong side"' since governments are "never" interested in helping the poor' (Hanlon, 1992: 208).

> commitment to the disability movement and transferring a degree of control to
> disabled people' (Stone & Priestley, 1996: 711).

Or more accurately, to western disabled activists. In the original version, that caveat was made in parentheses and is an indicator of my mindset at the time: I was more afraid to step out of line with the western disability movement than to be directly accountable to research participants who were still, in July 1995, a silent and faceless number. That position became untenable during nine months of work, research and life-sharing with Chinese people and in the light of my growing awareness of the criticisms levelled at western or western-trained intellectuals whose emancipatory theorising is deemed conceptual and methodological imperialism when transferred across cultures (see Humphries & Truman 1994). What 'need not run counter to the goals of emancipatory research' risks running counter to the goals of non-imperialistic research.

> 'Even accounts that at the time were aimed at championing the values and rights
> of oppressed people are now seen as fundamentally racist in their assumptions'
> (Wilson, 1992: 181).

Criticisms abound wherein western feminist representations of third world women assume that western feminisms can be transferred to non-western situations (Amos & Parmar 1984; Humphries & Truman 1994 *inter alia*). In the area of disability research, Miles has been highly critical of the transfer of western theory and praxis into developing countries. He attacks the: 'largely monocultural western or westernised disability evangelists' who have 'exported community slogans, muddled with the rhetoric of individual disability rights, to third world countries having minimal formal service structures' and he reminds potential western sociological imperialists like myself that the 'inutility to developing countries of much western social science has been documented angrily by people who have tried it' (Miles, M., 1996: 488, 496).

Given my intial intentions (subsequently altered) to base my thesis on a critical exploration of the export of western rehabilitation concepts to China, I could hardly participate in the wholesale transfer of western social model concepts with impunity. And so I found myself steering between the Scylla of emancipatory research which would leave me open to charges of irrelevance and imperialism, and the Charybdis of jettisoning the western-evolved social model to calls of treachery by those who have fought long and hard to get due recognition for it.

In the end, I came to two conclusions. First, that it is insupportable to seek sanctuary in the social model of disability when engaging in cross-cultural research. Secondly, that the responsibility for balancing fidelity to respondent analysis with my own insights and perceptions as an outsider lies on my shoulders as the researcher. It is an unpassable buck, a burdensome obligation that might be associated with expertise or researcher independence. To understand my arrival at these conclusions (which seem to fly in the face of emancipatory research) a few more fieldwork illustrations are required.

Where the Social Model Falls Short

The social model of disability should inform and direct the formation of research agenda and specific research questions. That much is clear from Abberley's criticism of the OPCS surveys for failing to ask questions commensurate with the social model and thereby compounding the oppression of disabled people by focusing on individual impairment (Abberley, 1992). In Britain, I determined to avoid that mistake only to find that in China the vast majority of participants conceived disability exclusively as impairment, as the result of individual fate or bad luck, as a problem for themselves, for their families and communities. This conceptual barrier was made even more evident by the linguistic barrier which renders 'social model' untranslatable in its entirety (inspite of the translation of Oliver's 1983 text on social work with disabled people). Where a text in Chinese reads 'disability is a social problem', the meaning is more that disabled people constitute a problem for society, not the other way round. Certainly, there are Chinese disabled people and sociologists who identify social and physical environments as being the locus of some of the problems faced by Chinese disabled people, but these individuals tend to be at the apex of the Chinese disability elite: those who have had a chance to participate in international events and thereby gain exposure to non-Chinese approaches (Ma 1993; Xi *et al.*, 1993). Yet it is telling that even at this end of the disability hierarchy, language does not allow for the divisions on which the social model in the west is premised: the definitive divisions between 'impairment' and 'disability', between 'individual' and 'social'. Hardly surprising, then, that I found myself formulating research questions in Chinese which conformed to emancipatory research guidelines but made little sense to disabled participants.

If the social model proved culturally and linguistically untranslatable in research questions, it left me in a practical and ethical minefield in terms of recommendations for action. In Heping and Shanlin, I was in a position to help make a difference in disability-related provision. I had not fully appreciated the dilemmas which can ensue from a position of influence, dilemmas which again bring into question the relevance of aspects of the western-evolved social model to the daily struggles for survival experienced by many in the third world.

In Shanlin County, the needs and aspirations expressed by research participants who had disabled children centred almost exclusively on western-style medical intervention. The training of a team of rehabilitation medics, the establishment of a medical rehabilitation centre (if not hospital), the availability of remedial operations – these were on the lists of all families interviewed as well as of several disabled adults. But if, in accord with grassroots wishes, the disability programme in Shanlin took on a predominantly western medical approach, might that not compound the medicalisation of disability and encourage the rise of an oppressive rehabilitation business in China as it has elsewhere? Another example, this time from Heping County, revolves around employment. In Heping, the vast majority of disabled adults in non-agricultural work are employed by social welfare factories in which half the workforce is disabled. The possible extension of welfare factories is welcomed by all the disabled workers interviewed who greatly value the opportunities afforded them by factory work. However, the social welfare factory perpetuates the separation of disabled and non-disabled in society and economy: as long as the institution of social welfare factories persists, disabled adults are likely to be consigned to low-skilled work in marginalised factories. In light of this, should I go with or against the opinions of research participants, should I recommend or not recommend the extension of social welfare factories in Heping and beyond? There are clear conflicts in both these examples between the researcher's allegiance to the social model and allegiance to research participants. Adopt the social model (which stands against medicalisation and against segregation) and you disempower research subjects, dismissing their opinions. Remain faithful to the analysis of your research participants (who want more medicalisation and view segregated employment better than none and, in some cases, better than non-segregated employment) and aspects of the social model must be set aside. Your choice is between oppression and oppression.

Navigating between Oppression and Oppression

'(I)t must be recognised that what we choose to observe, what we consider to be data, what we write about and how will always be affected by our personal and institutional values and the underlying assumptions absorbed through our training' (Wilson, 1992: 181).

My underlying assumptions are drawn from the social (oppression) model of disability. In view of this, I have had to make a conscious effort to examine and re-examine the nature and development of my research, to ensure that the enlightenment I have derived from the social model does not outweigh a personal and professional commitment to my research and research participants.

Research into indigenous concepts of and responses to disability is a vital but frequently neglected part of researching disability in developing countries (Murthy, 1991; Dalal, 1993; Prabhu, 1993; S. Miles, 1996; M. Miles, 1996 *inter alia*). To do this properly, the researcher should not be a slave to outsider theories or socio-political movements. Definitions need to begin with individuals, families and communities at the grassroots and not with outsiders. That said, there are times when the researcher must accept the weight of responsibility that comes with the job. Even Chambers, who has been the foremost advocate of listening to the voices of the marginalised rural poor, notes that the researcher's role is more than listening to, noting down and reporting the words of those interviewed:

'the rural poor are dispersed, isolated, uncommunicative, rarely asked their views, frequently masked by others, selectively perceived, deferential ... direct approaches distort impressions' (Chambers 1983: 141).

The academic and the practitioner must make inferences from what is said and observed and only then report and recommend. A clear case for analytical detachment (independence? expertise?). I would add that where differences remain between researcher and research subjects (as they must where there is no shared epistemological or ontological base) then these need to be made explicit. The point is to make sense of difference not distort or disregard it.

In short, caution is vital when a researcher moves across cultures with a theoretical guidebook that was written by and for another country, another people, another set of social, cultural and economic structures. In my opinion, this means that any outside theoretical or practical approach, the social model included, must be critically explored rather than reified. I doubt that anyone would dispute this. Equally inadvisable is an unquestioning acceptance that the knowledge of research participants is beyond reworking or reinterpretation. Nothing is holy, nothing is beyond inquiry.

CONCLUSION

I have used my experiences of doing disability research in China to inform and to illustrate discussion on three issues: the status and identity of the researcher, the social relations of research production and the use of the social model of disability. It is clear that my initial fear of not being able to square my research within an emancipatory research paradigm was fully justified. The reasons for this centre on my decisions to form multiple partnerships in the field and to reject the social model as the sole referent in my research and recommendations. Thereby I forfeit claims to working to an emancipatory research paradigm which requires that disabled research subjects control research process and outcome and that agenda, analysis and action are premised exclusively on the social model of disability.

My decisions *not* to reverse the social relations of research production and *not* to defer to the social model as sole referent in theory and practice were taken with a view to increasing the relevance of my research to the lives of all those involved, whether disabled people, families with disabled children, local government cadres or international organisations. At times, these decisions have resulted in alienation for research participants but this is balanced with the increased likelihood that my research can make a practical contribution to disability-related interventions and evaluation in China, thereby improving the material and social situations of at least some Chinese disabled children and adults.

I conclude that emancipatory research, narrowly defined (and I think it would be unwise to broaden definition), is practicable and necessary only in certain contexts – notably where a unitary relationship can be formed with disabled research subjects and where researcher and researched share an epistemological and ontological framework grounded in the social model. Once research crosses cultures and the researcher forms multiple partnerships which reflect rather than reverse real world hierarchies, then scope for realising the ideals of emancipatory research is severely restricted.

If the emancipatory paradigm is of limited practicability, does that render it less necessary and less desirable as a framework for all disability research? Many say not: better that research which cannot conform to the paradigm be left undone. In my opinion, the emancipatory paradigm provides invaluable guidance in making the disability researcher think through all the implications of research but I disagree with those who would make the paradigm the sole measure of worthwhile disability research. The fact that I have not remained faithful to the emancipatory paradigm does not mean that I am parasite or oppressor (contrary to my initial beliefs). My work has made several significant steps towards participatory and action research in China and it should prove of practical and academic worth. For me, for the time being, that is justification enough.

REFERENCES

ABBERLEY, P. (1992) 'Counting Us Out: a discussion of the OPCS disability surveys', *Disability, Handicap and Society*, 7 (2): 139-155.

AMOS, V. and PARMAR, P. (1984) 'Challenging Imperial Feminism', *Feminist Review*, 17: 3 - 19.

BARNES, C. (1996) 'Disability and the Myth of the Independent Researcher', *Disability and Society*, 11 (1): 107-110.

BURY, M. (1996) 'Disability and the Myth of the Independent Researcher: a reply', *Disability and Society*, 11 (1): 111-114.

CHAMBERS, R. (1983) *Rural Development: Putting the Last First.* Harlow: Longman.

DALAL, A.K. (1993), 'The DABB Research Project', *ActionAid Disability News*, 4 (2): 33-34.

DEVEREUX, S. and HODDINOTT, J., eds. (1992a) *Fieldwork in Developing Countries.* London: Harvester Wheatsheaf.

DEVEREUX, S. and HODDINOTT, J. (1992b) 'Issues in data collection', in S. Devereux and J. Hoddinott, eds., *Fieldwork in Developing Countries*. London: Harvester Wheatsheaf.

FRANCIS, E. (1992) 'Qualitative research: collecting life histories', in in S. Devereux and J. Hoddinott, eds., *Fieldwork in Developing Countries*. London: Harvester Wheatsheaf.

GOLD, T. (1989) 'Guerilla Interviewing Among the *Getihu*', in P. Link, R. Madsen,   and P.G. Pickowicz, eds., *Unofficial China: Popular Culture and Thought in the People's Republic*. Boulder: Westview Press.

HAMMERSLEY, M. and ATKINSON, P. (1983) *Ethnography: Principles in Practice*, London: Tavistock.

HANLON, J. (1992) *Mozambique: Who Calls the Shots?*. London: James Currey.

HARRISS, B. (1992) 'Talking to traders about trade', in S. Devereux and J. Hoddinott, eds., *Fieldwork in Developing Countries*. London: Harvester Wheatsheaf.

HODDINOTT, J. (1992) 'Fieldwork under time constraints', in S. Devereux and J. Hoddinott, eds., *Fieldwork in Developing Countries*. London: Harvester Wheatsheaf.

HUMPHRIES, B. and TRUMAN, C., eds. (1994) *Re-thinking Social Research*. Aldershot: Avebury.

LOCKWOOD, M. (1992) 'Facts or Fictions? Fieldwork relationships and the nature of data', in S. Devereux and J. Hoddinott, eds., *Fieldwork in Developing Countries*. London: Harvester Wheatsheaf.

MA, H.L. (1993) *Huigui: Canjiren yu Shehui de Xiangsi* (Coming Home: Disabled People and Social Lovesickness). Beijing: Huaxia Publishing House.

MANION, M. (1994) Survey Research in the Study of Contemporary China: Learning from Local Samples, *China Quarterly*, No. 139.

MILES, M. (1996) 'Community, Individual or Information Development? Dilemmas of concept and culture in South Asian disability planning', *Disability & Society*, 11 (4): 485-500.

MILES, S. (1996) 'Engaging with the Disability Rights Movement: the experience of community-based rehabilitation in southern Africa', *Disability & Society*, 11 (4): 501-517.

MURTHY, R.S. (1991) 'Community Based Rehabilitation – Is There a Need for Research?, *ActionAid Disability News*, 2 (2): 17-20.

OLIVER, M. (1992) 'Changing the Social Relations of Research Production?', *Disability, Handicap and Society*, 7 (2): 101-114.

PRABHU, G.G. (1993) 'Symposium on Research and Evaluation in Community Based Rehabilitation - Summary Proceedings: 3 May 1993, Bangalore, *ActionAid Disability News*, 4 (2): 21.

SHAKESPEARE, T. (1996) 'Rules of Engagement: doing disability research', *Disability & Society*, 11 (1): 115-120.

STONE, E. and PRIESTLEY, M. (1996) 'Parasites, pawns and partners: disability research and the role of non-disabled researchers', *British Journal of Sociology*, 47 (4): 699-716.

TRUMAN, C. and HUMPHRIES, B. (1994) 'Re-thinking social research: Research in an unequal world', in B. Humphries and C. Truman, eds., *Re-thinking Social Research*. Aldershot: Avebury.

WILSON, K. (1992) 'Thinking about the Ethics of Fieldwork', in S. Devereux and J. Hoddinott, eds., *Fieldwork in Developing Countries*. London: Harvester Wheatsheaf.

XI, C.Q., LIN, Q.H. and CHEN, Y.F., eds.(1993) *Canjiren Shehuixue* (Disabled People Social Studies). Beijing: Huaxia.

ZARB, G. (1992) 'On the Road to Damascus: first steps towards changing the relations of disability research production', *Disability, Handicap and Society*, 7 (2): 125-38.

INDEX